Praise for the UK edition of *Dusty*

"Karen Bartlett's *Dusty* may well be the most definitive biography yet of the iconic Sixties singer, frank in its examination of Dusty's personal life and rightly demonstrating how, in so many ways, she was way ahead of her time."
—*Choice* magazine

"You may well have heard of the demons that drove the Hampstead-born, convent-educated Mary O'Brien to become the soul diva Dusty Springfield, but this biography does a good job of telling the complete story."
—*Sunday Times Culture Magazine*

"A definitive biography of the singer." —*International Express*

"A well-researched and revealing biography . . . Those last few years, however, make for a heart-breaking read, but [are] handled sympathetically and without sensationalism." —*Record Collector*

"Karen Bartlett's biography sends you back to the music—to the extraordinary, dusky vulnerability of her voice. I'm re-touched every time I hear it."
—Helen Brown, *Daily Telegraph*

"Bartlett's compassionate biography uses an unadorned style to succinctly distil Springfield's tumultuous life." —Brendan Daly, *Sunday Post*

"This is fertile rock biog territory and Bartlett spins the tale adroitly, never surrendering to the impulse to sensationalize. There's a rich seam of self-destructiveness that comes alive on every page. Rather than merely cataloguing Springfield's mishaps, however, the author's chief concern is to locate the shy frightened woman behind the iconic exterior." —Ed Power, *Irish Independent*

"An insightful delve into the troubled, conflicted mind of the UK's soul queen . . . It's an incredibly sad story but Bartlett gets the balance right, celebrating a talent with few equals, while never shying away from the pain involved."
—*MOJO*

"*Dusty* is a fascinating read, desperately sad and painful though it is to discover its heroine's Californian dark night of the soul." —*The Tablet*

"A lucid biography." —*Sunday Business Post*

"[*Dusty*] is rich with information on some of her most significant personal relationships . . . paints a vivid portrait of a tortured soul." —*Out in the City*

Dusty

AN INTIMATE PORTRAIT OF A MUSICAL LEGEND

KAREN BARTLETT

LESSER
GODS

For Elizabeth B. Reed

CONTENTS

INTRODUCTION

NO EASY WAY DOWN

When Dusty Springfield heard Dionne Warwick sing "Don't Make Me Over," she sat down suddenly on the edge of her bed in the Capitol Motel—her breath taken away at the realization that there was someone out there already one step ahead of her and, as she thought, doing it so much better. Dusty was recording in Nashville, on her first trip to the country she had dreamed about for so long. But she was worried that she was already too late. "'Don't Make Me Over' changed my life," she remembered. "Nobody can sing Bacharach and David music like her. Nobody. It's total gossamer."

By April 1964 both women were well-established in the music industry, but when they met in London for the first time, delighting locals with a sing-song in an East End pub, Dusty and Dionne already had a history. After several fruitless attempts, Warwick had secured a British top ten hit and had flown in to promote it. For years she had fumed while white British singers covered the songs that had been written for her, and which she had made her own. Cilla

Black's copycat version of "Anyone Who Had a Heart" had deprived Warwick of a place in the British charts and Dusty, with her version of "Wishin' and Hopin'", had done much the same. "If I had, during the course of the recording, coughed or sneezed, that would have been an integral part of what they recorded," Warwick said frostily.

With Burt Bacharach agreeing to hold back "Walk On By" and release it simultaneously on both sides of the Atlantic, Warwick was finally guaranteed the US and British hit she deserved—but hard feelings remained. "I feel Dionne did resent me," Dusty said later. "I tried to get along with her but I always found her a little cool." Superficially, they were two burgeoning stars about to enjoy a day out in London—for the benefit of the press—but while Warwick bristled with self-assurance (no matter who cheated her out of a hit, she *knew* she was the best), Dusty was already feeling wrong-footed by her own insecurities.

By all accounts, Warwick had a whale of a time, singing lustily along to the piano in an East End pub, the City Arms—"Dionne just had to get up there and sing along and as her hostess I had to join her," Dusty recalled—before they went on to snack from a cockle and whelk stall and banter happily with the barrow boys in Petticoat Lane market. Warwick came from a family of distinguished gospel singers, but her humble origins in East Orange, New Jersey, and the color prejudice she faced every day in the 1960s, meant that she could easily relate to ordinary people. Dusty, who emerged from a family of Irish immigrants in the London borough of Ealing, was fraught with middle-class hang-ups, never leaving the house without first donning the fully made-up, hairsprayed persona of "Dusty Springfield"—a creation which confused her for her entire life and led to endless fretting over which character, Dusty or her birth identity, Mary O'Brien, was the "real her."

The truth is that Dusty did not want to copy Warwick and her hits; she worshipped her, and the black soul and Motown singers who would always make her feel inferior. Her greatest thrill, she would later say, was standing in the wings at the Fox Theatre in Brooklyn, New York, waiting to sing backup for Martha and the Vandellas. Standing in the same spot, and working with the same musicians as Aretha Franklin, literally struck her dumb during the 1968 recording of what should have been her greatest musical triumph, *Dusty in Memphis*, and she retreated, alone, to a studio in New York to finish work on what *Rolling Stone* named one of the greatest records of the twentieth century, but which Dusty herself dismissed as "such a *white* album."

Underneath her cheery exterior, Dusty desperately wanted to be the best. With her ear for music, and her demand for control over the recording process, she often stretched the music business of the 1960s to the limits, and beyond. But perhaps even more than wanting to be the best, she wanted to be someone else. "She wanted to be straight and she wanted to be a good Catholic and she wanted to be black," remembered her lover Norma Tanega. Ultimately she was none of those things, but she was a star. The convent girl who shrugged off what she considered to be the unappealing "dull librarian" look of dumpy red-headed Mary O'Brien transformed herself into Dusty Springfield—and was propelled on a trajectory that would take her to the heights of fame and success, before stumbling to the kind of rock-bottom low fueled by struggles with misdiagnosed mental illness, drink, drugs and depression worthy of a Hollywood legend. Unlike many, she survived, recovered—and restored her reputation as one of the greatest female singers Britain has ever produced, and the greatest blue-eyed soul singer of all time. She remains in all respects a definitive musical icon, the voice of her generation—and a woman who was always ahead of her time.

1

MARY O'BRIEN

"Our house was full of ambivalence. Raging ambivalence," Dusty later remembered of her childhood home. "We none of us wanted to be there."

When Peter Miles first met Dusty she was still Mary O'Brien—a petite teenager with auburn hair, curled up in the living room at Kent Gardens, Ealing, gazing out of the window.

> *There is Mary—sitting alone in an armchair. She would come home from school, very straight, and very plain, no makeup, and of course very aware that she was a teenager and had to obey Mummy and Daddy; and she'd sit back in the armchair in the lounge. She'd sit back like Toad of Toad Hall in* Wind in the Willows. *He was thinking of his latest passion—"Oh, motor cars. Oh, motor cars!" Mary was in a dreamworld too from the age of puberty, very early on.*

An American magazine was open on the floor with an article about music on one page, and a picture of a skyscraper on the other. Even then Mary was slightly elusive, taking part, but slightly apart. Daydreaming. "All that she went through in her life was music," says Miles. "Inside her guts, there were two things she was obsessed with: music, and her doing it, and also the word 'America.' Those two things were an obsession. I don't know where she got it from."

Peter had met Mary's brother Tom, then called Dion, through another mutual friend at a local youth group where Dion played table tennis. The two young men seemed to have a lot in common; both were musical and had grown up in Roman Catholic families in post-war English suburbia. To be a Catholic in 1950s England was still to be distinct from the majority Protestant population.

Dion, good-looking and fun, soon invited Peter to come round to his house in the evenings and play music with him in the kitchen long after most other residents of Kent Gardens were asleep. Sometimes Mary would drift in and sit listening to them—keen, but hesitant about taking part. "It was quite a large kitchen— there was a nice table there. Dion, who sang with us, would have one leg up on the chair, playing guitar," Miles says. "Mary would come in and watch sometimes, but she never joined in with the blokes, although she liked doing a solo, or duets."

One day Mary grabbed Peter by both arms and said, "I know you are deeply fond of my brother, and I know you are deeply in love with music. I think you and I ought to make a record together," her usual shyness replaced by a startling confidence. "She had been watching us," Miles says. "She knew I sang a melody perfectly in tune, I was good at timing. She just came up to me and said, 'Let's go Monday week, I'll come round, we'll go at three, and it'll be over by half past four.'"

Miles discovered that Mary had arranged everything, and was in control of the whole process. They caught the bus to a rented studio in Bayswater where budding singers and musicians could cut a record for a small fee. With Mary playing her guitar, and Peter ad-libbing between some of the verses, they hammered out a passable rendition of "Can't We Be Friends." Miles recalls:

> *Listening to what we recorded—the first lyrics between the chorus line from me are totally unprepared. She didn't know they were coming, I didn't know they were coming, but they worked one 100 percent. I was using the story of the lyrics as if I was the singer and she was the singer talking about it—"Can't we be friends," and at the end of each chorus, I slipped in a medley.*

Mary's voice already carried the distinct genesis of the sound that would make her famous. When they parted company at the end of the day they had a record to their name, and Peter had made a surprising discovery—the quiet Mary O'Brien knew what she wanted, and when it came to music she wasn't diffident about getting her way. "She was on the ball so quickly—she inspired me. We rehearsed and then it was so simple to do."

Despite their friendship, Peter never lost the sense that both Mary and Dion were at heart unknowable, with a strangeness about them that was hard to identify. "With their parents, they couldn't really be themselves. They were both kids who had this insular feeling about them, which a lot of stars have in music. They can't have successful marriages, they want to be themselves but can't be. They want to be private because they give everything to music." Later Dusty would attribute this to a peculiar family upbringing, driven by terrible tension and family rows. Peter Miles saw no such rows, and remembered both her mother and father as being very polite, but with an obvious incompatibility that made them seem like "two islands" with nothing connecting them except their children. "With the parents it was as if two strangers were together. Mum would talk to Mary as if he wasn't in the room, and he talked to Mary as if Mum wasn't in the room—it was a very strange atmosphere." To Peter it seemed almost as though they were not Mary and Dion's parents, "just two mature people living" with them.

No one could ever fathom what had brought Gerard "OB" O'Brien and Catherine "Kay" Anne Ryle together, except for the fact that they were both music-loving Catholics, neither of them in the first flush of youth—and they were stretching at the boundary of marriageable age. Miles recalls thinking, "How on earth did they get married? It was as if they had no love between them."

Kay was born in Dublin and grew up in a large family of three sisters and four brothers in Tralee. Her father, Maurice Patrick Ryle, was a prominent journalist who edited the *Irish Independent* and the *Evening Herald* in the 1920s, on one occasion taking his daughter to London to sit in on a session of Parliament. Ryle became extremely well known, reporting for the Irish Parliamentary Party as a prominent "Redmonite", a nationalist political movement that campaigned peacefully for Irish home rule but threw its support behind Britain in the First World War. Ryle died in 1935, four years before his famous granddaughter was born.

Hoping for a career on the London stage, Kay escaped her respectable rural roots to head for the big city to have a good time. But by the time she reached thirty the dream of a career in entertainment had evaporated. Amateur dramatics was the only remaining outlet for Kay's creative urges, and she could no longer hold off her family's expectation that she settle down and have children of her own. Peter Miles remembers Dusty's mother as chirpy and bird-like and "full of Irish crack"–chat. Yet she was an unfulfilled woman who believed that marriage and family, and convention, had stifled the life she should have led—leaving a residue of restlessness and disappointment that played out in her own relationship with her daughter, and overshadowed many of the decisions Dusty would make. "Mother blundered through life," Dusty told the *Radio Times*. "Nothing bad ever happened to her until she married. She wasn't cut out for it and would like to have been a flapper forever." Sometimes she would disappear to the south of France, sending back postcards to OB that read "Having a great time . . . Regards . . ." "It was never 'Love,'" Dusty added meaningfully.

Gerard O'Brien was Irish and Scottish, but grew up in a family of well-to-do colonial expats in India. For much of his childhood he shuttled back and forth between the subcontinent and a boarding school in Derbyshire. Although OB claimed to have travelled back and forth during the holidays, family life must have been limited as the boat trip took so long. Dusty later said he must have had time "only for a plate of curry before it was time to turn around and go back to school again." Once he left school, OB pursued a career as an income tax consultant who also gave evidence in court cases. Overweight, bespectacled and balding, he was undoubtedly an intelligent man—but his professional progress was limited by his refusal to take accountancy exams. According to his daughter, this stemmed from the fact that he thought taking exams was "beneath him," but perhaps his ambivalence also stemmed from the fact that music, not tax, was his true love. Just as his wife Kay was an unfulfilled actress, OB was a frustrated musician.

"My parents didn't get on," Dusty told Jean Rook in the 1980s. "My father was an income tax consultant who really wanted to be a concert pianist—a very bitter man, with a foul temper. By the time I was at school my mother thought he was repulsive."

At different times in her life, Dusty remembered her parents with varying degrees of harshness. Later she often recalled their unhappiness, and their faults. Dusty's long-term partner in Los Angeles, Sue Cameron, says:

She grew up in a house where there was no emotion expressed. Her mother was always drunk, but very properly drunk. She would sit at the table and have tea, but there would always be liquor in the tea. Absolutely no one was at home, she was off in her own universe. Her father was nice, but cold, mechanical.

Earlier in her career, however, when life was treating her more kindly, Dusty often visited her parents, invited them to her parties and took them with her on foreign tours. Singer Madeline Bell remembers how, in the mid-1960s Dusty would drive down in the middle of night to visit them in Hove, stay for a few hours and then drive home again. They could be amusing too, and shared a wacky sense of humor. Mike Hurst, who joined Dusty and Tom in The Springfields, recalls a trip to Ireland when the band were appearing on the Gay Byrne TV show, and Kay and OB were in the audience. "Now, Mr O'Brien, Byrne told him before the show, 'We'll be asking you something like 'How do you feel about being back in Ireland?'" OB cheerfully said, "I've never been!" Alarmed, Byrne warned him that whatever his answer was, it mustn't be that. The lights went down, the show started and Byrne enthusiastically introduced Dusty's parents. "How do feel about being back in Ireland?" he asked. "I've never been!" OB replied.

Dusty's friend Vicki Wickham remembers, "We were always going round to their house, and her mother would be preparing dinner and have two different radios on to hear when they would play the next Dusty song." Kay, she adds, was always "the last one standing at a party—still going and still drinking at five o'clock in the morning." Within a few years, though, Vicki noticed that Dusty was visiting her parents less often: "I can't explain. Later she didn't bother to go home and visit when she should have, and could have. I don't know why she didn't."

As Dusty grew older and became more self-aware, her view on her parents changed, yet she never stopped wanting their approval. Were they a happy or unhappy family? Riss Chantelle, who knew Dusty and her family well from their early days together in the Lana Sisters, says, "The unhappiness is the real answer." Yet whatever her eventual verdict on their family life, Dusty could never deny that her parents had instilled in her a deep appreciation of music that added a depth and sophistication to her entire career.

The O'Briens' first child, a boy called Dion, was born four years after their marriage, on July 2, 1934. Five years later their daughter arrived. Mary Isobel Catherine Bernadette O'Brien was born in a nursing home in West Hampstead on April 16, 1939. It was a suitably Irish Catholic name for a family where the local priest was later often in situ, clutching a strong drink. The family lived in comfortable middle-class circumstances in an apartment block called Lauderdale Mansions. Later, interviewers would tease Dusty about her posh "Hampstead blues" upbringing, but in truth the family lived only one step removed from the large Irish community that had settled around West Hampstead and Kilburn —and were a world apart from the wealthy liberal intelligentsia of Hampstead proper.

Mary O'Brien was born only months before the outbreak of the Second World War, and the O'Briens soon decided to abandon London and move to the relative safety of the Buckinghamshire town of High Wycombe—first to a flat in the basement of a pub and then to their own house on a suburban road in an area of town known as the Sands. Deep in the English countryside and the rolling Chiltern Hills, High Wycombe represented quintes-sential suburban middle-class life. The sense of respectability it conveyed—of drawing a rather prim veil over unpleasant matters, of speaking well and knowing good manners and being "nice"—was one that Dusty liked to play with for the rest of her life. Indeed, she did speak well and have good manners, and her "niceness" was a deep-rooted and genuine part of her personality. And the people she liked, and was attracted to, usually embodied those qualities too (one of her unlikely infatuations, whom she passionately fancied, was the politician Shirley Williams).

But there was another side to Dusty, and there were signs that there was another side to the O'Briens. Superficially they were a traditional family: Kay kept a spotless house, her husband commuted to the City for work, and the family took their summer holidays in the genteel south coast resort of Bognor Regis. But not everything could be tamed. They were restless—never unpacking in case it delayed their move back to London. OB let the garden become overgrown, and it didn't matter how bitterly the neighbors complained—he refused to cut the grass on the grounds that there could be snakes hiding in the undergrowth. Dusty later told the *Radio Times*, "They were trapped into being suburban without having suburban minds."

Inside, life could be just as wild. Dusty remembered her mother carefully making a trifle, and then smoothing the top with a spoon, smoothing it and smoothing it, until suddenly she started hitting it so hard it flew out of the basin and splattered all over the walls. "That way you'll get it quicker," she angrily told her daughter. The wrong remark at the dinner table could lead to a bowl of potatoes flying past someone's ear and full-scale food fights often ensued, with the remnants of meals lurking behind radiators and curtains for weeks until they were discovered and eventually cleaned up. "They could be really naughty sometimes as a family, throwing food at each other and all of that. The first time I saw that I couldn't believe it, but that was the family," Madeline Bell says.

Sometimes Dusty would recount these incidents as being humorous—those crazy O'Briens letting their tempers get the better of them again. The truth, however, was often far from amusing. "I can't remember a thing about my room at home except the raised voices coming from the next-door room—the intense bitterness," she said. "I'd feel embarrassed to go out with my parents because the arguments still continued. I never invited friends home because I cringed about the rows."

Her parents were good people, she concluded, but "their very Irish 'staying together for the sake of the children'" mentality drove them to extremes. "They had a lousy marriage. They tried hard but they never got along. My mother always discouraged me from thinking about marriage." Regardless of her sexual orientation, Dusty told her secretary Pat Barnett that listening to her parents bickering and fighting and throwing things had put her off marriage for life.

Growing up in the midst of such tension, and overshadowed by her blue-eyed and rather brilliant brother, Dusty struggled to be noticed. No one, she believed, paid much attention to her—nor to some of the distressing things that were happening to her: "Because I was so unhappy as a kid, I used to go into a corner and cling to the hot water pipes in my bedroom until they were cold, to prove I really existed." "She was a very feeling, alive person," Sue Cameron says, "but she looked around in her childhood and nobody was feeling anything, everybody was oblivious." Cameron believes Dusty's story about clinging to the scalding hot pipes was the most revealing fact about her childhood.

> I'd never heard of someone having to hug a water pipe and burn themselves to know that they're alive. That's the most telling thing of her childhood, and she talked about it a lot. She felt there was something wrong with her because she had all these feelings and she was surrounded by cotton wool. So she hugged it to know that was real.

Dusty believed she was both ignored and abused—and the world turned its face away in ignorance of this. Her mother Kay could be distant and unaffectionate, Dusty remembered. Kay favored Dion, who always seemed to be excelling in all his school work and activities while Mary, nicknamed "Pudge" by her family, lumbered along. "Her parents did nothing to get excited about her. Nothing," Peter Miles says. "They should have got more excited."

"I was a nothing kid. Not particularly good. Not particularly bad. Maybe it was the middle class coming out in me but I never had the courage to be really bad," Dusty said. Even if, as her brother told her, their mother bounced her on her knee when she was a baby, Dusty said she never remembered being hugged or loved. OB, meanwhile, could be violent, lashing out at his daughter. Many years later, Dusty claimed, she built up the courage to confront her father and ask him why he had hit her—but he looked blank, and "denied it had ever happened." "She always thought she looked like a boy," Dusty's former Alcoholics Anonymous sponsor Suzanne Lacefield says. "Her father was verbally abusive, he called her stupid and ugly, which can be so harmful and is so eroding of someone's nature. I know when she talked about her father her face would change and you could see the sadness. And when she talked about her brother, which was rare, you could see a lot of anger there."

At the time it was not uncommon for children to grow up with disciplinarian fathers, and parents trapped in a loveless marriage, but Dusty would later hint to friends that she had also been sexually abused—and that she was always tortured by the memory of it. "In a roundabout way, it was implied," says Lacefield. "In her session with me about it, it was implied. She did not reveal herself even though she revealed herself." If true, it would go a long way towards explaining the silence and secrecy she extended over much of her life, and her self-loathing.

Whatever demons Dusty carried with her from her childhood, the O'Briens were profoundly different in positive ways too: they were musical. While the rest of England tuned in to Dame Vera Lynn and tea dance music, OB came home in the evening and played long hours of classical music and jazz. "A quick burst of Mozart can transform your day," Dusty later said. But classical music had a less direct influence on her life than the jazz and blues of artists like Jelly Roll Morton whom her father exposed her to.

Morton was a black Creole musician called Ferdinand Joseph LaMothe who had started out playing the piano in a New Orleans brothel as a fourteen-year-old. His later claims to have "invented" jazz were widely scoffed at, but he was the first jazz arranger to demonstrate that an improvised genre could be written down and retain its original spirit. His 1915 work "Jelly Roll Blues" was the first published jazz composition. Up in New York, Billie Holiday, who would go on to influence Dusty's style, was carving the pain of her own tortured history of rape and prostitution into classic renditions of "God Bless the Child" and "Strange Fruit," while another of Dusty's favorites, Ella Fitzgerald, brought together jazz and pop by recording songs by the likes of Cole Porter and Duke Ellington in what became known as the Great American Songbook.

Such fusion, and moving across genres, laid the groundwork for the kind of artist Dusty would eventually become, but as a teenager she was still driven by imitation, not innovation. Dusty started to sing when she was very small and, after the family left High Wycombe and moved back to London in 1950, Mary told the nuns at St. Anne's Convent School in Ealing that she wanted to become a blues singer. It was a shocking ambition in several ways. She had already recorded a ragtime selection on a Philips reel-to-reel in the garage, including "When the Midnight Choo Choo Leaves for Alabam'" and "Pretty Baby"—intuitively interpreting the phrasing and feeling of the music, even if she did not yet understand the meaning of many of the words. Jazz and the blues were sensual, soulful—and sometimes downright dirty ("jelly roll"was the nickname given to women's genitalia in the New Orleans brothel). Such earthy physicality could not have been further from the virtues preached in a good Catholic education, where sex was forbidden and all bodily functions appeared to be nonexistent.

When Mary formed a schoolgirl band with classmates Angela Patten and Jean MacDonald, their rendition of "St. Louis Blues," complete with purple lighting, was banned from a school celebration of St. Stanislaus's feast day. "They thought it too raunchy," Angela Patten remembered. Even then Dusty took music very seriously, becoming irritated when Angela and Jean did not pay enough attention to their practice sessions.

Jazz and the blues were also very "black" genres—signifying an otherness that intrigued and attracted Dusty from an early age. "'Blues singer' had a certain exoticism to it," she said, "and it also meant 'black.' I was fascinated with black faces, and black voices." Jelly Roll Morton had faced the deep discrimination of being "colored" in the American South in the first half of the twentieth century, and almost died after a white hospital denied him medical treatment for a life-threatening stab wound. But, as a Creole, he was also a double outsider—not white, but not "colored" enough to be fully accepted by the African American community either. Dusty would always identify with outsiders.

Dusty's announcement that she wanted to be a blues singer pointed to her deeper desires. Everyone else in her school class wanted to do sensible things—"like become a radiographer," she sniffed. But underneath what was still then a rather unprepossessing exterior lurked what she dramatically described as a "seething mass of ambition, ready to claw my way to the top."

In an unpublished 1973 interview with *Rolling Stone* magazine

Dusty recalled another musical influence: "I was very interested in film musicals—especially 20th Century Fox. My brother and I would set up a broadcast system, neighbors would come in and sit in one room, we'd sing and play piano in the other room." Her mother was constantly finding various instruments strewn across the floor and, indeed, while OB instilled musical knowledge in his children, Kay was equally responsible for laying the foundations for Dusty's career, according to Pat Barnett: "She loved her mum for taking her to late-night musicals, and that's where her love for musicals came from. It was her mum that really said she should have a musical career."

While Dion was musically gifted, and a talented composer, it was his sister who possessed the precocious, strangely adult—and slightly eerie—voice. "There is a sadness there in my voice," Dusty said. "I don't know why, it didn't grow on me. I was born with it. Sort of melancholy. Comes with being Irish-Scottish. Automatically melancholy and mad at the same time."

It helped that there was at least one thing that she could do better than Dion, with whom she remained locked in fierce competition: "It was too much for me, I used to get very upset that I wasn't good enough," she told the *Daily Mail* in 1990. "The feelings of inadequacy followed me through my life. Now I'm grateful to my brother because it was he who unwittingly started me off singing. I started because he started, and I wanted to be better than him at something."

2

YOU'VE GOT WHAT IT TAKES

ary O'Brien left St. Anne's Convent in Ealing in the summer of 1955. When she returned a year later she was in look, if not yet in name, some way towards becoming Dusty Springfield. The transformation from an awkward, unprepossessing schoolgirl into a high-heeled, heavily made-up vamp left her former classmates speechless. "She walked in and we just couldn't believe it," one former school-friend, Liz Thwaites, told writer Lucy O'Brien. "Fully made up . . . dressed in high-heeled shoes. Nobody had seen her, really, since she left. We were whispering to each other, 'Have you seen Mary O'Brien?' It was as if she was in [costume]." In many respects, she was.

"I was destined to become a librarian at that point," Dusty said, looking back on her transformation in the 1980s. "I had awful glasses, unstyled hair and thick ankles, which I still have. And one day I went to Harrods and came back with this black dress on, and my hair had been done in French rolls, with endless pins in it. I just suddenly decided, in one afternoon, to be this other person who was going to make it." Like her idols June Haver, Peggy Lee and Doris Day, Dusty later took her transformation a step further and became a platinum blonde. "I just decided I wanted to become someone else . . . so I became someone else," she explained, demonstrating what seems like remarkable self-awareness and determination for a sixteen-year-old. "I had to change Mary O'Brien to become successful."

Upon their parting, a small group of St. Anne's girls had agreed to meet five years later in Trafalgar Square. "I'll be there as long as I'm not in rehearsals," Mary had joked. Only a year later, that dream was—to everyone's surprise—in the process of coming true.

Dusty had not enjoyed being a schoolgirl, saying, "I didn't think they were the happiest days of my life, and I still don't." She disliked taking part in sports, and played for a undistinguished year on the hockey team. Undoubtedly intelligent, she passed her eleven-plus on the second attempt and eventually sat six O-levels, passing four: English grammar, history, French and geography. Her love of America was to blame for her failure in English literature, she claimed—there was little chance that she would become enchanted with *Mansfield Park* when she was engrossed instead in movie magazines and Budd Schulberg's writings about the glamor, and disillusion, of Hollywood life. "She was bored stiff with the school, with the routine," Peter Miles says. "They [Mary and Dion] were extroverts and wanted to get things done in the world and be themselves and not be goody-goodies. So she sat there and did her homework, but she couldn't open up. She was just waiting until she could do music. It was that simple."

In addition, Mary already knew that she was attracted to girls. She'd experienced her first crush on one of the nuns at St. Anne's, something many girls experienced but that Dusty realized, for her, was something more. Later, she told her lover Sue Cameron, she would watch, transfixed, while the girl across the road in Kent Gardens undressed in front of the window. Like many other aspects of her true self, this had to be concealed at all costs— hidden beneath a new persona, which was best enacted through show business.

The O'Brien children had been obsessed with show business since their earliest years, banging out Carmen Miranda songs on frying pans and maracas, while Mary also slipped away and spent many afternoons in the cinema with her mother. "My mother was so tired, poor thing. She was never meant to be a housewife so she would sit through the afternoon showing twice, which made it even better," Dusty said. In her teens, Mary's attraction to drama grew even stronger when she started going to see plays at the Old Vic, and snuck into the West End to watch foreign films at the Curzon movie theater in Mayfair.

At first, however, employment came in a more mundane form, including working in a laundry, and then at Bentalls department store in Ealing, where she sold train sets and trash cans. Yet, even at that time, Mary saw that the life of a shop girl who grew up into an ordinary suburban wife was definitely not one she wished to pursue. She was determined that her future was as a performer and, after shyly trying some acting classes at the local Jane Campbell Acting School, she concluded that music offered her more opportunities. "I was miming, my first serious try at acting. I learned that I was not a good mime, that I couldn't open a window without the window being there."

Peter Miles, by then an aspiring actor himself, remembers calling her up and inviting her over to his apartment to record some comedy on a reel-to-reel tape machine. Mary arrived, with her mother in tow, and they sat together on the sofa while Peter tried out some of his lines. Mary responded and improvised the part, but Peter remembers a certain caution, and a look in her eye that seemed to be holding back.

> *She clammed up because her mother was there. We put the tape on and I said, "You and I are in a big aircraft in flight and you happen to be next to me on the seat," so, as would happen in a plane, if you can think of any ad-libs that would get a laugh of some sort—something going wrong—a stewardess spilling something or a kid saying something, you know, let's go for it, just open yourself up. But, although she joined in, you could see that she was a little bit worried—in case she wasn't good.*

The question of whether Dusty could have made a successful transition into acting hung over the later stages of her career—but she was always afraid to make the leap.

As a teenager, singing along with her brother in what she called her 'strange little voice' was a far easier entry into the business. Dion had breezed through grammar school, passing nine O-levels and working his way through a succession of jobs in the City and the army, eventually joining the Intelligence Corps and serving two years as a Russian translator. When he was away, Mary often wrote to him asking for a favor here and there. "Oh yes, I was her favorite brother. I was her only brother," Tom told Pat Barnett. "And when I was in the forces, guess who used to write to me and ask me if I could send her some money?"

Like his father, Dion was a frustrated musician. During his time in the armed forces he sang in the Russian choir at the Joint Services School for Linguists, and then played piano in the Navy, Army and Air Force Institute's jazz band. Back in civilian life it wasn't long before he was playing at night in small clubs in Sloane Square and Chelsea too, and Mary spent long hours practicing with him in their garage at home. When her parents took her along with them one evening to the club, her brother suggested to the manager that he should hear her sing. The manager looked "disbelieving;" Dusty recalled, "I suppose he'd never seen such an awkward-looking teenager before." Nevertheless, when she took the stage and started singing along to her brother strumming on the guitar, the audience stopped talking—and then applauded. Mary was offered her first paid job in entertainment, earning seventeen shillings and sixpence a night.

Working in drinking clubs was a relatively thankless entrance into the business. The O'Briens sang up to a hundred folk and Latin songs in an evening, playing in small smoky rooms to audiences that sometimes included movie stars such as Jack Lemmon, but more often consisted of hordes of bored debutantes who Mary always felt looked down on her. Sylvia Jones, the owner of a Belgravia supper club, the Montrose, remembers asking permission from OB and Kay for Mary to perform. "She was terribly young, but extremely good," Jones told *The Mirror*. "She was sixteen, self-possessed and had lovely auburn hair. With Tom she'd play at debutante parties in Eaton Square, which she loathed because, although the mothers were friendly, the daughters were vile." Dusty herself said, "It was a rotten job. It really was a rotten job. But it was a way of earning a buck."

Catapulted into an adult world, Mary was still living in a hybrid cocoon—somewhere between being a girl and an adult. Although she looked like an enticing worldly young woman—far older than her years—she remained innocent. Her fierce Catholic upbringing still burned strongly in her (at one point she had briefly toyed with the idea of becoming a nun) and she had experienced none of the teenage pleasures of going on dates, or holding hands at the movies. The truth was that, despite later claiming "I regret that I didn't have a silly youth," and summoning up a supposed girlhood crush on a blond German prisoner of war in High Wycombe, she seemed to have little interest in men—or romance.

Mary was still young enough to wait for her father to arrive and escort her safely home on the last train, but she was eager to grow up and become more independent—circling adverts in *The Stage* for girl singers and performers. In 1958 she applied to join an all-girl vocal trio. The act's founder, Riss Chantelle, had worked first as a Redcoat at Butlins, and then learned her trade playing guitar in the all-female Ivy Benson Band before deciding to go out on her own. "I'd seen the Hedley Ward Trio and I thought they were very good," Chantelle says, "so I thought on that scale. I played guitar, a girl played piano and another girl played the mini bass. Originally we were instruments as well as vocal. Then I found out the harmonies were getting quite strong, so we left the instruments behind and just went out as a sister act."

When one of the girls dropped out to look after her sick mother, Chantelle advertised for her replacement. Mary arrived to audition with her red hair up in a French braid. She seemed polite and well educated. "She was nicely spoken and she was well brought up, or so I thought at the time," Chantelle says. More to the point, Mary's audition, at a rehearsal room in Leicester Square, revealed that she could also sing. "When we sang together the sound blended perfectly," Chantelle recalls.

At that stage, Mary was "more or less the same as a lot of other girls I had in, but what I liked about her was her speaking voice, and that is her singing voice really. Very often you don't get that, but in Dusty you did, you got a speaking voice and her singing voice was there. I liked her because she had a nice tone in the bottom range." Chantelle took a few days to think it over, and then offered the part to Mary O'Brien.

Despite singing in clubs, Mary knew very little about performing or stagecraft, and in joining Riss and Lynne Abrams she embarked upon a brutally steep learning curve. "She was very amateur when she came with me," Chantelle says, "and I had to sort of knock her into shape." Yet Chantelle could also see that—if pushed—Mary was hard-working and disciplined.

> *She was so pleased to be in it. That was the nice part of it—that she was so pleased I'd had her. She worked like mad on things, like the harmonies. Lynne used to do the harmonies and give them to her at first, because Dusty didn't have a clue about anything then, but gradually she went in with Lynne and they did them much better together.*

The group rehearsed every morning in the old Metropolitan Theatre on Edgware Road, with Chantelle putting the trio through their paces and ridding Mary of habits including whistling in the dressing room—an unlucky show business omen—and dropping crockery.

All-girl groups, such as the Beverley Sisters, had already proved to be hugely popular, and the trio adopted the same style of close harmonies and cheerful pop—wearing tulle skirts with a drawstring that were whipped away to reveal tight silver lamé trousers. One day Mary fell down the stairs and when she whipped back her skirt in performance the knees of her trousers were all torn. "She thought that was very funny, but it wasn't to me because I'd had to book it and everything else, but she was rather like that," Chantelle remembers. "She took it for granted that things were going to be funny, but sometimes they weren't."

Chantelle remembers finding Mary's jokes less than hilarious on other occasions too.

> *We were doing a television show, doing "Buona Sera" with Cyril Stapleton's orchestra. Just as we were on, she put her foot between my feet, so I went head first. And that's a live television show. There's nothing you can do about that. It*

was just her sense of humor, and that isn't a very good sense of humor when it comes to a television show.

Mary loved neither the look nor the songs, but she was a "happy girl, laughing and joking," Chantelle remembers, and she appreciated what she was learning, meaning that she was soon ready to make her debut appearance at the Savoy cinema in the seaside resort of Clacton-on-Sea. Rejecting Kay O'Brien's suggestion that they call themselves the Twister Sisters, and picking an alternative from the phone book, the newly named Lana Sisters were partly managed, out of what Dusty described as a "sleazy little office," by Evelyn Taylor, who worked for Joan Collins's father Joe and also managed Adam Faith. Taylor booked the trio as a support act for Nat King Cole ("That was the biggest show that Dusty did with us," Chantelle says), as well as Tommy Steele and Faith. They appeared twice at the Royal Albert Hall Festival of Music, as well as touring Ireland and US airbases in Europe.

On one occasion, Riss was about to drive Mary home after a tour of Germany. "Dusty said, 'How terrible, you've got a flat tire.' And I'd got another flat tire, and another flat tire—four flat tires. How could I have four flat tires?" The O'Briens had let down the air in her car tires to stop her from leaving—they did it apparently because they appreciated what Chantelle and the Lana Sisters were doing for Mary, and they wanted to stay up all night and have a long chat. Resigned to staying over, Chantelle remembers, "We were going to have a meal but we never had it. We had some Ritz crackers, 'Get you something to eat in a minute.' We knew what that would mean . . ." It usually meant nothing, as Chantelle knew the O'Briens ate late, if at all. Chantelle added that she never saw any of the legendary food throwing, as usually there was no food in the house to throw.

Crucially the Lana Sisters were also signed up to Fontana,

a subsidiary of Philips Records, paving the way for Dusty's recording career: "We didn't have hits," she said, "but we did have records." At that time, finding a song to record was easy and Chantelle remembers driving down to Denmark Street in 1959, then the hub of London's music industry, while publishers came out and handed them demos through the car windows.

Recording with the Lana Sisters was a very different experience from what Dusty would demand later in her career. "When we recorded, we were very lucky we got anything at all," Chantelle says.

> We stood in the booth all round one mic and had to have an internal balance that meant you couldn't turn one down and then turn the other one up. So you were stuck if one was lower than the other, but we weren't, we'd get a very good internal balance. Do the rehearsal, and then do it once or twice, and that was the record. And then of course we got three mics, and that seemed wonderful!

The group's debut single, "Chimes of Arcady," was based on a 1930s original by the Frank Luther Trio and was followed by "Buzzin'," which the girls promoted on the BBC's hugely popular *Six-Five Special* music show, launched only a year earlier. After "Buzzin'" the Lana Sisters recorded "Tell Him No," which sold poorly despite their appearance on the BBC's *Drumbeat*. The group also recorded "Seven Little Girls (Sitting in the Back Seat)." Other songs followed, including "You've Got What It Takes," which had a more Latin tempo, "Someone Loves You, Joe" and "Two-Some," but none quite made it. "We got a couple of near hits," Chantelle says, "'I Want That Boy' and 'Seven Little Girls (Sitting in the Back Seat)'—we were just beaten by the Mudlarks on that."

Mary's mother Kay took an active interest in the group and

the music they sang. Every night, at about 2 a.m., Kay rang Riss Chantelle and woke her up to talk about the latest American record that she'd heard on the radio, or some such matter. One night Chantelle fell headlong down the stairs trying to get to the phone. "Are you all right, Riss?" Kay asked her. "Not really, Mrs O'Brien, I've just fallen down the stairs and I think I've hurt myself," Chantelle told her. "Oh dear," Kay said, and then proceeded to discuss the latest record. After that Chantelle had a phone line installed in her bedroom.

Although she liked the O'Briens very much, Chantelle often marvelled at the difference between Mary's family and her own more conservative parents. When the two sets of parents sat together at the Nat King Cole show, Chantelle said to her mother afterwards, "They are unusual, the O'Briens, aren't they?" Chantelle's mother replied, "Yes, they are," and didn't say any more. "It must have been frightful," Chantelle says, "because my mother was so conservative."

Chantelle also remembers Kay O'Brien telling her how she sat down and played the piano for a visiting plumber. "I said—'But Kay, you can't play the piano.'" Chantelle shuddered at the strange thought of Kay thundering away, while the plumber listened, bewildered, to some tuneless cacophony. Chantelle said, "Please don't tell me you played to him like that!" Kay said, "I did, and he listened."

Later, Chantelle would often pop around to help out, and she remembers Kay getting scolded for gambling with the little boy next door. "The next door neighbor said: 'You're not to play with my boy any more, because you're playing snakes and ladders, and taking his pocket money!'" Shocked, Chantelle asked Kay, "You're not gambling with that boy, are you?" Kay laughed and said, "Yes, he likes it!"

Despite her mother's interventions, joining the Lana Sisters was Dusty's first move to becoming more independent from her parents, and she would soon move out, never to return. Taking her first stage name, Shan, Mary O'Brien had become a professional performer, with a recording contract and TV appearances, in only a year. "She knew the studios, the touring, the ups and downs," Chantelle told Lucy O'Brien. "A lot of people think it's going to be easy, but she saw it as a job, like an accountant."

With such a cool-headed view, however, Mary could also see the limitations of the Lana Sisters, and she was restless to move on. By 1960 the Lana Sisters had become successful enough to be voted seventh Favorite British Vocal Group by *Melody Maker*, but Chantelle and Abrams were aware that their partner was disenchanted, and neither was terribly surprised when she announced that she was leaving to join another group—this one fronted by her brother.

Dusty later acknowledged that the Lana Sisters felt a little used and abused by her, but elucidated the pleasantly concealed ruthless streak that propelled her career: "I hated it when they implied that I was letting them down, but I had to move on. Sometimes you have to let people down in order to get on, particularly in show business." More plaintively, she added that such focus came at a cost: "I was only eighteen years old. My life was so busy, and in a way, so narrow."

3

THE SPRINGFIELDS

The line of young men with slicked-back hair and guitar cases waiting for their turn outside Quaglino's nightclub in St. James's was long, and Mike Hurst could see that at least one of the musicians was already a well-known guitarist for the singer Lonnie Donegan. The simply worded ad had advertised, "Wanted: Young Singer/Guitarist from well-established group," but in the face of such stiff competition there seemed little hope that Hurst, a nineteen-year-old earning four pounds ten shillings a week as a trainee insurance broker with Lloyd's of London, would get it. Fortunately for him, his mother had applied on his behalf. "My mother applied for the audition, without telling me. My mother was always in show business—and she didn't tell me because if they didn't reply, she didn't want me to be disappointed. Which I thought was incredibly sweet of her," Hurst says.

When his turn came, he nervously walked onto the small stage, and was blinded by the spotlight. "Are you going to sing us a song?" a voice eventually called out from the darkness. Hurst struck a sultry pose, strummed—and sang "A Mess of Blues." "Yeah, very good, very good," the voice said. "Can you sing any songs in a foreign language?" Nothing in the ad had mentioned foreign languages, but Hurst's grandfather was Italian and he thought he could remember a plaintive Neapolitan folk song. "Very good, you'll hear from us," the voice said at the end. Hurst breathed out, and heard a seat creak. For a brief moment a wisp of white-blonde hair shimmered across the edge of the spotlight. There was something about it that seemed familiar. Hurst thought, "I've seen her somewhere before."

A few days later the letter arrived, politely telling him he had been accepted into The Springfields—the number one group in Britain.

Hurst, whose real name was Mike Longhurst Pickworth, was taking the place of Tim Feild, the original band member who was leaving the group after two years. Now Dusty and Tom were looking for something different. It was February 1962. With the youthful John F. Kennedy still commanding the White House, the first rumblings of events that would define the decade were under way: in Memphis, the city council ordered the racial deseg-regation of lunch counters, while astronaut John Glenn orbited the earth, and the US military pondered how to respond to what they believed was a communist threat in Vietnam. Despite an unsuccessful recording session, back in Britain The Beatles were playing in Liverpool's Cavern Club—to much excitement. Sensing the shifting mood, Dusty and Tom hoped their new recruit would inject some much needed rock 'n' roll into their folksy formula that, while unique, was in danger of going stale. Tall, young and dark haired, Hurst could be the teenage heartthrob that girls seemed to be looking for. His arrival seemed fortuitous—almost immediately the group recorded their biggest ever hit, "Island of Dreams."

Picking Hurst was probably a joint decision, but one of Dusty's greatest strengths was the chameleon-like instinct that enabled her to sense changing times and public moods innately, and to harness those changes to strike out in a new direction, both in terms of her music and her look, even if that meant leaving people and established success behind. "I was a calculating bastard," she later said of herself—although "astute, determined and ambitious" would have been a more forgiving way of putting it.

It was that instinct that had led Dusty to leave the Lana Sisters and team up with her brother in the first place. After only one year as a professional, she knew that she had wrung all of the experience she would ever find useful from the all-girl trio, and that their syrupy 1950s persona was on the cusp of becoming outdated. When her brother arrived to see her one evening in the spring of 1960, his proposal offered a new world of opportunity.

The Lana Sisters were playing a week-long engagement in Taunton, Somerset, when Dion, as he then still was, came backstage to speak to Mary after a performance. He had been playing in a folk group with Tim Feild, an old Etonian singer and adventurer who had once taught Elizabeth Taylor's children to water-ski. The two men had met at the High Society club in London after Dion's regular partner fell ill, and Tim stood in. Despite some success in the clubs, both men realized they needed a charismatic female lead to go further.

Dion suggested Mary join him in a trio with Feild, but, despite seeing the immediate advantages and thinking "two men and a girl would make a novel group"—and one that would push her, as the only female, more into the limelight—she fretted about how she would break the news to the Lana Sisters. For the remainder of the week she secretly snuck away to practice in a field with Tim and her brother, while continuing to perform with Riss Chantelle and Lynne Abrams at night. It was torture, and she could hardly sing. As Chantelle admitted, Mary was always an "honest girl" who would never say things behind your back, "she'd always say them to your face." Nonetheless, things took an unpleasant turn when Chantelle spotted Dion in the foyer of the theater and asked him why he was there. Dion fudged, and Chantelle felt hurt that she had been deceived. She was equally nonplussed when later she discovered that The Springfields were ringing around trying to use all of her contacts.

The reality was that, however uncomfortable parting ways with the Lana Sisters would be, Mary's mind was made up—and she would later describe her fledgling week with Dion and Tim, practicing in that sunny field in Somerset, with a wistful nostalgia that conjured up all the hope, enthusiasm and innocence she had once possessed. "We'd had such fun being The Springfields," she said, "ever since that idyllic sunny day when it all began." She rarely expressed such sentiments about any other point in her career.

That field in spring may have inspired the group's name, but it is just as likely that they named themselves after the many cities and towns called Springfield in the US—which was the fulcrum of music as far as the O'Brien siblings were concerned, and an important force in influencing their sound. Dion and Mary were also heavily influenced by world music, using guitars, piano and conga drums to craft a unique sound that melded folk, pop, and country and western with some of the Latin American rhythms that Dion had loved from an early age. They were definitely not a pop group, but Dusty considered The Springfields not serious enough to be a true folk band either. Nonetheless, she admitted they "very much admired" the Weavers, the famous US folk group with Pete Seeger that was undergoing a renaissance during the folk revival of the 1950s—and The Springfields were indeed to cover many of the same songs.

Despite, or perhaps because of, what Dusty considered a lack of serious folk credentials, The Springfields' fresh sound made them almost immediately appealing in the space that opened up in British music and light entertainment in 1961, with a crossover appeal that extended well beyond a folk audience. The later part of the 1950s had seen an incredible turnover of musical styles and genres as the growing generation of teenagers fueled a rise in record-buying and popular music, competing directly with the easy-listening, big-band based style still in favor with older generations. The Springfields filled a gap somewhere between the end of the first wave of American-inspired rock 'n' roll and the rise of The Beatles and the Rolling Stones. "The Springfields happened at the right time," Dusty said (*Rolling Stone* 1973). "We were an extraordinary mixture of pseudo-country, folk . . . indescribable, I would put it. There were two guitars and me, in the middle, trying to find room to move my arms. I felt like I was directing traffic."

With their folk harmonies, cultivated American twang and new names—Dion became Tom and Mary became Dusty— the Springfields practiced intensively and were soon ready for their first engagements. But like many other issues in her life, how Dusty became Dusty was never entirely clear. Sometimes she said it was because she had sold dustbins (trash cans) in a department store, other times she said it was a childhood nickname relating to her red hair, or because she was always a tomboy covered in dust. Perhaps weary of the discussion, she later admitted, "I'm still looking for the bugger who gave me that name." Whatever its origin, somehow the name suited her unspoiled, girl-next-door charm.

"She was so *natural*," her secretary and friend Pat Barnett remembered. She felt—as many people did—overwhelmingly protective towards Dusty from the first moment they met in a small office off Bond Street. Pat Barnett began her career working with scriptwriters like Frank Muir and Dennis Norden for the literary agent Kavanaghs, "And I dealt with people like Spike Milligan who used to come up behind me, I'd be typing a whole load of figure work and he'd hammer on the keys and the whole thing would be gone," she says. By 1960 she had moved on and was running the office for entertainment agent Emlyn Griffiths. "He was like a Peter Sellers character," Mike Hurst remembers. "He was actually called Captain Emlyn Griffiths and he wore a monocle! And he was about six foot three—large, wonderful grey-white military moustache—and he was the manager. He stuttered: perfect."

One day The Springfields appeared in the office. "I heard this noise, lots of chattering and clumping on the stairs one day, and then suddenly the room was full up. Tim and Tom and Dusty burst in," Barnett remembers. "Dusty said, 'Is Mr Griffiths in?' I said, 'Yes . . . I think he's on the phone.'" Griffiths was in and, as Barnett knew, asleep in his office after meeting clients at Quaglino's and downing a few pink gins. Barnett's usual tactic was to wake him either by calling him on the phone or by knocking loudly on his door. "I bet he's been down to Quag's and he's passed out," Dusty said, hammering loudly on his door and shouting, "Griff! Griff!"

Barnett had never heard of The Springfields, but she thought they were a nice group—polite and very well spoken—and she was struck by Dusty's bright enthusiasm, but also something else: "I thought she was very vulnerable," Barnett says. "There are a lot of sharks in show business, and somehow I wanted to protect her from them."

Under the auspices of Emlyn Griffiths, The Springfields were immediately booked for sixteen weeks of touring Butlin's holiday camps in a cramped VW camper van. For this they were paid fifty-five pounds a week between them, minus expenses and agent's commission.

In 1960 the popularity of Butlin's holiday camps was at its height. Founded by Billy Butlin in 1936, each of the ten camps provided a range of activities and family entertainment, all within the single cost of the holiday. It was still an era when most Britons vacationed at home, enjoying the austere pleasures that a week in a Butlin's chalet in rainy Clacton could bring—and considered it a good deal better than a vacation in a seaside boarding house where they'd be locked out of their lodgings after breakfast. A photo taken at the Butlin's Ocean Hotel in Saltdean, Brighton, shows Dusty, still with auburn hair and looking much as she did in the Lana Sisters, laughing and having a drink with Tom, Tim and Redcoat Carol Lupton. Dusty reportedly spent most of her weekly wages playing cards, and exploring other activities away from her parents—later telling friends that she'd lost her virginity at a Butlin's camp during that tour.

Touring Britain in the early 1960s had little rock star allure: "There weren't any motorways, nothing was open after the show. It wasn't that much fun to tell you the truth," Dusty told *Mojo* in the mid-1990s. Traveling over 1,200 miles the length and breadth of the country in a camper van with two men was a challenge, even if one of them was your brother. Tim Feild told a reporter to try traveling the same distance in similar conditions with his dearest friend, "and see if that person is still a dear friend at the end of it." He recalled that Tom and Dusty would often grate on each other's nerves—and lash out whenever differences over musical style arose. Yet both were also more willing to accept the simple food, and night after night in grim lodgings, that life on the road entailed: "On a journey they were quite happy to pull into a transport café for a plate of steak and kidney pudding," Feild said, admitting that he preferred something "more elaborate." Feild was also riled at being made to carry Dusty's ornate dresses and costumes, which "required at least fourteen stiff petticoats" and were wrapped up for transport in an enormous triangular tent-like construction—calling her a "grande dame" who marched on ahead imperiously while he struggled behind.

Dusty retaliated that, although this was true, she had spent many afternoons sitting on station platforms "guarding the guitars . . . while the boys went and had sandwiches in the buffet." After a show, the group usually emerged into a dreary English evening in a provincial town where all the cafés and restaurants were shut up tight, and they would return to a shabby guesthouse where, as the "girl," Dusty would have a single room with a three-bar electric fire, but would be forced to share a bathroom with numerous other people on the same floor. Out of the spotlight, life was far from glamorous, but they were young and the group's growing popularity made such inconveniences easier to bear.

Following the summer season at Butlin's, The Springfields began a nineteen-week run at the Churchill Club in Mayfair, an exhausting season that saw them finishing in the early hours of the morning and catching the night bus back to Ealing, before walking the long final stretch home. London's clubland famously brought "high society" into contact with the organized crime gangs who ruled the West End and Soho, and Dusty remembered a depressing twilight world where weary hostesses sat backstage every night smoking and waiting to be called to one of the tables for some paid conversation with a "lonely" but wealthy gentleman. The Churchill Club had originally been set up by Bruce Brace, Harry Meadows and south London gangster Billy Howard. When Meadows took sole control of the club Brace and Howard set up a competing hostess club across the street called Winston's, so named to wind Meadows up.

Life in the London clubs was as far from the family-friendly ambience of Butlins as could be imagined. One hostess, Lisa Prescott, remembered a terrifying incident when she was taken to a flat in Barking in December 1966 to have paid sex with a gangster called Frank Mitchell, who was associated with the Kray twins. On Christmas Eve, Mitchell was taken to a van outside the flat and shot by the Krays, who thought it was an easier solution than trying to control him—and Prescott was told to go back to hostessing and forget she'd ever met him. Later she often found herself under duress to have sex with the man who'd killed Mitchell, and who she believed wanted to kill her too. Dusty's experience in hostess clubs stood her in good stead later in her career when she sang the theme song for the film *Scandal*: Christine Keeler worked nearby as a hostess in Murray's Cabaret Club.

After the Churchill, The Springfields moved on to a succession of bookings at variety halls, playing to half-empty houses alongside magicians, second-rate Spanish dancers and a female fire eater. Having been exposed to the seediness of the clubs, Dusty was now having her eyes opened to life on the margins of show business, getting ready in a dressing room packed with the frayed tempers and jealousies of entertainers who were eking out a living, but would never really make it. Unlike most of the people she was coming into contact with, however, Dusty and The Springfields were on their way up. Word of their growing popularity had spread and in April 1961 producer Johnny Franz invited them in for an informal audition at Philips Records. Franz, a Cockney with a pencil moustache, had joined Philips in 1954 as head of A&R (Artists and Repertoire) after working as a pianist for, amongst others, singer Anne Shelton. Famously, he had perfect pitch and could look up from a crossword, or anything else he happened to be doing, and name any note that had just been played. He was also a notoriously good talent spotter (when an unknown Shirley Bassey performed for him he immediately said, "Yes, good singer.")

That day The Springfields sat on the edge of his desk and sang a playful version of "Dear John"—a reworking of the American Civil War song "Marching through Georgia." "It was a new sound. A fresh sound," Franz told *NME* in 1966. "I signed them on the spot." The love life of soldier John Maguire was soon recorded at Philips' Stanhope Place studios by The Springfields, who were, according to their promotional material, "Britain's most popular new singing group." Released the same month, the song failed to make it into the charts but was noticed by radio DJs and critics, who enjoyed it but puzzled over whether the sound was pop or folk. More importantly the recording brought together the formidable combination of Franz and Ivor Raymonde, a former jazz and classical pianist who had also been musical director for Wally Stott at the BBC before joining Philips. Franz oversaw contracts, booked and produced sessions and added his critical thoughts on the product while Raymonde managed the musical direction.

By Dusty's definition, much of what The Springfields produced was "incredibly fast, incredibly jolly, and often out of tune," but their enthusiasm and clean-cut looks would take them far. In July 1961 their second single, the jaunty "Breakaway," made it into the top forty for an eight-week run. The song was the first hit for Tom Springfield as a writer, one critic describing it as "brisk and energetic with an easy to follow tune."

"Bambino," The Springfields' third single, was an old Italian carol ("Tu scendi della stella"), inspired by their summer holiday in Italy that year and with new words written by Tom. Dusty said, "An Italian friend introduced us to the song and we fell for it the first time we heard it." She added that although the song had originally been in waltz time, "the melody hasn't been altered at all, it's far too nice to be tampered with." Released in time for Christmas, "Bambino" shot up to number sixteen in the charts and stayed there for three months. That summer the group also recorded a series of Christmas songs, including "Jingle Bells," which weren't released in the UK until Christmas 1963.

Three cheerful hits—"It was terribly important to be cheerful,"

Dusty said—guaranteed The Springfields maximum exposure and a series of mainstream TV appearances on *Thank Your Lucky Stars* and *The Benny Hill Show* as well as on radio music shows like Saturday night's *Parade of the Pops* and *Easy Beat* on a Sunday afternoon. By the end of 1961, the trio had surged into the public consciousness enough to win *Melody Maker*'s Top Vocal-Instrumental Group, and had been voted Best Vocal Group in *NME*'s end-of-year popularity poll.

Tom expressed amazement at the result, and said that since they'd heard the news "our feet haven't touched the ground." But in truth, the group's charisma owed much to Dusty's stagecraft and years of pop apprenticeship. Her awareness of how to appear, both on stage and television, now extended to dying her auburn hair platinum blond: On black and white television, "My natural red came out black and I looked as if I was wearing a giant busby [the tall, full-dress fur hat worn by British soldiers]!" she said. Reflecting on the TV appearances, she remembered that she was already impatient with the rushed and harried nature of the shows that left her struggling to remember the lyrics to songs—and were far from the perfection she always sought.

After their Christmas hit, The Springfields recorded their fourth song, "Goodnight Irene," which was released on January 23, 1962. Despite the fact that the song had been a number one hit for the Weavers in 1950, attempts to turn it into a more pop-oriented tune led to a sound more akin to a "back street market in Cairo," according to one review. Proving that the folk-pop mixture did not always work, the record did not do well—nor did the Springfields' first album, *Kinda Folksy*, which was released the following month. The album mixed folk songs such as "The Green Leaves of Summer"—one of the best tracks on the album according to author and Dusty fan Paul Howes—with the Latin-influenced "Tzena Tzena Tzena," a music hall rendition of "Row, Row, Row" and popular numbers including "The Black Hills of Dakota," which Dusty infused with a "lusty enthusiasm."

"The Black Hills of Dakota" symbolized the country and western direction the group often veered towards, despite their protestations to the contrary. In April 1962 they were to secure their US breakthrough with "Silver Threads and Golden Needles," a song that flopped in the UK but reached number twenty in the US charts and number two in Australia. Dusty always she said she preferred "Silver Threads" to other Springfields hits, including "Island of Dreams" but, at the time, Tom was quick to point out, "the trouble is that Americans now want us to go over there and cut a country and western album and we're not too keen on this. You see 'Silver Threads' is a C&W number but we don't want to become labeled as a C&W group." Hearing their twanging harmonies, US audiences were completely unaware, at first, that The Springfields were British.

The eminent Nashville producer Shelby Singleton heard the record and immediately invited the group over to record an album. Tom admitted that US offers were now "coming in like a whirlwind," and that it was surprising how much an American hit "can set the wheels turning." Before that could happen, though, The Spring-fields had a series of engagements at home to fulfil and—in a sign of things to come—Dusty's voice collapsed due to the strain, leading the first hospitalization of her career. The collapse, she said, was due to trying to force her song into the unnatural style of the group. "Seems like I do everything all wrong when it comes to singing. Experts have told me that I'm straining this and fracturing that . . ."

In the summer of 1962 the group was fracturing too, with increased arguments about musical direction and personal problems leading Tim Feild to announce that he was leaving. "We'd row over this, row over how a song should be sung, what engagements should be accepted . . . finally I decided to chuck it all in." His final outing would be on "Swahili Papa," a novelty record complete with war whoops that Dusty recorded, but loathed. The record bombed, and Feild made his exit, performing his last set with the group at the Coventry Theatre on December 1.

Feild had contributed much to the success of the group, and Dusty always credited him for his formative work. His replacement, Mike Hurst, was still wet behind the ears, but about to innocently embark with The Springfields upon a period of phenomenal success that would see them become one of the top groups in Britain. "I know why they picked me," Hurst says.

> They'd come up through that cabaret circuit, and they wanted someone who could play guitar as well as sing, with a more "rock" attitude and a proper 1960s attitude. Which, of course, I had. They dressed me up in the same suit which I detested. God I hated it! Beige, who wears a beige suit?! I really hated it. And the awful tie and everything—oh God! They wanted me for the younger girls in the audience and someone who looked a bit more like a Beatle. That was it, that's what I was there for.

Soon Hurst was rehearsing every day, putting in long hours and piecing together how Dusty and Tom worked: "I could see that she was the creative force and he was principally the business force, even though he wrote the songs . . ." In rehearsals, Tom took charge musically. "When you are doing three-part harmonies you have to get your harmony locked into your brain like the melody line of that song—for you, that's the melody, but it's not, it's your harmony. Tom was very exact, and very good with harmonies, and that taught me a lot."

In two years, Hurst noted, the group had already become a smooth professional act. "We used to rehearse in front of a wall of mirrors, so we could see how we looked, and I thought that was ridiculously funny: having to smile at the right time. Tom and Dusty were very big on smiling to convince the audience that they are there to have a great time."

While Dusty told Tom whether she liked his song choices or not, the atmosphere was professional:

> *It was very business-like. It wasn't "I've been doing this too long now. It's been at least an hour, I must have a break and go and get a drink." No, we went on and on and on. It's work and you've got to get it right. And we did—we were a polished act. Of course, we were old-fashioned now you look back at it. A lot of people's criticism today would be that it was a bit cabaret, and it was a bit.*

4

SOMETHING ABOUT LOVE

"I know . . . something . . . about love" came blaring out from the speakers outside the Colony Music Store in Times Square and Dusty was gripped. It was a freezing night in December 1962, and Dusty was shaken awake to the possibilities of what she could, and should, be doing. It was "the attack" of the song, a one-hit wonder called "Tell Him" by The Exciters, that seized her. The way it "sort of got you by the throat . . . out of the blue comes blasting at you" made her realize, "That's what I wanna do." And this to her, "a little white convent-educated Irish teenager," was an amazing thing.

Dusty was where she had always wanted to be: in America. For days she ran around New York City, marvelling at the hotel and the bright red wall-to-wall carpeting, staying up all night eating shortcake in Broadway diners, catching Earl Scruggs play bluegrass at Carnegie Hall, and then waking up early to watch Shari Lewis and Lambchop on color television.

"They put us in this hotel that no longer exists called the Americana, which was a new build," says Mike Hurst.

Every floor was named after one of the states, so we are talking fifty storeys. We were staying in Wisconsin. You could have heard the shouts from each room. The first thing I did when I went into my room was look at the menu by the bed—room service—bloody hell! What's room service? I didn't know a thing about it. Unbelievable! You could get this food twenty-four hours a day and they'd send it up. We called down: "We'd like a cheeseburger." They'd say, "What's that?" We'd say, "We'd like a cheeseburger." Then they'd say, "How do you spell it?"

Beyond the Fringe, with Peter Cook and Dudley Moore, was playing on Broadway, and Dusty, Mike and Tom went along. Hurst says, "I knew Peter Cook, and we went to their dressing room after the show. You could see how everyone had absorbed American culture—they were watching television in their dressing room. We couldn't believe it. Television in their dressing room! It was wonderful. The British invasion was a lot of fun."

A first for any British vocal group, The Springfields were on their way to Nashville to record a country and western album—but it was not the soulful, black-influenced music Dusty loved. If The Exciters shocked her into hearing how it could be done, it was hearing Dionne Warwick singing "Don't Make Me Over" on the radio in Nashville that really took the wind out of her sails. The Exciters were part of the Uptown sound—a New York version of what black R&B musicians played in the South, but more urgent and less masculine. The Uptown sound was largely crafted in the Brill Building near Times Square, where the writers of "Don't Make Me Over," Burt Bacharach and Hal David, were also hammering away every day in another small smoky room. Dusty had yet to visit the Brill Building, which housed many of the songwriters who would play such an important part in her career—including Carole King and Gerry Goffin, and Barry Mann and Cynthia Weill. All she heard was how far she had come from her days with the Lana Sisters, but how far she still had to go.

There was ice on the wings as Dusty peered out of the plane window on the tarmac in New York and waited to take off for Tennessee. The Springfields had left London in the grip of a terrible smog, while New York had dipped into an unusually somber cold snap, the sense of wintry silence aided by a city-wide newspaper strike that was to last for 114 days.

Landing in Nashville, Dusty, Tom and Mike were ushered in to meet the great Shelby Singleton, who looked like an archetypal country and western producer with his black hair oiled back in a quiff, and a cigarillo between his lips. "He had those great suits, smoked Nat Sherman cigarillos, little brown cigarettes," says Brooks Arthur, who worked as a sound engineer with Singleton, and later as Dusty's producer. "He was a vision of sartorial splendor, that's all I can say, and he really knew how to dress. He had his style, he was Shelby S. Singleton, man. I guess S was for style!"

Born in Texas, Singleton had cut his teeth working on hugely popular radio shows like *Louisiana Hayride* in the 1950s, and was now the creative lead at Mercury. Never a musician himself, Singleton had the "ears of a record buyer" according to his friend, and successor at Mercury, Jerry Kennedy. In 1962 he had turned "Chantilly Lace" and "Hey, Paula" into stratospheric hits, and was then to be responsible for resurrecting the careers of Jerry Lee Lewis and Roger Miller, before buying Sun Records in 1969 and marketing Elvis's back catalog. He was also well known for his open-mindedness about race, using black and white musicians in recording sessions long before it was common practice in the South, and putting up black musicians at his own home when local motels wouldn't accept them.

Meeting the Springfields for the first time, Mike Hurst recalls, he enthused to the group about how much he loved their music, and told them he had some great songs for them to record.

> *Shelby Singleton threw all these songs at us and said, "These are the songs you've got to do." And then Tom said, "I write all the songs." Singleton puffed his cigar and flicked off a column of ash and said, "Not any more." I knew why he wanted us to do these songs—and they weren't great, some of them were really old corny country hick standards like "Wabash Cannonball." He wanted us to do them because he didn't think we were worth any more than that. They all thought when "Silver Threads" hit the top ten in the States that we were Americans. The public thought we were Americans. When they discovered we were British, they were really upset.*

Despite the disappointment, Hurst remembers his sense of wonder at being in America for the first time, and in the South where people cruised the freeways in enormous gas guzzlers and went shooting in the woods.

> *In the hotel in Nashville this man accosted me and it was Sheb Wooley, who was in the TV series Rawhide with Clint Eastwood. He fancied Dusty, and he came to me, thinking I was the way in, buttering me up saying things like "Do you want to see my gun?" I said, "Yeah!" So he pulls the suitcase out and brings out the gun and asks, "Would y'all like to try it? It's not loaded." So I took this gun, was pulling the trigger; popped it about three or four times and on the fourth time it fired—he had a bullet in the chamber. In the*

hotel room. Straight out of the window. We laughed and
laughed. I said, "The police will be here any minute." He
said, "Are you kidding? The police don't give a damn."

While Hurst enjoyed himself, however, Dusty and Tom remained aloof. When Shelby Singleton invited them to his home for dinner Hurst readily agreed, thinking it was good for business if nothing else. Tom and Dusty declined. "Shelby invited us all to his home. They wouldn't come, but I went. His wife was a country singer—and his kids were fairly objectionable. But, they had this television set that was color! I said, 'Where did you get this?' It was incredible to me. I was quite happy doing those social things but they never wanted to." Tom and Dusty also hated their American tour manager: "They hated Shelly Turk. Shelly was [imitates] 'Up up up! Gotta get outta here, bus is late!'—a bit like being in the army. It was very funny, they hated him. They really hated him. I didn't, he was all right."

In truth, they all had mixed feelings about the trip, which concluded with a short promotional tour around a few states. "We went on a road trip, a small tour of Ohio, Kentucky, and other places in Tennessee, ending up in Maryland and Washington doing dreadful television shows," Hurst remembers. "It was the pits. So bad—American TV was appalling! It was so child-like. I don't want to sing a song with this clockwork toy jumping up and down in the background. It was weird." In addition to the tour, Tom said that they'd acted like characters out of *The Beverly Hillbillies*. But Hurst at least came away with some positive memories:

In Nashville I met people from my dreams. We had
Bill Black playing bass. Bill Black, Elvis's bass player! Bill
Black taught Elvis how to do karate. He was a madman.
As a bass player, though, this guy had almost another set of

*knuckles because they spent their time punching their fists
into buckets of gravel to harden up their hands. In the two
or three weeks we were there Bill Black was teaching me
karate. And we had Jerry Reid on guitar—and Johnny Cash!*

Meanwhile, Dusty had displayed the nerves and insecurities around working with other musicians that would plague her next trip to the South, to record the *Dusty in Memphis* album in 1968. Feeling out of her depth, she said, "It was a disastrous experience for us. They didn't realize it took three weeks for us to rehearse one verse (at home). In Nashville they'd write a song in the morning and we'd record it in the afternoon!" Dusty was struck dumb with laryngitis, fretting that "here we are in Tennessee singing country music that the people here were born to . . ." Not "being born" to country music hadn't stopped "Silver Threads" selling more than a million copies in the US, but often it seemed that little could offset Dusty's deep sense of inadequacy, however unfounded.

For a session she had described in such unpromising terms, The Springfields recorded nineteen tracks, with Tom delighted to see veteran musicians, and elderly lady fiddle players, clapping along enthusiastically to their work. Nor did Shelby Singleton doubt the potential of the group he had liked so much upon first hearing, nor that the star was Dusty: "I thought she had the most unusual sound of the three," he told Lucy O'Brien in the late 1980s. "She was doing country and western, which was something she didn't want to do. She had become more 'black' with her voice, and she felt restricted within the group."

When released in April 1963, the album cover for *Folk Songs from the Hills* showed Dusty wearing a tartan dress perched on a hay bale, while Tom and Mike strummed a banjo and a guitar behind her. It was neither the look nor sound she coveted, and Dusty did indeed feel frustrated. She was becoming a star, but through recording the kind of easy-listening, country-style songs that she knew were going to be left long behind by the transformation of music in the 1960s. Producer Brooks Arthur, who worked with Dusty later in the 1960s and 1970s, claims, however, that although the album was country, it was more than competitive with other sounds of the times:

> They did have an arranger named Jerry Kennedy on those dates and he's country. It doesn't get much more country than Jerry Kennedy, so it had that kind of a vibe—but it sounded pretty competitive '60s and rock 'n' roll. It was bigger arrangements than what might have been needed, but I can see why she might have not been happy.

The revolution in '60s music was yet to unfold, but its first strains could be sensed. At the same time as the group were wandering wide-eyed through the streets of New York, Bob Dylan was down in Greenwich Village recording five songs for the *Freewheelin' Bob Dylan* album, while the top spot in the US chart was about to be seized for the first time ever by a British record—"Telstar," an instrumental smash by The Tornados. Nevertheless, it was a life-changing experience for Dusty. Pausing to complain at the time that the trip had "channeled us into doing country and western music without us knowing it," she also had to admit, "It changed everything for us." She had visited the Mecca of music and the country she had dreamed about for her entire life. She returned inspired by the sounds of black America, shaken by its energy, and more convinced than ever that she could produce a different sound. Later, her life and work would bring her back full circle to Nashville, and she would reflect on that first trip, pondering that if she had stayed, "I'd either have become incredibly rich, or I'd have blown my brains out."

Back home, The Springfields' absence had meant that their latest single, "Island of Dreams," had sunk down the charts. They had recorded the song in October, and Mike Hurst had made his first appearance with the group singing it on *Thank Your Lucky Stars* on November 24. Arriving back in England a day before Christmas they embarked on a new round of publicity, which sent the record, based on an old Irish melody sung with an American lilt, rocketing back up the charts to become their biggest hit. It helped that they performed it nightly around the country on tour with Del Shannon, part of a show that included other performers who would be important to both Dusty and Tom, including American dancer Pepe Borza and British singer Kenny Lynch.

It was always galling to Dusty that she sang "Island of Dreams" flat: "I wince every time I hear it," she said. "I had a sore throat when we recorded it and I knew that I sang out of tune." The group recorded take after take, finally settling on releasing take nine, she remembered: "We were about to give up and send everyone home when we decided 'one more time.' We were really too tired and the finished result meant that we were singing flat all the way through," Dusty told *NME*. With no disrespect to the many people who bought the single, she later added, "I never liked it at all."

Flat notes aside, Dusty's voice soared through "Silver Threads" and "Island of Dreams," adding an unmistakable poignancy and class to songs that now sound dated. The Springfields continued with their folk/country/Latin recordings but, even breaking away in only one line of a song, Dusty had demonstrated that she was heading in a different direction.

As Tom noted at the time, "Island of Dreams" expressed a wish to escape that he and Dusty shared. "We always wanted to get away," he said, "I wanted to go to Brazil, Dusty always wanted to go to Hollywood." They were both restless souls, Dusty later admitted, saying that their family motto was "There's always another motel down the road." So far the road had not taken her to Hollywood, but she had got as far as New York, and was adopting a sleeker, sexier, more show-business persona. The layers of stiff petticoats and neat blouses were replaced by form-fitting sheath dresses, while Dusty's hair got longer, blonder and more teased. In some recordings she appeared wearing sunglasses.

In all respects, Dusty was growing up. She had left home for good, moving into a flat in Baker Street owned by a Scottish couple above an ABC bakery, and she now embarked upon her first love affairs. "It was a man that hurt her badly, really badly," Pat Barnett says. "When she was very impressionable, right at the start of her career. We always used to tell people it was an Italian that hurt her; it wasn't an Italian, unfortunately he was an Englishman, and he's still alive now. I often wonder, did that . . . make her think 'I wonder if being with a woman is better?' Because she certainly didn't want to know men after that for a while."

A life in entertainment, and touring on the road, had already given Dusty exposure to gay men and women—to a far greater extent than the population at large at the time. By 1963 she knew that, as she quaintly put it, she was "as capable of being swayed by a girl as a boy." In truth, however, she was almost exclusively swayed by girls, and almost never by boys, but such feelings caused her far more anguish than that carefree-sounding admission revealed.

As a committed and practicing Roman Catholic, Dusty regularly stopped the tour van to go to confession when she was on the road, and scouted out the local Catholic church in every town she performed in. Maintaining the persona of a good ex-convent girl, she wrote for the school newsletter about her experiences in show business, reporting that "an average day begins at about 8 a.m., with a hairdressing appointment (I am writing this at the hairdresser's). After this probably a press interview, a hasty snack lunch and then afternoon rehearsal and recording session." Life in the industry was enjoyable, but "entails much hard work," she added. In 1964, the newspapers were delighted when she returned to open the school fete at St. Anne's in Ealing, printing a big picture entitled "Dusty and her swinging nuns."

Yet Dusty knew that she was also committing a grave sin in the eyes of her religion. She was never to come to terms with the unhappiness of her childhood, and the self-loathing that she later said her father had instilled in her. Now her growing attraction to women added to the guilt and self-hatred. According to her friend and former musical director Doug Reece of The Echoes, "the Catholic Church has a lot to answer for" in causing Dusty's struggles with herself.

The shame over her sexuality went deeper. Lesbians in the 1950s and 1960s faced utter rejection by a society that emphasized femininity at all costs. Women were encouraged to wear makeup, corsets and high heels for their men. Any work they undertook was menial and badly paid, and should be given up as soon as possible in favor of family life. Above all, women must marry, and marry young, to avoid a life on the shelf. Four fifths did so before the age of twenty-five. Somewhere in the shadows in this oppressively sunny view of family life, there were lesbians—usually presented as manly creatures, ridiculed and scorned for their secret perverted desires and sad lonely lives. The 1950s were the "worst time ever to be a lesbian," according to American activist Lillian Faderman. With no information available through the media, girls who suspected that they might be attracted to women gleaned slivers of information through novels like Ann Bannon's *Odd Girl Out* in which two sorority sisters at a US college fall in love and run away to Greenwich Village, or films like *The Children's Hour*, released in 1961, in which Shirley MacLaine and Audrey

Hepburn share a passionate, but doomed, friendship. With no opportunity to be open about their lives, gay women employed "deeply ambiguous concepts, such as the "career woman" or the 'bachelor girl' to simultaneously indicate and mask a lesbian identity," writes Rebecca Jennings in *Tomboys and Bachelor Girls: A Lesbian History of Post-War Britain*. Sometimes these categories allowed women to "partially pass," and remain 'respectable' in society while exploring their own desires. It was a tactic that served Dusty well through the 1960s, but one she grew tired of.

A worse fate was perhaps only to be had by gay men, who were often sent to prison for acting upon their feelings. Although the Wolfenden Report of 1957 had suggested decriminalizing sex between men, it was not implemented for another decade, during which time arrests and persecution of gay men increased. For either a man or women to be gay was considered at best a pitiable affliction, and possibly an actual mental illness (one that was still treated with "aversion therapy," including electric shocks and hypnotherapy by psychiatrists).

No wonder such a life made Dusty feel uneasy and tormented. Her ultra-femininity—her carefully applied mask of make-up—disguised the fear that someone would discover her terrible secret, and accuse her of really being a "big, butch woman," as she put it when she first discussed the subject several years later. Unless it was explicitly spelled out, such a revelation rarely crossed anyone's mind in the early days of her career. The vast majority of her fans would have been astonished to discover that Dusty preferred women, although she had taken it light-heartedly when her brother and Tim Feild shouted out "Dusty's a lesbian! . . . Dusty's a lesbian!" to surprised fans waiting outside for an autograph one night after a show.

Mike Hurst himself had no idea that the woman he was rehearsing and touring with every day might be gay.

I was as red blooded as any nineteen-year-old male, and although I didn't absolutely fancy Dusty, there were times when you are thrown together and you think "Oh—hey!" There was a sort of vague attempt on both our parts which came to nothing. I thought about that originally as "Oh, she obviously doesn't have anything for me, so what the hell!" and that's that. But of course that was part of the reason— perhaps the whole reason. She wished, I know she did, that she was straight. She really did.

With a shrug, Hurst also remembers that, to his dismay, a trail of good-looking girls always seemed to be heading towards Dusty's dressing room rather than his own. "All this time she used to have girls coming to her dressing room—nothing wrong with that—but I mean normally it's the girls coming to the guys' dressing room, but she always had one in every place we went to, it seemed to me, always one."

It was only after The Springfields had broken up, however, that Hurst heard about Dusty.

I went into the kitchen at my mother's house one morning to make a cup of tea and there was a plumber under the sink unblocking the pipe. He said, "Hey, aren't you one of them Springfields?" I said I was. Then he told me that he was also Dusty's plumber and said, "She's a rum old bird, that Dusty." I didn't have a clue what he was talking about, but he said, "I done her pipes . . . and you know . . . you know! . . . Her and that bird . . ." and then he mentioned a woman singer I knew she was close to. I said, "What are you talking about?" He said, "Oh come on, son, come on!" It dawned on me. I was stunned.

Peter Miles also remembered discovering Dusty was gay at about this time. Tom had paid for Kay and OB to move to a house near Richmond-upon-Thames, in south-west London. One afternoon Miles rang and spoke to Dusty and arranged to come over, but when he arrived he discovered that Tom and the O'Briens were out. "We sat in the living room and she asked me how I was." Then she got distracted and went back into the kitchen. "She was giggling and laughing" back there with a woman who was obviously her girlfriend, according to Miles, who sat alone for some time before realizing that Dusty had completely forgotten he was there.

At the time when they worked together, Mike Hurst's feelings were also of exclusion, and of being politely shut out of something he didn't understand.

> *I think that clique—it is a clique—the clique all working together with their private jokes and this, that and the other—I sort of find that unhealthy. I don't like that. If you are not in the club, you are really out, you know? They made that perfectly clear—they made that perfectly clear to me in 1964 actually. Because I didn't belong to the club. I just think that's terribly unfortunate.*

He recalls going to a party that Tom and Dusty were throwing in a suite at the Mayfair Hotel. Newly rich with his earnings from The Springfields, Hurst pulled up outside in his convertible E-type Jaguar. Inside he found lots of people throwing food around. In the bathroom people were hurling chocolate at Pepe Borza, who was shrieking and laughing in the shower in his underpants.

> *I thought, "It's not right!" I didn't like this at all, I didn't understand. But everyone was taking photographs of him*

53

covered in chocolate so I thought, "No, no, this is not for me." So I made my very brief excuses and I left. Anyway I got downstairs and my car was covered in chocolate cake—they had thrown the stuff out of the window, and they were up there about five stories up, laughing their heads off. I thought to myself at the time, "You stupid little buggers."

Dusty had inherited her food-throwing habit from her mother, and it emerged in the early days, usually in the form of one her notorious pranks, and then later in temper.

Usually quiet and diffident, often pausing mid-sentence with an uncertain catch in her voice, Dusty could also be temperamental. At first, this manifested itself in heated arguments with Tom over song arrangements, with Tim Feild eventually smoothing over differences and suggesting the band tried it both ways. As she grew in confidence, however, Dusty spoke and acted out more often, especially when she thought people were foolish or wrong. "She didn't suffer other people gladly. You know, someone changing the time to go on stage. She would do things that really left you in so much difficulty," Mike Hurst remembers.

Driving up to the De Montfort Hall in Leicester on one occasion, Hurst recalls, Dusty discovered that the Lana Sisters were on the same bill, and was seething, rather irrationally, that the Lana Sisters were taking part. At that time she and Riss Chantelle had fallen out, although later they would be reconciled and become very good friends again.

We got to the theater, and Dusty said to the stage manager, "Have you got a boy who could run an errand for us?" So a lad came up and she said to him, "Could you go to Woolies and buy two sets of the cheapest crockery you can find?" The kid came back with two boxes and that's when I realized how weird all that was. She liked the sound of breaking crockery. She used to just throw them down the concrete stairwell. Just to hear the smash.

Dusty had already introduced Hurst to her penchant for throwing plates the first time they performed together in Weymouth. Now, enraged by the Lana Sisters, Dusty sent out for crockery again: "What had annoyed her and Tom, and to a lesser extent me, is that the Lana Sisters had done their run-through first, and were apparently singing the song 'Scarlet Ribbons'—which was one of ours. So, because they had got in there first, we had to adjust our running order. Dusty really didn't like this," Hurst adds. "She swore they had done it on purpose."

The show went on, and Hurst watched from the wings. "There is one point where, before 'Scarlet Ribbons' is on, Riss steps forward, and in this awful faux-dramatic event says, 'Ladies and gentlemen, at this point in the show we would like to do a most beautiful song—one of the most beautiful songs.'" Hurst felt a sharp dig in his side:

Dusty is standing there with two trays, one on top of the other, with tea services, and she goes, "Nudge me." I said, "Are you kidding?" "Nudge me!" I said, "No!" at which point she throws them all up in the air! Crockery every-where. Then Dusty looked at me and goes, "He pushed me!" at which point the stage manager rushes up and says, "You, out!"

Only after an intervention by Emlyn Griffith was Hurst allowed back into the building to go on. "They wouldn't allow me back in: that's what Dusty did."

Riss Chantelle was livid with Dusty. "She was hiding in the restaurant when I came offstage. I said, 'It's no good you hiding, Dusty, that's a really childish thing to do.'" Dusty never changed, Chantelle says. She got older, and more sophisticated, but inside she was still a little girl. "That's why I've never really been able to be terribly cross with her," Chantelle adds.

On another occasion Hurst remembered appearing for a rehearsal at the Blackpool Winter Gardens when Harold Fielding, one of the country's leading theater producers, stood up in the stalls and objected to the group's new amplifiers, three feet high. He shouted out, "What are those boxes?"

"They're amplifiers for the guitars," said Dusty.

Fielding replied, "They'll have to go, they ruin the look of the act."

"They are not going anywhere, they're part of the act the way they are."

"I'm not having it," Fielding shouted back.

"You bloody well are, because they are part of our act!" Dusty told him.

Then a woman popped up and said, "Don't let them talk to you like that," at which point Dusty replied, in front of the auditorium, "And you can tell that bitch to shut her mouth as well!" "That bitch" was Harold Fielding's wife. Outraged, Fielding told them, "You'll never work in one of my theaters again," Hurst remembers, "and we didn't."

Young, inexperienced, and swept away with his sudden success, Mike Hurst looked up to Dusty and Tom from a distance. Benefiting from the groundwork laid by Tim Feild, Hurst stepped into what had become Britain's number one best-selling group—voted best British group again in the *NME* 1962 poll and earning £1,500 a week on tour, the equivalent of £25,000 a week in 2013, and nearly 100 times the average weekly wage at the time. In a short time The Springfields had risen to even greater heights, but Dusty was keen to temper any suggestion that this was due to the new band member. "It is true our record success has been tremendous since Mike joined us last November," she said in 1963, "but as far as our makeup goes we are the same group that operated with Mike's predecessor Tim Feild." Later Hurst heard the rumor that Dusty had not particularly liked him, and found him arrogant. "I was nineteen years old. I'd suddenly walked into something that was Big Time so—sure I was arrogant," Hurst admits. "But I wouldn't have thought that was a "be-all and end-all" criticism of a nine-teen-year-old boy: that he was arrogant. I couldn't have been so arrogant that I gave them a problem, because I wasn't in control—Tom was in control." Regardless of Dusty's feelings towards him, Hurst says he never had negative feelings about either her or Tom: "I always liked her, although sometimes I liked her more than others."

From their first meeting Dusty and Tom had treated him with scrupulous fairness, cutting him in for an equal third on every-thing—something that would be unheard of now, and was unusual even then. Hurst says:

> I was treated so well by them, business-wise. It wouldn't have crossed my mind at the time—to ask what the deal was for me financially. But they made it perfectly clear from the first meeting that it would all be split three ways. When I think about that today I know what would have happened: someone joins a group that's already established, you're put on a salary, and the others who are already there take the split. So it was incredibly generous of them, and I've never forgotten it.

Yet, as Dusty's teenage friend Peter Miles has also expressed, Hurst found both siblings somewhat unknowable and unreachable, saying, "Tom and Dusty were a very odd couple and their upbringing must have contributed in part to that." On Dusty, Hurst adds:

> *There was always a wall, always. There was with Tom too. It was the way she would look at you, the way she would talk to you. It was, "I'm not going to let myself out. I'm behind this wall." So, she'd enter into the humor, you'd laugh together, she'd enter into musical conversation about this, that and the other. But when it came to anything else, anything more personal, or anything like that—no. I couldn't talk to her or Tom on a level of wanting to ask their advice. That would never have happened. It might have saved me a lot of headaches if it had.*

Dusty's sense of aloofness was probably born of a natural reserve and the need to conceal vital experiences and parts of her personality, and was felt by many who encountered her. "Dusty was very difficult to get through to," agrees Jean Ryder (now Westwood), one of Dusty's first backing singers.

> *She was a very private person. She was a difficult woman to get to know even when you knew her. I think the big problem was her sexuality. I don't think she was sure of what she wanted to be for quite a long time and in those days, way back, it wasn't good to be homosexual or lesbian, and I think she was terrified that if it came out it would ruin her career and her fans would leave, so she refused to talk about it. She wouldn't give interviews to press or anything and there were so many rumors going round about her. But she was very, very wary of everyone, even the people around her, so this made it difficult to penetrate this outer shell— and yet, inside, I think she was a very nice person.*

Even those who warmed to Dusty straight away and became her closest friends, like Pat Barnett, felt she was holding something back. Barnett believed that sense of withholding would melt away over time as the two got to know each other—and she often wondered why it never did.

> *Dusty was terribly shy. In all the years I worked for her I never saw her completely naked. I was always helping her dress and everything, but she was always shielding her body. And one day I thought, "This is getting ridiculous." I'd been staying overnight with her, and I thought, "There is a way to kill this," and I went and had my shower and I came out into the room to talk to Dust about something, starkers [naked]—I'd got the towel round me because I was just pretending to dry. I thought, "If she sees that the body doesn't mean anything to me, maybe she'll relax." She did after that, but not as blatantly as I did. It was always sort of covering up "bits" and I thought, "That's the blasted Catholics again, you mustn't show your body."*

In all the years they knew each other, Dusty rarely discussed her relationships with Barnett. "She wouldn't talk to me about any of the people she was in love with. That was always terribly private. Dusty once said to me, 'I'm really lucky, aren't I, because I've got it both ways.' That's the only time she ever sort of acknowledged her sexuality to me."

Later, Mike Hurst was always amused to hear Dusty described as the icon of the Swinging Sixties scene, as he never remembered her attending any of the famous parties he loved going to with other well-known figures like Jean Shrimpton. Dusty kept herself to herself, and whatever she did, she did not discuss it with her bandmate.

Onstage, though, Dusty was not shy: she gave everything. Before a performance her nerves would be so intense that the skin across her chest would flush bright red. But it was Tom's stage fright and terror of the audience, not Dusty's, that Mike Hurst remembers most clearly. "He used to say, 'I hate them, I can't do it,'" Hurst recalled. "I'd say to him, 'But they're our fans! They don't hate us.'" Sedated with sleeping pills to calm his nerves, Tom's eyes would close in a semi-stupor onstage, while he strummed and sang with a rictus grin. Next to him Dusty sang with her notable charisma and stage presence, while Hurst would be positioned with his nose stuck into her hairsprayed-solid beehive, which he claimed was usually unwashed to preserve its shape, and often quite smelly.

After the success of "Island of Dreams" The Springfields released the single "Say I Won't Be There," a reworking of the French song "Au clair de la lune," and starred in their own BBC TV specials, in which Dusty took the lead, speaking in her slightly breathless and clipped tones. Hurst says:

> Her ability to present herself and talk to an audience, I personally felt that let her down. I'll be shot down in flames for that, I'm sure, by a lot of fans, but I didn't think she was that good at presenting herself. She was a voice to me, a great voice. As a singer, she was always fantastic. Wonderful. I admired her voice tremendously. I still think she had one of the best voices of the last century. She wanted to sing like a black singer, but the great thing about Dusty is that she didn't let it go to her head in that you couldn't hear the melody of the song. Dusty always sang the song.

If her singing voice was spectacular, her nerves always got the better of her when she was talking, perhaps because it was harder to maintain the separation between "Dusty Springfield" and the insecure, uncertain, Mary O'Brien. As she both longed for and feared, Dusty was becoming a personality, distinct from The Springfields. In DJ Alan Freeman's TV show *Here Come the Girls*, her vulnerable charm was emphasized when she was filmed at a mock recording session, balancing on a pile of phone books to reach the microphone.

"Say I Won't Be There" reached number five and stayed in the charts for fifteen weeks. It was followed in July 1963 by "Come On Home," which was Tom's attempt to fuse country and western with a more R&B sound that included him playing a twelve-string guitar and a guitar solo for Mike Hurst. Dusty's voice took on a grittier edge, but the record was not what fans expected, and sold relatively poorly. "A lot people say it's not us, but it is us," Tom said. "I wrote it myself and, because I was a bit frightened the group would get stuck in a groove after our last two hits, I decided to go for a rhythm and blues number."

The song was their attempt to move towards an edgier, funkier, sound, driven by what they were hearing from other groups, according to Mike Hurst:

> *The country thing sort of came and went, then The Beatles happened and Dusty wanted to get more rhythm and blues, more rock 'n' roll than the old Springfields. If you listen to a song like "Down and Out"—it was still written by Tom, but very much more like a Liverpool group. We even do the "Oooh!" on there. We knew the tide was turning in musical terms, so we knew we had to change.*

In truth, once Dusty and Tom heard The Beatles they knew the game was up. In early 1963, The Beatles released "Please Please Me" followed by "From Me to You," which shot to number one in April of that year, and was followed by "She Loves You" in

September, which went on to become the best-selling single of the decade. "We saw The Beatles coming and we weren't rock 'n' roll," Tom said. "Our group had gone about as far as it could. We were also quite fed up with each other." Tim Feild told reporters that he had guessed the group might break up when he left ten months previously, saying, "I reckon they've reached the stage when, like everyone who lives in close contact, they are getting on each other's nerves." The Rolling Stones, who Dusty also expressed excitement about, were hot on their heels too, having played their first gig in July 1962 and released "Come On" in July 1963, followed by "I Wanna Be Your Man."

The revival of British music, influenced by the US but unique, was something that Dusty had long been waiting for. She knew that the time was right to take the gamble on her solo career, the ultimate breakaway that she had been planning for years. Her mother Kay was dismayed to hear that Dusty would be going it alone, crying that she had become used to seeing her daughter's name in the papers. Dusty reassured her that she hoped it would be back there soon.

It was a gamble, as Dusty admitted at the time: "Everyone tells us we're mad. Well, we've always been mad. It's a big chance and we're taking it. It's better to gamble while we're at the top than when we're on the way down."

To help organize her solo career, Dusty asked Pat Barnett to become her secretary. From the beginning, Dusty had realized it was Pat, not Emlyn Griffiths, who made sure the group had the essentials—like a piano—when they needed one. One day Dusty had emerged from Griffiths's office and said, nonchalantly, "When I go solo I'm going to ask you to be my secretary." Barnett had thought little of it, but when the time came Dusty was back. "You remember I asked you to be my secretary when I'm solo?" she asked. "Well, will you?" She asked how much Barnett was paid, which was not much, and then confirmed that she could manage to pay her the same.

"I *did* think twice about it," Barnett says. She initially accepted, and then "I thought, 'What have I done? I've got a safe job here, I don't know if this girl is going to ever make it on her own. But I've got faith in her—I think she will make it, and I think she needs someone around who isn't going to change her.'" Barnett thought the "very vulnerable" young woman she liked so much would need her by her side to protect her, as a companion as much as a secretary.

> I did all the secretarial work, but I went with her and kept people at bay when they were nasty . . . and I was glad I was around, quite honestly. She shielded me a lot, she always seemed to think of as me as terribly naïve . . . but she forgot I'd worked twenty years in show business, and I wasn't that naïve.

It was Dusty's girl-next-door nature that brought out Barnett's protective instincts, almost from the beginning: "We were protecting each other . . . I think it was because of her down-to-earth way, not at all star-like. She picked totally the wrong people to be friends with."

Dusty and Tom later said they had always put a three-year time limit on the life of the group, but Mike Hurst was unaware of it. Sitting backstage in Blackpool one day in October 1963 he was gobsmacked when Tom suddenly said, "Why don't we break up?" Dusty paused and replied, "Yeah, why not?" Hurst remembers:

> I said, "Yeah, fine." Because I thought nothing of it—I thought, "I've been at it a couple of years now—I'll be fine." Of course, afterwards I realized, she already had that record in the can, the first single of her solo career. So it was all

*fixed. Fixed by the record company, fixed by management
and everything else.*

Looking back Hurst realized that Dusty and Tom had already
agreed to break up long before, but the conversation had been
engineered in such a way as to avoid hurting his feelings. "They
didn't want to offend. I know they didn't. And if they had—would
I have been annoyed? No, not in the slightest. I was too arrogant.
It didn't faze me at all." In fact, the idea was far from horrifying to
him. His sudden success had come so easily, he believed he would
easily go on to solo success of his own.

Soon after, photographer David Redfern arrived backstage at
a TV show in Bristol, on assignment to shoot The Springfields.
Redfern, who shot most of the stars of the 1960s and was friends
with many of them, always found Dusty particularly tricky to
work with. That day she was in devilish form, and long negotiations began about whether Redfern could get the shots he needed.
For reasons unknown to him at the time, The Springfields were
refusing to be photographed, but Redfern knew that he could not
return to London empty-handed; he simply would not get paid.
He recalls:

> *I did have a bit of a run-in with her. They were doing a
> thing for HTV. When I got there Dusty was jumping up
> and down that I was there—"No, you can't take pictures.
> It's impossible"—and I said, "You know, I've come all the
> way down here from London to get pictures; it's all been
> arranged with the record company." Anyway, to cut a long
> story short, she actually turned round to me and said, "Oh,
> take your fucking pictures then." So I took the pictures
> and got some nice pictures of them all performing—they
> were miming to a couple of numbers. Next day, front page*

of the Daily Express, *as you would have it in those days:
"SPRINGFIELDS SPLIT." So I have the last set of pictures
of Dusty with The Springfields, so that was quite good!*

Later, Dusty spotted Redfern on set on *Ready Steady Go!* and
pointed him out, saying, "Watch him! He's the evil one, he always
gets his picture!"

The Springfields took to the stage to give their final performance on *Sunday Night at the London Palladium* in October
1963, then the biggest television program of the day, where they
were presented with a trophy by emcee Bruce Forsyth. Dusty
cajoled her brother into singing "So Long, It's Been Good to
Know You," a song he found indescribably corny. Dusty, who
always had a feeling for her audience and a sense of what made
good show business, had picked the right song, but she had not
counted on being overwhelmed with the emotion of the moment.
Breaking down in tears midway through, she saw Tom shoot her
a look of incredulity. "In the middle of the song I started to cry.
I remember Tom throwing me a look of complete amazement as
I sniffed beside him." He believed her crying was part of the act,
but in fact her tears were real.

It was the perfect moment for Dusty to go solo: she had already
been voted eighth in Top British Female Singers by *Melody Maker*
readers, despite still being part of The Springfields, and she had
added to her profile through a series of solo TV appearances
talking about pop music. Bravely she said about the breakup, "I
have no regrets, now is the time to look forwards, not back . . .
our decision is quite irrevocable," but inside she was terrified. She
was twenty-four years old and for the first time in her life success,
or failure, would be her own: "I was scared of the way ahead," she
said. "The way alone."

5

A GIRL CALLED DUSTY

Cramped, grey, dirty Britain was just beginning to peel back its layers and bloom into something youthful, fragile and colorful. Somewhere in the London night a long sleek car was speeding its way through the city: out of the West End with its newly developed concrete offices, tourist hotels and four-lane highways, beneath the new high-rise apartments that symbolized modernity, past the all-night Italian coffee bars, and teenagers perched on spotless scooters listening to R&B—out into the sprawl of the northern suburbs with their roads of what John Fowles described as "peeling, pitted, endlessly dirty houses, children playing in the streets . . . junk shops, cheap grocers." The driver of the eye-catching silver Buick Riviera had become the icon of these changing times— the Queen of the Mods with her sharp blonde bob, heavily lined eyes, and cool soulful intonations.

Dropping off her bandmate Doug Reece, of The Echoes, Dusty would eventually pull over to the side of a quiet street in north London, and the two of them would sit and talk for hours. "We were both war babies," Reece says, "we could both remember looking up and seeing the bombs falling." Reece had grown up in a big family in a Dickensian house near Camden Town, an inner city district of northwest London. Since then the family had moved into an apartment in Brecknock Road, Tufnell Park, and Reece had followed his brother into playing with the silver band that practiced in the community center across the street. Sitting with Dusty outside his mother's apartment late at night, they'd talk about music, about Dusty's childhood and her struggles with herself, and about cars. "Dusty loved cars," Reece says, remembering how she would tear out pictures from magazines to show him—promising that one day they would drive all over the Continent in a Lamborghini. They both loved her Buick Riviera with its long American silhouette, thrusting Wildcat V8 engine, Silver Cloud paintwork and interior done out in vinyl and blue cloth. Unlike those who found hard her to know, Reece felt immensely close and protective towards this young woman he'd begun rehearsing with only a few months earlier, but who was already a star.

Dusty had been itching to start her solo career long before The Springfields announced that they were disbanding, but she needed the right single to kick it off. Since that cold night in New York in 1962, she'd been captivated by the sounds coming out of America, and from Detroit in particular. At weekends she went down to the West End and bought all the Motown and soul records she could find, playing them over and over again in her apartment in Baker Street. Should she start her career with a version of Berry Gordy Jr.'s "Money (That's What I Want)"? The only problem was that the Beatles had covered it on their latest album, and Dusty feared the comparison. Then she toyed with the idea of Burt Bacharach and Hal David's "Wishin' and Hopin'," already a B-side hit for Dionne Warwick. In total, nine songs were considered, recorded at the Olympic Sound Studios in London—and rejected.

Inspired by the success of "The Twist" and "Dancing in the Street," Dusty insisted she wanted a song people could dance to. "Dusty was all into black American soul-type music and I think she was not keen to do a pop song," says Jean Ryder, "but Johnny Franz said to her, 'Look, you've got to establish yourself as a solo artist, if you want a hit record this is what you've got to do,' so she went into the studio and recorded 'I Only Want to Be with You.'"

"I Only Want to Be with You" was written by Ryder's husband, Mike Hawker, and Ivor Raymonde, who'd worked on all The Springfields' recordings. Hawker was already well known and had penned hits for Helen Shapiro. Inspired by his recent marriage to Jean, a trained opera singer who sang with Margot Quantrell and Vicki Haseman in the group The Breakaways, he'd written "I Only Want to Be with You" as her song, and hoped that she would record it. Ryder remembers:

> When Dusty said that she was leaving to go solo, a lot of the music business and the press and everything were all saying, "She'll never make it on her own because she's just not glamorous enough and she's not good enough, she's okay in a group but she's not a good enough solo singer," and so she was being knocked. So, Johnny Franz rang up Mike and said, "Look, we need something that is going to put this girl into the charts, because everybody is knocking her, everybody is saying she'll never make it—have you got a song that's a guaranteed hit?"

Hawker and Ryder put together a very rough demo, with Ryder playing percussion on a biscuit tin lid, and sent it to Franz, who immediately heard the song's potential. In the end Ryder's role was to be a support vocalist, for as soon as Dusty heard the demo she wanted the song. "It's a great tune," she told Hit Parade. "It wasn't really a difficult choice." Later she admitted she had paid little attention to the meaning of the song: "I just knew it was a hit, and did it. I didn't think about the lyrics at all" (*Rolling Stone* 1973).

Remarkably assured, and bursting with energy, "I Only Want to Be with You" submerged Dusty's voice under some of the "wall of sound" distortion she was eager to achieve. In the US, Phil Spector had created a reverberating ambience unheard of in British studios using one microphone placed in the middle of the studio with musicians and singers playing into it. Working with Franz again as producer, Dusty had recorded on a four-track master tape, with Raymonde pulling in as many members of the London Philharmonic Orchestra as he could find. At the time many musicians still only recorded on two track, and cranked out three sessions in three hours. Dusty worked differently, with a deliberation that would become her hallmark, and with the four tracks giving her more of the flexibility she needed. First the musicians would rehearse together in the studio and record on three of the tracks while the singer recorded a fourth vocal track in a soundproof studio. When the instrumental tracks were mixed together, Dusty would then rerecord the vocal track over the top. In a way of working that would later cause her problems, Dusty wanted everyone else to lay their track down first—she had to be last. "We'd make the records very important-sounding with a huge band," Raymonde later told Lucy O'Brien, "then we'd take the record acetate and deliberately distort it."

The song had some classic Dusty elements, a rhythm section and horns—and a breakaway string section that was simpler than, but similar to, what producer Bert Burns had used in 1959 to revolutionize R&B on The Drifters' records. If Dusty could recreate a "wall of sound" ambience, with some of the flavor of R&B, and a unique British melodic soulfulness, she would be some way nearer to the sound she wanted. The result was somewhere between Gerry and the Pacemakers and Carole King, she told *Disc*.

Dusty and Raymonde did not get on particularly well during the recording, Jean Ryder remembers. "Dusty didn't gel with him, unfortunately. He was a lovely man, full of fun, very outgoing, very gregarious, but he did write very, very busy arrangements and Dusty argued with him about it. Mind you, she argued with everybody about music!"

Creating the sound she could hear so clearly in her head was to become an obsession for Dusty, but Phil Spector had listened to, and approved of, her first attempt. "He said he thought it would do well in the States because it had a good 'white' sound," she said. Despite such praise, Dusty subjected herself to fitful agonies of self-doubt before the single's release on November 8, 1963. "I didn't think I had the right image and I didn't think I had the face of a pop singer. I waited in agony for six weeks, hardly daring to appear in public in case people asked me about the record." Yet the hook of "I Only Want to Be with You" was immediate, strong enough to send it flying up the charts to number four, where it was halted by The Beatles, the Dave Clark Five and the Swinging Blue Jeans.

If Dusty's career with The Springfields had been like cruising along the freeway driving a beautiful smooth automatic, she had now leaped into a roadster, ripped the top back, and revved up and down the gears. Laying to rest the eternal debate about what kind of music The Springfields produced, Dusty had firmly stamped her own identity on her first recording. "I Only Want to Be with You" was definitely a *pop* song, and Dusty was on her way to becoming a pop star. *Melody Maker* proclaimed: "Dusty Springfield is now a solo star." Her success had been propelled further and faster by her appearances on the cult music show *Ready Steady Go!*

Ready Steady Go! burst onto the air with a pilot program filmed in early 1963, and the show's anarchic, youthful energy threatened to do for music programs what *That Was the Week That Was* had already done for satire and comedy the previous year—puncturing the stiff and formal mold of British light entertainment forever. On *RSG!* presenters and bands turned up in a slightly better version of their ordinary day clothes, and spoke to each other, and the audience, as if they were all dropping in to the same party. After appearing on the pilot (with Dusty rehearsing in dark shades) The Springfields were booked to take part in the first show that autumn. A few weeks before the date, however, Dusty appeared in the Kingsway offices of the production company, Rediffusion, and said that The Springfields were breaking up, and she was going solo.

Dusty started chatting with the program's young editor, Vicki Wickham, and they immediately struck up a friendship. "We started talking, and then we left and went over to my flat and started playing music," Wickham says. "I remember liking her and realizing that a lot of our references were the same. We weren't that far apart in terms of school and background and so on, and from that day on we became friends." Wickham adds that, without talking about it, "from day one I knew that she was gay. That was another thing we had in common—we never sat down and had a serious discussion about 'why are we gay?' We just laughed about her girlfriends, and my girlfriends . . ."

Wickham asked Dusty if she wanted to emcee three *RSG!* shows. The job fit in nicely with the weeks that Dusty was waiting for her first single to be released, and it would be a useful boost to her visibility, laying the groundwork for the idea of her as a solo star.

On the night of her first show on October 4, 1963 (two days before she made her final appearance with The Springfields on *Sunday Night at the London Palladium*) Dusty appeared on screen, friendly and well spoken, with the slight air of nervous uncertainty that added so much to her charm. Tucking her head to one side shyly, and hiding a little behind her blonde bob, she spoke directly to the camera: "Hello there . . . Yes, folks, it's the all-talking solo Springfield . . ." before introducing The Beatles.

When, shuffling her feet, Dusty later conducted her first interview with the Fab Four, she politely asked John Lennon if the marks on his face were from being shot at when he was scrumping apples as a kid. "No, they're scabs," he replied in down-to-earth Liverpudlian tones, before teasing Dusty about the marks on her own face. Embarrassed, Dusty backed off. Their clash of cheeky seemingly working-class upstart versus polite middle-class established singer symbolized the spirit of the '60s.

Across Britain there was a growing air of discontent with the "established order." The 1950s had ushered in an era when the advent of hire purchase meant that televisions, washing machines, and, in some cases, even cars were now within the reach of many more Britons. But largely the economy lingered in the doldrums, while even Japan and Germany seemed to be surging ahead. Increasingly, as the 1950s gave way to the 1960s, the country was beset by strained labor relations, a dissatisfied working class and sexual scandal, all threatening to bring an end to thirteen long years of Conservative Party rule.

Two weeks after the start of Dusty's solo career, the once seemingly unflappable Prime Minister, Harold Macmillan, resigned. He had been finally brought down by an inaccurate cancer diagnosis, a series of brutal by-election defeats and the fallout from the "Profumo affair," when the Secretary of State for War, John Profumo, had been caught lying in Parliament about his relationship with the much maligned "good-time girl" Christine Keeler, and her additional liaison with a naval attaché at the Soviet embassy. The "Profumo affair" was later to play a significant role in Dusty's life with the film *Scandal*, but at the time she noticed only a series of lurid newspaper headlines describing a world she was still too innocent to fully understand. "They said things like 'lovenest,' and I didn't know what a 'lovenest' was," she told TV interviewers in the 1980s, and at the end of that decade she told *NME*:

> *I have no real clarity about the scandal because I was very obsessed with what I was doing. I didn't understand things like call girls and naughties because I was brought up in a very sheltered way. But I remember seeing all these tabloids and I could tell people were going "Naughty! Naughty!"*

Success was propelling her into a world she sometimes felt inadequately prepared for, and, as ever, her insecurities rose to the surface: "I was very sheltered and suddenly I was taken out to these little clubs off Sloane Street. I didn't know what people were talking about and I didn't know anything about the food they were serving. I was raised on potatoes." In fact, Dusty's middle-class accent immediately signified to the whole of Britain that she was far from being a girl who had grown up on potatoes. In a country obsessed with parsing every slight nuance of social class, any working or middle-class person would understand that Dusty was clearly "posh." She was not nearly "posh" enough, however, to have access to the world of Cliveden, the country house where some of the Profumo frolicking had occurred, the aristocracy or the English establishment—and as an Irish Catholic, she never would be. Despite her proclamations of innocence, however, Dusty's days of singing in hostess clubs meant she probably knew a good deal more about the world of Keeler and Mandy Rice-Davies, the two former showgirls at the center of the scandal.

Dusty's show business background had already exposed her to

many types of people and circumstances, something Kiki Dee was also familiar with. Dee remembers arriving in London in 1963 as an innocent sixteen-year-old from Yorkshire: "When I moved to London I didn't know what gay was. So you can imagine the naiveté I had about all the people I was meeting in the music industry. I was a slightly overweight teenager with wonky teeth and, to me, all these people just seemed fabulous." Sudden immersion into the entertainment industry had a way of opening your eyes to all types of activities.

Still, in the pre-pill, pre-summer-of-love, early 1960s everyone understood the code of good girl versus good-time girl—and the "Profumo affair" demonstrated that there was a very high price to pay for transgressing the rules. Many thought that Christine Keeler (the good-time girl who was used and tossed aside, and rarely had anything approximating a good time) was treated most harshly of all the participants, in part because it was revealed that she liked black men, and had conducted a series of affairs with black American airmen. Crossing the color bar was the ultimate transgression—and in the US it was the basis of an FBI investigation against her.

In the early 1960s, "sexual misconduct" still sometimes involved prosecution. The Italian owners of a Soho café called Milan were prosecuted in late 1962 for permitting disorderly conduct when a police constable testified that he had witnessed two couples kissing and embracing, with the girl sitting on the man's lap—and a "beatnik girl" dancing with a man near a jukebox. Richard Davenport-Hines describes in *An English Affair* how "'the girl was wearing a low cut blouse' reported Constable Thomas Jones, 'and the man put his fingers under her bra at the back and pulled it.'"

Even without the threat of a court case, sex—for women at least—could easily lead to general disgrace. The *Sunday Pictorial* of 1962 issued instructions for how a good girl might gently refuse to have sex with her boyfriend until after marriage, asking, "IS this really necessary to win him?" (the answer is NO), while a woman drinking alone in a bar or hotel drew frowns, and signs in Wimpy bars prohibited two unaccompanied women from eating together for fear that they might be prostitutes.

"The '60s were a very naïve time really," says Vicki Wickham; "we were all growing up, with no knowledge of what we were growing up into." Dusty was still a good girl, turning down propositions from men, and laughing when other musicians left her a note saying, "Hey Dusty, let us know when you decide to lose your virginity." But another part of her was yearning to explore what she might want. Until then, feigning chastity remained a good disguise for not knowing what she really wanted.

October and November of 1963 proved to be momentous and tumultuous months for Britain, and then for the world, culminating in the assassination of President John F. Kennedy. For Dusty, however, it was the point at which she was ready to debut her first solo single on *RSG!*, and hand over the reins of the emcee's job to Cathy McGowan. By now both she, and the show, were cemented at the center of pop culture, and Dusty was a Mod icon.

Taking their name from the "Modernist" art movement, Mods believed that they were as refined as Rockers were rough and greasy. Mods thought of themselves as more middle class, and more educated, and at weekends they slicked back their hair, picked up their girls and flocked into Soho on scooters, leaving behind the monotony of London's post-war suburbia to listen to jazz in smoky dives, hang out at the Marquee club, and listen to unreleased R&B at the Scene club on Wardour Street. Some partied all week long, fueled on "purple heart" amphetamines, with one teenage Mod called Denzil reporting that he only took Thursday nights off to wash his hair.

Gravitating to *RSG!*, the program was a place where they

could dance away right next to their favorite acts, and where cool but surprizing guests, such as Muhammad Ali, turned up just because the production team liked them. The show had become the Mods' spiritual home— the program that, according to one teenager, you just couldn't miss. Wickham remembers dispatching the production team to various clubs across outer London to find the best dancers for the Friday night show, and being mobbed by Mods wanting tickets. She was sometimes asked to dance with them so that they could show off their moves—which was tricky as Wickham was an embarrassingly bad dancer.

RSG! plugged directly "into the center of the scene," said the jazz musician George Melly, transmitting information about clothes, dances and slang to the whole country. "It made pop work on a truly national scale." At the heart of these early performances was Dusty: a natural fit with an audience who dug her love of European film, her deep connection to black American music, her sense of style— and her air of always being slightly apart. She was the epitome of cool, and the fact that she never felt so only added to her allure.

Appearing on *RSG!* was a chaotic experience. Performers, artists and journalists arrived on Friday lunchtime and spent five hot and exhausting hours hanging around backstage, and on the studio floor, during rehearsals. Dusty would appear, already immaculately made up, carrying her own clothes in plastic wrappers, with her hair loosely pinned up under a scarf. While the cast and crew waited, she would launch into a series of *Goon Show* jokes (always her favorite) or entertain everyone with exploits using one of her wigs. Eventually, the show commenced with Dusty weaving her way onto one of the small stages amidst groups of dancing teenagers, trying to remember her lines, and watching out for the enormous studio cameras that rumbled across the floor— sometimes leaving devastation in their wake. The resulting sense of jerky, spontaneous, amateurish fun only added to the appeal—and

Dusty would finish the show and depart, sometimes carried out over the heads of screaming fans who, on one occasion, danced on the hood of her car in stiletto heels. In person, Dusty was fun and friendly, but professional. "She was serious about it," said one person who sang with her on *RSG!* "She did the show, and then she wanted to get home."

Dusty's strength lay in the fact that she treated the other artists as her equals, Vicki Wickham believes: "She didn't treat them as a fan, which Cathy McGowan was much more inclined to. It was musician to musician." Despite her obvious intelligence and glamor, however, Dusty was always happier to be singing than speaking. "I'm not a natural interviewer," she later admitted, saying she had "little cards" hidden behind her beehive to read things off. It had been a nice way to spend three weeks, but she "much preferred singing to interviewing."

Soon the hiatus was over, and Dusty began her solo career in earnest, piecing together a tight-knit team who would support her for years, if not decades. In addition to Pat Barnett, Johnny Franz and Ivor Raymonde, all of whom had known Dusty from her days with The Springfields, she replaced Emlyn Griffiths as her manager with Vic Billings, hired lighting director Fred Perry and then, later in 1964, added The Echoes as her backing band.

Vic Billings had found it hard to break into the music industry, moving to London in 1954 as a trainee for Rank Entertainment, working his way into theater management, and eventually becoming assistant controller at the Victor Sylvester Dance Studios. Now thirty-four, he had worked for one of The Springfields' occasional booking agents, Tito Burns, and had set up on his own with an office on South Molton Street. In 1963 he had just signed a promising young singer, a sixteen-year-old Yorkshire schoolgirl called Pauline Matthews, and transformed her into an up-and-coming star renamed Kiki Dee (Pauline's father had refused to allow his first suggestion, Kinki Dee). "I was singing with a dance band in Leeds and got an audition with Fontana Records, based in Marble Arch," Dee says. "I passed the audition. It was quite an interesting time because it was the early 1960s, The Beatles were just about to happen and the whole '60s pop scene was about to happen. I was put in touch with Vic Billings's management through the record company."

Three weeks later, Dusty announced that she was going solo, and Dee's hopes of being at the center of Billings's attention were to be thwarted for the next five years. "Maybe there was a bit of rivalry. I don't know really. I suppose in a way for me the timing wasn't that great because the manager who had taken me on suddenly had this star on the books who was happening. I was always quite pragmatic—I just got on with it." Dee adds, "I just instinctively knew that my time wasn't there yet, and hers was." Despite the disappointment, Dee looked up to Dusty: "I was a huge fan of her and The Springfields—particularly those big dresses she wore. 'Island of Dreams,' those songs had great vocals. She seemed very grown up and sophisticated to me. She was only seven years older, but I was quite awestruck by her.

As soon as Billings heard that The Springfields were splitting up, he quickly rang Dusty and told her she needed a good agent. After meeting him in a café for a preliminary chat, Dusty coolly said, "I'll think about it," before announcing to everyone that Billings would be representing her, some time before she actually informed him of her decision. In the early days they made a formidable team, learning the business together, with Billings providing the right degree of soothing and cajoling that Dusty needed. His sense of direction for Dusty's career, and advice about song choices, was impeccable, and he was able to judge perfectly when to give in to one of her whims and when to stand firm. As Vicki Wickham put it, "He understood Dusty, and he knew her insecurities. He also knew everyone in the business and I think he made the right choices for her, what shows to do and what concerts to do. And she had more top ten hit singles than any other artist, so he can't have been too far off."

Mike Hurst said, "Dusty adored Vic Billings," and many believed that the charming, fair-haired Billings, who was also gay, would have proved the perfect partner for Dusty in a *mariage blanc* (a marriage without consumation), providing her with the kind of security and reassurance she craved. Together with Vicki Wickham, Dusty and Billings formed a tight-knit social group—"We were a crew," says Wickham—going to the Talk of the Town together, giggling at Danny La Rue's costumes at his club on Hanover Square, and organizing dinners at Billings's apartment around the corner at which Dusty would appear bare faced, without her usual hours of carefully applied makeup.

Dusty, Billings said, would have been a perfect Garbo-esque movie star, "lounging in bed all day," occasionally reaching over for a chocolate. His job, he believed, was to cut through her languor and nerves, and make sure she arrived at all her engagements as planned. Wickham remembers one notorious fight when, early in her career, Dusty had protested about a Sunday rehearsal for *The Billy Cotton Band Show*, complaining to Billings on the phone that "I don't see why I have to go there now, the rehearsals aren't that important." *The Billy Cotton Band Show* was not trendy like *RSG!* but it captured the wider, older audience that Dusty also appealed to. When Billings appeared in person to get her out of bed and escort her to the studios, he met Wickham, who was lodging with Dusty at the time, in the flat and they picked up Dusty's dog and carried it downstairs. "As we walked down Baker Street he was telling me how mad at Dusty he was—and would literally pass the dog to me, which luckily I caught and then gave back to him, and to 'illustrate his fury' he would keep doing the same thing," Wickham says. "That day Vic definitely could have killed her—because it sounds silly but it was a big deal, a big show, and she obviously must have had a record out, and she needed to plug it."

Dusty's lateness was to become a recurring issue in her career, whether it was missing the 8 a.m. tour bus, or fraying Madeline Bell's nerves as she watched Dusty spend three hours putting on her makeup while a car waited outside to drive her to Blackpool. Pat Barnett would inevitably be stationed in the wings at a venue to correct any last-minute problems. "She was always last minute, but she was always there just as they played her cue, and she'd step out. I used to be thinking, "Oh my God, she's going to miss it, she's going to miss it," because I was always at the side with a little lipstick and compact so she could do it quickly . . ." On one memorable occasion things became so hurried, Barnett had to run onstage alongside Dusty, trapped in her hairpiece.

> I had a dress with little buttons, and it [the hairpiece] caught round the button, and I actually had to run onstage with her. I couldn't get it off her hairpiece, and I just had to wrench it off. Everybody went, "Ooh!" I was so embarrassed, but she carried on as if there was nothing going on. Later she said, "Did you actually come onstage just then?"

Fred Perry, Dusty's lighting and stage manager, also knew the other side of the woman he worked for—calling her "Aunty" and then "Madam," a nickname she tolerated rather than loved. Like Billings, Perry met Dusty for an introductory chat in a café called Jaegers on Bond Street where she appeared, looking chic and dramatic in a turban and snakeskin coat, and offered to pay for his cheese salad sandwich. They had met before when Dusty was with the Lana Sisters, but now Dusty had turned blonder and radiated a new aura. "Dusty was very glamorous with her hair teased within an inch of its life, Perry said. Like Pat Barnett and Vic Billings, he accepted the job and remained devoted to his employer for twenty-five years—despite many ups and downs and falling outs—giving her a favorite T-shirt that she often slept in which read "This is no ordinary housewife you're dealing with!" Although he was gay too, Fred Perry was in love with Dusty, according to Doug Reece. Many of the men in her entourage were.

The first task of her new team was to promote Dusty and "I Only Want to Be with You" as much as possible. After performing for British troops in West Germany, Dusty began her first British tour the day after the single was released, starting with two shows a night at the Halifax Odeon. Performing on the bill with Brian Poole and the Tremeloes, The Searchers and Freddie and the Dreamers, Dusty played the Liverpool Empire and Cannock, before moving south to Tunbridge Wells and Brighton, and concluding in the Midlands. Her act included "Rock Me in the Cradle of Love" and "Hallelujah I Love Him So," in addition to "I Only Want to Be with You."

Dusty was nervous about appearing onstage alone without Tom and Mike for the first time. "At first it was awfully hard," she told American reporter Louise Criscione in 1965. "I was used to having two boys with me and at first there was so much space! I didn't know what to do with my hands." She suffered from terrible stage fright, she admitted, something that was to get only marginally better as her career progressed: "If I'm doing a week somewhere I'm nervous the first night. But if I'm doing a big occasion, then I'm nervous the whole time."

Before her first appearance alone on *Sunday Night at the London Palladium,* Dusty's hands were shaking so violently she squirted hair spray over all those around her. She was overwhelmed by the feeling of "They're waiting for the big mistake . . ." "I do think she was actually petrified," backing singer Jean Ryder says. "She was of a nervous disposition, you could see that when you were working with her. She would get very edgy and twitchy nervous, and we were just laidback and calm with her, and she seemed to respond to that."

The strain of stepping up to becoming a solo act, and the intense glare of publicity, were taking a toll, and Dusty blamed the backing band on her first tour for not helping her achieve the standard she was looking for. Dusty was supported by Dave Berry's Crusaders, who worked very well with other acts. Nevertheless, Dusty raged against them, calling their combined efforts "abysmal"—and determined to find her own dedicated backing band.

Bass player Doug Reece was already an established member of The Echoes, playing in support of artists like Gene Vincent and Jerry Lee Lewis. When Reece's mother told him Dusty was advertising for a backing band he thought it would be a good opportunity, and rounded up his bandmates to go to the audition at the Granada in Kennington, south London. Reece says:

> I had a call from my agent, George Cooper. He told us that we had an audition to do the next day for Dusty Springfield and to be sure that an organ was in the group as that was the particular sound that Dusty wanted. I contacted all the group but I got a real shock when I spoke to Ray, who told me he was leaving the group and had sold his organ and was going back to Scotland. I tried to talk him around but he had made up his mind. I called Peter back, who knew of an organ player who could do the audition with us, but without any rehearsal anything could have happened. His name was Mickey Garrett. So The Echoes are just about to do their first audition with a drummer and a guitarist that had done about seven jobs, and an organ player who had never played in the band at all.

Like Fred Perry, Reece had met Dusty before while she was on tour with the Lana Sisters, but remembered little about her. He was immediately impressed with the petite, pleasant woman who greeted him at the audition and asked him to play some Ray Charles. In the end, Dusty did not seem to mind too much that The Echoes had a brand new organist, and the band began a relationship with her that would carry them through the high tide of her career to the end of the 1960s.

Dusty would pull up for rehearsals at drummer Bob Wackett's house in Friern Barnet—out in the furthest reaches of north London. "She parked her sports car outside, came in and wanted a cup of tea. That made us all feel very much at ease," Reece says. "I think that Dusty was more relaxed there with no pressure. She seemed to enjoy trying different things with the group."

While she had no affectations of stardom, it became immediately clear to The Echoes that when it came to music, Dusty knew exactly what she wanted. "She told us about the drumming," Doug Reece says. "In those days the fashion was to go hell for leather, but Dusty wanted a much more open and full sound." Dusty also wanted the bass "fills" that were used on soul and R&B recordings—and asked Doug Reece to come up with musically challenging arrangements:

> She had told us the kind of things to listen to before the rehearsal so we had some idea what she was after. Being the bass player I had to do a lot of listening as most of the things she wanted me to play were not readily available in Britain—it was a style played on soul and R&B records in America. Also a lot of the songs she wanted were very full arrangements so I had to come up with a way for a four-piece group to sound like a forty-piece orchestra.

Dusty later added a brass section, with trumpeter Derek

Dusty and the Lana Sisters wearing the 1950s outfits she soon abandoned © Riss Chantelle

Riss Chantelle, Lynne Abrams and Dusty during her year with the Lana Sisters, looking "terribly cheerful" © Riss Chantelle

Dusty goes solo, shortly after splitting with The Springfields © Getty Images

The Springfields © Getty Images

top left Dusty on the beach near her parents' house in Brighton © Getty Images

top right Dusty and her parents flying to New York © Getty Images

middle Dusty with her friend Martha Reeves – a deeply influential figure in her life both professionally and personally © Getty Images

bottom left Dusty, Tom Jones and the Beatles © Getty Images

bottom right Dusty returning from her aborted tour of South Africa, with Doug Reece and The Echoes © Getty Images

top left Dusty at the height of her powers, performing at the NME poll winners' concert at the Wembley Empire © Getty Images
top right Dusty with Einstein, the teddy bear she kept with her for the rest of her life © John Adams
bottom left Dusty back to back with Madeline Bell © Carole Gibson
bottom right Dusty in her imported Buick Riviera after a performance in Blackpool © Carole Gibson

A backstage photo of Dusty © Carole Gibson

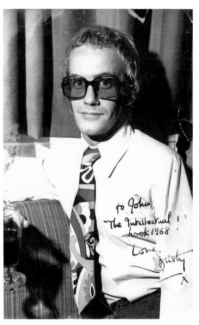

Dusty's hairdresser John Adams,
with a note from Dusty © John Adams

Dusty, John Adams and Norma
Tanega © Carole Gibson

Dusty and Norma Tanega on the balcony of the flat in
South Kensington before they moved to Aubrey Walk
© John Adams

Hope all is going well for you — come back to England for a visit soon! Corinne is a gas! What a character! We're staying in St. Thomas a big island about an hour's sail over the bluest sea I've ever seen — having a really healthy uncampy time — we stayed in a cottage at first till Norma saw a tarantula on the kitchen floor — EEEK! We moved the next day to the safe HILTON!! Much love Dusty XX + NORMA x

FERRY AT DOCK
Cruz Bay, St. John
Virgin Islands

Bermuda Postcard, Hamilton, Long Island, U.S.A.

POST CARD

Address
JOHN ADAMS
c/o 28 LINDEN WAY
CASTLECRAG
SYDNEY
N.S.W
AUSTRALIA

top Dusty sends John Adams a postcard from a beach holiday with Norma Tanega © John Adams
bottom left Dusty's photo session with Peter Rand before her trip to Memphis © Getty Images

top right Dusty, Vicky Wickham and John Adams at Heathrow en route to New York, 1968
© John Adams
bottom right Dusty with Peppi Borza, a great friend of her and her brother Tom. She later visited Peppi at the hospice before he died of AIDS in 1989
© Associated Press

Dusty dressed as Shirley Temple for "Talk of the Town." She was delighted when the photo made the front pages © Getty Images

top right Dusty and Burt Bacharach
© Getty Images
top left Dusty and brother Tom singing
"Morning Please Don't Come" on *Top of
the Pops* for their last public performance
together © Getty Images
bottom right Dusty and Lulu singing
together on *It's Lulu*, London, September
1970 © Getty Images
bottom left Dusty and Sue on holiday at
Eleuthera in the Bahamas © Sue Cameron

Dusty's Jenson Interceptor and Sue Cameron's car parked outside their Laurel Canyon home
© Sue Cameron

The pool at the Laurel Canyon house into which much furniture was thrown
© Sue Cameron

Dusty's cats Sister Mary Catherine and Fortnum (named in tandem with her other cat—Mason) at her house in Laurel Canyon © Sue Cameron

Dusty in hiding on the plane to St Maarten
© Sue Cameron

Dusty arriving at St Maarten airport on holiday © Sue Cameron

Wadsworth, and percussion—and rehearsals moved to a studio where Doug Reece would take charge: "Because I understood what she wanted, I would take the rehearsals and direct the band whenever we worked. Rehearsals were fun, hardly ever any dramas. Just good musicians playing good music."

They key to their relationship was that The Echoes listened with complete seriousness to Dusty's politely iterated demands, and delivered. Her ear for picking up on different sounds, and backing arrangements, was unparalleled. Reece says, "I changed the way I played when I worked for her. Dusty had a way of making every song her own." His goal was to make her relax "and trust us." Trust was not something that came easily to Dusty, but in time she grew to rely on Reece, and they spent many evenings in her apartment on Baker Street, listening to music—and Dusty really made people *listen* to music—and sometimes talking until dawn. Early the next morning they would walk around to the Golden Egg café on Oxford Street, or drive out to Heathrow to eat breakfast and watch the planes land.

Doug Reece and Dusty had affectionate feelings for each other that at one point tipped over into Dusty's one real "foray" into being with a man, and she remained immensely fond of him. He was a "sweet guy," she told friends, but she concluded that being with men wasn't for her. Reece says:

> Dusty and I were very good friends. I understood her and most of the things she did. She understood me. When she moved out of the flat in Baker Street and into her own place she would have a few close friends around to play records, talk a lot and have a few laughs. She would break up listening to comical musical records like Jonathan and Darlene Edwards or the Goons.

The Echoes became like family to Dusty, Reece says. "She would get upset if one of the band said that they were leaving. I think that she felt safe with us, she could relax a bit and not be on show." Madeline Bell remembers:

> Dougie was great and he had so much patience because he used to drive her all the time in the early days. I remember us stopping at one of the services on the motorway, and when she walked in everybody knew who she was and she got her food and she sat down to eat, and people started coming over to her wanting autographs and Dougie would stop them. He would be like her bodyguard as well.

Although they were not such close personal friends, Jean Ryder was another musician who liked working with Dusty, and appreciated her vulnerable side. "When she spoke she had a very quiet voice," Ryder says, "almost like a little girl's voice when she was talking and trying to explain things, and she seemed to be very reticent about letting go, and you were always wondering what was going on inside—and we would try to draw her out and make her laugh and things like that. She was a really nice girl, but I always felt sort of protective of her." A couple of years older than Dusty, Ryder would try to encourage her. "I would try to give her a bit of confidence and boost her a bit, saying, 'Oh, that sounded great, Dusty,' and she'd go, 'Oh, did it really? Oh, did it? Thanks,' and she just seemed so eager to get it right and do things properly."

Despite the extraordinary success of "I Only Want to Be with You," Dusty was modest. It was wonderful, she told reporters, "but foolish to think it will last." She added that eventually she "was bound to flop." Vic Billings certainly didn't think so, yet he was also cautious about declaring Dusty's stardom too soon—"stars" were usually christened as such after three hit records, and Dusty had only achieved one. It was clear that she faced stiff competition. In addition to The

Beatles, groups like the Rolling Stones, and then The Animals and The Yardbirds, were adapting their own version of soul and R&B, while other female singers stalked Dusty's domain. Kathy Kirby, who had come up through singing with the big bands—and whose life was to prove even more torturous than her rival's—beat Dusty to the top spot as *Melody Maker*'s Best British Female Singer for 1963, while Cilla Black's modest success with the Lennon/McCartney song "Love of the Loved" was about to be eclipsed by her second offering—Burt Bacharach's "Anyone Who Had a Heart."

Much to Billings's chagrin it was initially hard to get Dusty bookings on big shows, such as *Sunday Night at the Palladium*, with the Beverley Sisters appearing on one occasion to cover one of Dusty's songs instead. Dusty was doing everything she could to launch her career, and the result was severe nervous exhaustion. In addition to her first tour, so fraught that Fred Perry said, "The lady wants to create an album every time she steps on stage," Dusty had followed up with a short tour of Dublin and Belfast ballrooms, a week at the Chinchilla club in Leeds, and a round of TV appearances, including one in Holland that had involved a car crash in the taxi on the way to the airport. After spending a few days with her parents in Brighton over Christmas, Dusty began 1964 by following the Rolling Stones on the first episode of *Top of The Pops*, which was recorded in a converted Manchester church on New Year's Day, and seemed more momentous in retrospect than it did at the time. (When reminded of this appearance, Dusty seemed amazed to discover that she had been the first solo performer on *TOTP*.)

Yet, once Vic Billings had managed to get Dusty into the limelight, he worried she was being pushed too far too soon: "Let her be top of the bill, when she's ready to be top of the bill," he said. Dusty was feeling the strain, and collapsed in mid-January following a bout of flu. Canceling three performances in Liverpool, Blackburn and Lowestoft citing voice strain, Dusty reported that she had been instructed to rest "on doctor's orders." Even then she admitted that she lived on her nerves—her constant striving for perfection in every performance and recording meant that her voice would fail her, and she would collapse again at various key points in her career. "I was completely run down," she said at the time. "I was so fatigued that I was able to catch anything and I did." Adding that she hated to let people down and miss her engagements, she said, "I'll have to take things at a less hectic pace in the future."

For her second single, Dusty released "Stay Awhile" on February 7, 1964, choosing another Ivor Raymonde/Mike Hawker song over the alternative, "Every Day I Have to Cry." It was less than perfect timing as "I Only Want to Be with You" was still in the charts, and the less melodic "Stay Awhile" reached only number thirteen. Despite stretching the "wall of sound" ambience even further, Dusty always claimed to dislike the song, claiming that, together with "In the Middle of Nowhere," they were her least favorite records. The major problem was that she lacked the courage of her convictions, she said. "If I think something is right for me and everyone else says I'm wrong, I end up with their line of thought." This sounded very improbable to anyone who knew Dusty, or had encountered her stubborn—and invariably correct—insistence on tour and in the studio. Later she conceded that both records had the right sound at the time, but insisted that the problem was that they "have made no lasting contribution to my career, and I have a real hate relationship with them."

"Stay Awhile" was excluded from Dusty's 1966 *Golden Hits* album in favor of other, less popular, songs, and for years Dusty refused to sing either "Stay Awhile" or "I Only Want to Be with You" in her performances. "I Only Want to Be with You" is now one of the most recorded songs in history. Jean Ryder says:

It's been recorded by at least about 400 different people all over the world, and Mike has won awards for it over the years and . . . Dusty refused to do it onstage and in her programs and everything, she wouldn't sing it. I don't know what went on with Dusty and Ivor Raymonde, as I say they didn't seem to gel . . . but to refuse to sing the song that gave her the biggest hit of her career was upsetting for Mike and Ivor. Unfortunately Ivor has died since, but Mike said, "We gave her those first two hit records and she won't sing them in concerts, it's like it's beneath her."

In her first few months as a solo artist, Dusty was further defining both her look and her sound. In December 1963 she had spent a few days in Paris with Vic Billings and Vicki Wickham seeing Dionne Warwick and Little Stevie Wonder perform at the Olympia Theatre. Even then the tension between Dusty and Warwick was palpable, but she went backstage with Wickham, who remembers that Warwick treated them "very graciously." Together they wandered the streets and drank hot chocolate in little cafés. Dusty returned with a renewed interest in French style, with her beehive getting higher, and her black eye makeup more defined. Ryder remembers:

She became very glamorous. She had short darkish-looking hair and she wore almost frumpy-looking clothes in The Springfields, I thought. But then she had all these beautiful gowns made for her and her hair was bleached blonde and backcombed, and she had that signature thing with the eye makeup, masses of black shadow and eyeliner and every-thing, so she had a definite look and it couldn't be anybody else but Dusty Springfield.

"She wouldn't have made it, if she'd stuck with those puffed-out dresses looking like she did with The Springfields," Pat Barnett agrees. "She wouldn't have made it, because that voice didn't go with that appearance, did it? She was a class act, and she acted like that when she was with her fans, all the time." Yet Dusty had also an intriguing quality that set her apart, and stopped her from being classified as a sex-bomb girl singer. She said later:

> It was amazing, when I first started singing on my own. There were crazy scenes, because it was sort of asexual. They didn't mind that you were a boy or a girl. They would come up sort of onstage. The minute I appeared onstage, girls would scream. Purely because they were so hyped up on the whole atmosphere of a rock 'n' roll show.

Even though Dusty disliked her appearance, disguising what she believed was a heavy lantern jaw with ever more elaborate wigs, having a series of nose jobs, and then covering up her legs and "OB's knees" with trousers or long gowns, she was undoubtedly a very attractive woman. Yet her appeal was as much to women— gay and straight—as to men. Later, her female fans would reminisce about how they had felt forced to conceal their ardent devotion to Dusty, knowing how far to talk about it in the office the next day, and when to stay quiet.

Dusty's trip to Paris was followed by welcoming the Ronettes to Britain a few weeks later, meeting them at the Granada in Harrow, where they were supporting a tour by the Rolling Stones. The Ronettes were then signed to Phil Spector, and had enjoyed a huge US hit in the summer of 1963 with "Be My Baby," before singing "I Saw Mommy Kissing Santa Claus," "Sleigh Ride" and "Frosty the Snowman" on Spector's iconic Christmas LP, *A Christmas Gift for You*. Dusty had heard the album, and was deeply impressed by it. In less than a month she had seen Dionne Warwick, Stevie Wonder and the Ronettes perform—and her appreciation of the sounds of black American music remained undimmed. A few months later she was to meet the Ronettes again, for what she long considered to be the highlight of her career—singing at the Brooklyn Fox in Murray K's Rock 'n' Roll Extravaganza.

In spring 1964 Dusty completed a 29-date UK tour, followed by twelve grueling days in Australia and New Zealand which had left everyone exhausted and stressed out. By contrast, the release of her first album, *A Girl Called Dusty*, in April made her jump around her living room with excitement, according to Vicki Wickham, who had been in the studio to hear her record it.

Freeing herself forever from the elaborate costumes she'd worn with The Springfields, Dusty appeared on the cover of *A Girl Called Dusty* wearing a blue denim shirt hanging loose over her jeans, her hair tossed to one side, and smiling—so young, so authentically herself, so perfectly of the moment. Wickham says:

> *She really enjoyed that first album. I remember when we got the pressing back she was jumping around—saying, "Well, I could have done this part better," but she was happy about it. For those first two or three albums she really enjoyed the process, then it got more difficult and she didn't enjoy it anymore.*

If Wickham had been impressed with Dusty on *Ready Steady Go!*, it was listening to her recording *A Girl Called Dusty* that really blew her away. "When I went to the sessions for that first album, I thought, *Oh my God, I really like the way she sounds. She doesn't sound like anyone else.*" Wickham noticed too how, from the beginning, Dusty was exerting her control: "She had picked the songs. It was the first time she'd been in the studio on her own. She wasn't a technician, but she knew about how to get sound and she could hear every single instrument."

In the US, Philips released Bacharach and David's "Wishin' & Hopin'" from the album as a single, reaching number six in the American charts—although it had never been intended as an A-side and wasn't released as a single in the UK. Burt Bacharach said Dusty's version had "knocked him out," adding, "Her performance of 'Wishin' & Hopin'" just walks right off that record. She really takes charge." Bacharach knew, however, that Dusty disliked the song, and later in her career she would sing it as a "joke" song, changing the lyrics. "The lyrics are so sexist that—I'm sorry, Hal—to this day I just can't do that song seriously. It's like, 'Wear your hair just for him . . . do the things he likes to do . . .'"

Dusty was happy too to have another hit single in July, also penned by Bacharach and David. "I Just Don't Know What to Do with Myself" reached number three in the charts, and would undoubtedly have gone higher if it hadn't stalled behind "A Hard Day's Night" by The Beatles and "It's All Over Now" by the Rolling Stones. Such competition reflected the feverish atmosphere being generated by British pop—something that Dusty admitted she also benefited from when she arrived for her stint at the Brooklyn Fox, a 5,000-seat art deco theater that was a Mecca for money-churning summer music shows. Dusty was the Fox's answer to The Animals, who were playing in another theater across the street. "In the early days I was pretty wild. I came in on the wave of Beatlemania, and they somehow associated me with the Beatles. [At the Brooklyn Fox] I only had to stick my head out in the street—and [*screams, high pitched*] AGGGGH!!!" As a one American commentator dryly noted, it was the time when "all an English band with a working class background had to do was turn up at the airport."

With six shows a day crammed into a ten-day run, playing the Fox was daunting, not least because the first show began at 10 a.m.—an hour when Dusty was rarely awake, let alone performing. After years of listening to, and emulating, black music, however, Dusty was in heaven; she was finally playing with some of the acts she so admired. "I would have *paid* to do it," she told a BBC interviewer. Also on the bill that season were The Ronettes, The Supremes, Martha and the Vandellas, The Shirelles, The Temptations and The Miracles. Dusty was the guest white artist, "the token honky" as she put it, and at first she wondered what she was doing there—recalling how she blundered around Harlem with her beehive, relying on her new-found friends to protect her from trouble. That summer, the US was seething with racial tension: Congress had finally passed the landmark Civil Rights Act but, a year after Martin Luther King Jr. had delivered his "I have a dream" speech at the March on Washington, three youth voters at a voter registration drive in Mississippi were abducted and murdered, while the lethal shooting of a fifteen-year-old boy by a New York policeman caused Harlem and the Bedford-Stuyvesant district of Brooklyn to erupt in race riots that spread across the country.

To many white people it seemed that the city was burning, but Dusty didn't seem to care about the danger she might be putting herself in; she loved New York—and even made her way up to the Apollo in Harlem on her own to hear Martha Reeves. "What are you doing here?" Reeves asked her, somewhat aghast. "I'm going where I wanna go," Dusty replied. Her answer was nonchalant, but Dusty found her performances themselves more challenging.

New York DJ Murray "the K" Kaufman organized the Fox shows to cater to a high turnover of teenagers, off on their summer break. As the day wore on the younger, whiter audience was replaced by an after-work older, blacker, crowd. Backstage,

Dusty sweltered in a tiny dressing room with temperatures soaring into the nineties. She had called her mother and flown her parents out to join her, but they waited at the hotel and went sightseeing while Dusty worked, and she usually finished late and then ran around doing a few late-night errands before bed. Professionally, Dusty was alone, without her close-knit entourage to support and buoy her up, and she suffered fits of nerves and despair.

At the beginning of the run, Kaufman pulled Martha Reeves into his office and asked her to go and soothe Dusty, whom Reeves soon found, in her dressing room, "having a fit and throwing teapots at the wall and cursing loudly." Reluctantly, Dusty opened the door, inch by inch, until Reeves pushed her way in, and kicked a few pieces of crockery around too. She was lonely, Dusty told Reeves, confiding that "she had no friends—that she had to do shows with people she didn't know, that Kaufman had forgotten to introduce her. She wasn't happy." Throwing crockery was both a way of getting attention and letting off steam for Dusty, but not all performers appreciated the distraction, nor the feat of picking their way back and forth offstage over broken teacups and saucers—with one calling her just plain "crazy."

The Brooklyn Fox was a turning point in Dusty's life in two other crucial respects. It was where she discovered alcohol, and it was where she had her first sexual experience with a woman.

Ominously, Dusty discovered that alcohol was effective in calming her fears and emotions. "I got laryngitis," Dusty said later, "and thought, 'I can't face it.' Then one of The Temptations gave me a cup of vodka. I drank the whole bloody thing and felt better." Soon Dusty was asking Martha Reeves to get a takeout bottle of vodka, and drinking it by herself. Reeves was later horrified when others pointed the finger at her for kicking off Dusty's drinking problem, writing in her autobiography: "If I turned her into an alcoholic it was not my design." Dusty always took full responsibility for her alcohol and drug problems, and never pointed the finger at others. Before long, she and Reeves had become close friends, with Dusty enthusing that The Vandellas had "a richness in their voice that some of the other groups didn't have."

It seemed that despite a rocky start, Dusty was having a good time, saying, "Everyone was partying, I was always very well treated." She came to love sharing her dressing room with The Ronettes—laughing at the incongruity of their two enormous black beehive wigs next to her blonde one, getting her hems turned up by Diana Ross's mother, and eating dinner cooked by Smokey Robinson's wife. She was in her element: nothing could compare with the spine-tingling thrill of standing in the wings listening to her own idols perform; sometimes singing backup with The Vandellas, tweaking her own vocal technique, and reveling in the sledgehammer beat of "Dancing in the Street."

Late one night she went out to a show with one of the women performers she'd become friends with. After a few drinks they went to bed—something that was not surprising given Dusty's earlier attraction to women. Nonetheless it was an important moment, and Dusty returned to London more interested in exploring a romantic relationship with a woman.

The Brooklyn Fox had deeply influenced Dusty, and some essential parts of her character had fallen into place. Although Dusty protested that she was never a political person, and took no part in the myriad of causes or political protests of the 1960s, she was inherently fair and open minded. She could hardly have chosen a more explosive time to become entwined with the American Civil Rights movement, and her experiences of performing with black artists impressed her deeply. While the friendships and relationships she forged at the Brooklyn Fox would mold the crucial years of her career and inspire the direction of her music, the discrimination that she had seen her friends undergoing was at the forefront of her mind when she reluctantly agreed to take part in the most controversial tour of her career, to South Africa.

6

DUSTY V. APARTHEID

Dusty organized no protests, staged no sit-ins and made no angry speeches, but her refusal to play to racially segregated audiences in South Africa rocked the cosy world of British entertainment, and ruined forever the possibility that entertainers could silently appease racism with a sly wink, while coining the profits. As far as Dusty was concerned, if it wasn't acceptable at home, it wasn't acceptable abroad—dismissing with a shrug the morally flawed compromise agreement that most entertainers signed up to which agreed to playing to some segregated houses. "I didn't particularly want to play to *any* segregated venues," Dusty said, as if this was the most obvious and acceptable reason in the world. Dusty was the first British artist to invoke what was effectively a non-apartheid clause, and paved the way for the future cultural boycott of South Africa.

Her deportation from South Africa, surrounded by a flurry of telegrams, front-page headlines, police escorts and a hastily arranged press conference back at Heathrow, suggested that perhaps she should never have agreed to the tour in the first place. After her experiences in America, and friendships with many black artists, it was unlikely that the brutal apartheid regime would be close to her heart. Both the Musicians Union, of which Dusty was a member, and Equity were debating the issue of racism, with the MU coming down on the side of banning its members from playing in venues that operated a color bar, and staging a strike at one British venue that attempted to enforce one. Equity was split down the middle, with resulting confusion.

At the time, public opinion was yet to conclude that apartheid South Africa should be an isolated pariah state, for there was racism aplenty in the world: in the US, in British colonies like Rhodesia and ex-colonies like Australia—and at home in England. South Africa was still a highly lucrative destination for British and US artists, who were almost always guaranteed sell-out shows in an otherwise culturally arid landscape. On the other hand, by 1964 the horror of the apartheid laws was certainly well reported, and no one could deny knowledge of a government that had segregated all public spaces, introduced pass books for blacks, declared whites-only areas and jobs, evicted nonwhite people from their homes and ordered the Sharpeville shooting massacre of 1960. As some form of appeasement, those entertainers who turned up their nose at such horrific racial oppression were guaranteed a special clause in their contract—usually a few shows to nonwhite audiences here, or a few mixed shows there.

Under the circumstances, Dusty was not keen to go to South Africa at all, and her agent, Tito Burns, said it took him "months to persuade her." Eventually, though, he believed he had succeeded, working with a South African promoter to discover a way around the law that ensured that Dusty would only play to multi-racial audiences. "What we'd done was to find a loophole in the South African law," Dusty explained, "that I could play to mixed audiences as long as I played in a cinema with a live show." Drawing further attention to the resolution, she spoke to *NME* before her departure and said that the clause was her "little bit to help the colored people there." Brian Poole and the Tremeloes had tried the same tactic, but unsuccessfully, she conceded, warning, "In the end they had to play some segregated concerts. If they try that tactic with me I'll be on the first plane home."

On such an ominous note, Vic Billings flew to South Africa a few days before the tour was scheduled to begin, to make sure that everything was in order. Naturally, it was not. Billings discovered that the authorities had already heard of Dusty's plan (perhaps by reading her threat to them in *NME*) and intended to put a stop to it. Billings was issued with an ultimatum: Dusty must not play to any multi-racial audiences.

Dusty and The Echoes landed unhappily in Johannesburg a few days later, aware that a storm was brewing. While the boys enjoyed the warm weather and some pool parties, Dusty fretted. Somehow she had to stay true to her conscience and the clause in her contract. But the apartheid government, hatchet-faced Afrikaners in black suits and pork pie hats who thought nothing of murdering their opponents should the need arise, had no intention of bending to the will of a diminutive, soft-spoken convent girl from Ealing. Their standoff began.

Before the first show on December 9, two government officials appeared and asked Dusty and Vic Billings to agree to a separate show for black and white audiences. Dusty flatly refused. That night Doug Reece was put in charge of making sure that she played before a mixed audience.

I peeped through a crack in the curtain before the show to see if there were any black, or nonwhite, people in the audience. If there were, the show could go ahead. If not, I'd have to tell Dusty and she would refuse to go onstage. We'd wait and then I'd look again, and a few minutes later some black people would have been mysteriously rounded up to appear at the front.

Uneasily the two Johannesburg shows went ahead, but although the audience reacted warmly, the two government representatives reappeared at the hotel to try and get Dusty to sign some papers saying the clause in her contract was void, and had been included by mistake. Of course Dusty and Billings insisted there was no mistake, and the officials left, this time issuing a menacing-sounding warning not to leave the hotel for fear that "there might be people around who won't be tolerant of all this." Two policeman were posted at the hotel entrance, although their purpose was unclear.

The next morning at breakfast two unknown men approached Reece and told him The Echoes could become big stars in South Africa. Reece was immediately suspicious. Alarmed by the conversation, he left, but it was only one part of a bigger plot to discredit Dusty by attempting to split her off from her backing group.

The sour, and sinister, atmosphere of the tour was intensifying, with lawyers' letters, telegrams and phone calls flying between London and South Africa as Dusty's team in the UK tried to find a resolution—but the South African government was intransigent. Dusty's South African promoter, Dennis Wainer—a Jewish lawyer already known and disliked by the apartheid government because of his legal aid work for black South Africans—reassured the group that the situation would be easier when they reached Cape Town, a city supposedly known for a more liberal attitude towards interpreting the race laws. The liberal nature of Cape Town was often overstated and, although the city itself had a high proportion of English-speaking whites (whose liberal leanings were also very much exaggerated) the surrounding area was a bastion of traditional Afrikaner culture.

As planned, the first show went ahead and Dusty and Vic Billings were elated to see young South Africans of every color waiting outside the stage door to tell her how much they loved her music—and Cape Town's mixed-race "Colored" population really did appreciate music, with a long and vibrant musical history. Dusty's relief was short lived, however, and, by the time she returned to the hotel, the situation had once again reached crisis point. Reece had noticed the now-familiar government officials sitting in the audience, still in their grey suits. The same two officials were there to meet Dusty again, informing her that since she wouldn't sign the papers nullifying her contract she could not leave the hotel—but she was free to leave the country.

Disbelieving, Dusty retreated to her room and sat around all night, feeling nervous and slightly hysterical, as Billings and her lawyers made one last attempt to resolve the situation. "I never want to see another tomato sandwich as long as I live," she joked, as the hours wore on. The next morning she sent a cryptic telegram to Vicki Wickham at the apartment in Baker Street, telling her that she would be returning sooner than planned, as "I don't think that the gents like 'Dancing in the Street.'" For three days the standoff continued. The South African government considered suing Dusty for breach of contract (something they did later to other entertainers) and then claimed she could leave on a flight to Rome, but without The Echoes, as there were only two seats left. Dusty refused, and eventually enough seats were made available for everyone on the BOAC flight back to London. "It got rather nasty," Billings recalled. "Dusty got very upset. We were scared and marooned in a hotel alone for three days, not allowed to make calls home to London and surrounded by people who were alien and opposed to us." Eventually, Dusty, Billings and The Echoes all left for the airport under police escort, without completing the tour—and having failed to observe the country's "way of life," according to the official report by the South African government.

White South Africans were outraged by her stance, writing in to the newspapers to complain that all other British entertainers, including wartime sweetheart Vera Lynn, had played in South Africa without causing any trouble. But Dusty's very personal protest was noted: as she crossed the tarmac to board the plane she was moved to see that the black porters, dressed in their blue boiler suits, had lined up silently to see her off, clutching their red berets in their hands as a gesture of respect. "Oh, you did notice," she thought.

Back at home, silent respect was not on the agenda, and Dusty landed into a melee, with newspaper headlines screaming "Dusty Ordered Out!" and "Showbiz Versus Apartheid." At a hastily arranged press conference at Heathrow she looked strained and tired, and spoke to the floor with her eyes downcast while reporters bombarded her with questions about why she had staged the protest, and why she couldn't play under the same conditions as everyone else. "I am not at all political," Dusty said, rather ingenuously, in her most clipped English tones, "I just think that people should be allowed to hear me sing irrespective of color, creed or religion."

The reaction to her comments was far from supportive, with other well-known entertainers more than ready to weigh in with bitter criticism. South African producer Albert Herbert accused Dusty of staging the protest as nothing more than a publicity stunt to drum up attention for her forthcoming American tour. Max Bygraves, who had a lucrative South African tour of his own on the horizon, wondered why she was making life so much harder for British entertainers. The actor Derek Nimmo spoke at up a meeting of Equity and said that, regardless of her intentions, Dusty had actually made life harder for black South Africans and achieved "an enormous step backwards as far as the cause of racial equality was concerned." Dusty never forgot or forgave such comments, railing against Nimmo in an interview as late as 1990 and calling him "a prat." The accusation that she had done it all for publicity cut deepest. "That was the biggest hurt," she said. "I cried for days." Anonymously, she donated her £2,000 appearance fee to a charity for black South African orphans.

While Dusty suffered, Tito Burns tried to counter the criticism by issuing a stream of statements in her defence, telling the press, "She has strong feelings about this color business—Dusty's a pretty deep-thinking girl." Others also stood up for her; Ringo Starr said, "Good for Dusty. I would have done the same thing. It's stupid to have segregated audiences." When a group of fifteen MPs praised Dusty's stance against "the obnoxious doctrine of Apartheid" the South African government responded that Dusty had not, in fact, been deported, but had left of her own free will as she had refused to apply for the correct "alien's temporary permit." To make the matter absolutely clear the statement went on, "Miss Springfield came to this country with the avowed object of defying the Government's stated policy in regard to multi-racial audiences." She had been warned twice to observe the South African way of life and was informed that "if she failed to do so, she would have to leave the country." The manager of the Luxurama Theatre, where Dusty played her final show, added that she had "waved a red flag" at the government with the aim of winning bigger black audiences in the US.

Dusty later seemed embarrassed and regretful about the entire episode, saying that she had been a naïve "idiot" for blundering into a situation she didn't understand, and had indeed made life harder for black South Africans by ensuring that they would be cut off from all visiting entertainment in future. The South African government quickly closed the controversial loophole that

Dusty had sought to take advantage of, and made it impossible for anyone to follow her course. Dusty's records were banned in South Africa for decades.

"There has been considerable reaction to what Dusty [and later Adam Faith] did," singing duo Peter and Gordon told the media after their subsequent tour of South Africa. "Theaters which had, up to then, been multiracial are now segregated. The trouble has started the government being interested in theaters . . . We decided to say nothing to anybody and, as a result, we played to multiracial audiences." Dusty responded that South Africa was a nice country—if you had blinkers on. Struggling with hypocrisy was something that would plague Dusty's life; it did not come naturally to her—and she never liked it. But just as she had once realized that ruthlessness was sometimes necessary in show business, so too were half-truths and double standards. Whatever other distractions she faced, Dusty had shown that she was ruled by an iron rod of conscience. She knew what was fair and decent, and she stubbornly refused to be moved.

Later, when Kiki Dee worked briefly in South Africa, she noted the second-rate British acts still making a living there—and thought of Dusty and the stand she had taken. When Dee played the same theater as Dusty, she saw that the audience was now entirely nonwhite, and thought that Dusty would have been delighted to see it. For Dusty, however, her trip and its consequences were a harsh lesson in how the press and public responded to "stars" dabbling in political issues. "Whatever your personal political feelings are," she said later, "if you become involved in them publicly you're bound to come out the loser." For the rest of her life, Dusty steered clear of publicly expressing her opinions. Occasionally, she would later be drawn into making supportive statements about people suffering from AIDS (many of her friends and fans were gay men, and privately Dusty supported them wholeheartedly) but when asked about a feminist slant to some of the lyrics to her songs she would airily dismiss the question, saying she'd never thought of it that way. And the topic of gay equality remained resolutely off limits—and thorny.

For reporters, Dusty's trip to South Africa was just another indication that she was living up to her growing reputation of being "difficult Dusty." Reflecting the more sensationalist agenda of the tabloids, a hardened press corps were less interested in her views on apartheid than they were in quizzing her about what they deemed another much more important incident that taken place just prior to her departure for Johannesburg. Dusty had been in her dressing room at the Gaumont in Hanley on December 6, trying to record a spot for a local hospital, when she was disturbed by the noise from the room next door. After asking the occupants to keep the noise down, the cakes from the buffet table started flying until the theater manager Gerry Bennett told the *Mirror*, "I've never seen anything like it." The dressing room was a shambles, and Dusty was billed ten pounds to pay for the cleaners' overtime. By the time Dusty returned from South Africa, the press were on her case: had she or had she not refused to pay the cleaners after hurling cream buns at her dressing room wall? If cleaners were paid ten pounds overtime, she'd be a cleaner, Dusty huffed—adding, more meaningfully, that she never expected anyone else to clean up her mess.

7

THE ICON

For a few brief years in the mid-1960s it seemed that music was at the center of the universe, and that Dusty Springfield was at the center of music.

One fifteen-year-old Scottish singer, who'd just burst onto the scene with "Shout," was agog to hear what Dusty could do. "I had admired her when she was in The Springfields. But when she went solo I thought, *Oh my God*," says Lulu.

> *I was very snotty and didn't like really British performers. I didn't think there were any British girls out there doing anything as good as American females, but I thought she really did it, and that got to me. That hit me in my sweet spot, that smoky voice of hers, and I felt that her heart was in her voice.*

For Dusty not only had the voice, but also a deep vulnerability that moved her audience in ways that were sometimes hard to identify. "Her vulnerability was such a magnet, and it absolutely let you believe her when she sang sad songs. You heard it in her voice, but you could also see it in her and you knew. If ever I felt shy I would hide it, but she couldn't."

Dusty had the elements to make her iconic in an era when pop stars could be just that. Fueled by the spending power of a new generation of teenagers, more records were bought in 1964 than had ever been bought before—or would ever be bought again. Pop stars were gods, their words hungered for, their hair and clothes slavishly copied, their music spiraling out in new directions—riding the wave of being the sound of the "new age." In the new age everything fast and modern was in, everything old and gloomy and established was out. Or so the story went: "This is the jet age," Deputy Prime Minister George Brown thundered, "the era of moving damn fast!"

Old bomb-damaged cities were pulled down and rebuilt along modernist lines, the economy boomed, and the newly elected Labor government encouraged the spirit of egalitarianism with ventures like the Open University striving for education for all in "classless Britain." No one wanted to be a civil servant, no one wanted to wear a black suit. Instead teenagers were encouraged to be engineers and scientists, with fashion designers, and then musicians, taking up the theme of living in a futuristic, multicolored, plastic world. The mood was summarized by Twiggy, who wrote, "Anything modern was wonderful, anything old was terrible."

Somewhere in this beguiling scenario, *The Telegraph* reported, young people were flocking to get into the hottest club in all of London (and therefore the world)—Ad Lib, a Soho nightspot frequented by The Beatles where only the trendiest and most famous grooved away on a dance floor of multicolored squares to a blasting soundtrack of "I Just Don't Know What to Do with Myself." Without even being named in the article, Dusty and her song had become the soundtrack of an era only a year after launching her solo career—ever present, even if she was rarely there in person. Although she was "very trendy" as one *RSG!* backing singer recalled, in other respects, she was an intriguingly unlikely '60s icon.

The spirit of music was sweeping towards amateurish groups springing up and finding their own, rougher, sound. But Dusty was already a smooth professional, who had been rigorously schooled in the entertainment industry of the 1950s. The new stars were now working-class lads and lasses who'd made their way to the big city and found fame and wealth, just as everyone was increasingly encouraged to believe that they could. Yet Dusty was as well-spoken as ever, complaining that her middle-class origins held her back as she couldn't lust for success in the way that she believed her contemporaries did, nor could she take to the stage with what she perceived to be the devil-may-care confidence of the aristocracy. As skirts got shorter, Dusty's gowns got longer and more elaborate, and when pop stars began wearing the kind of outfits that anyone could replicate on the high street, Dusty took to endless fittings at a high-society couturier, Darnell's of London. The more people began to let it all hang out, the more Dusty hemmed it all in, devoting hours of her day to makeup sessions, hair appointments at Vidal Sassoon, and dress fittings. In a candid moment, Dusty reflected that creating the myth required much effort, and that "I was my own Svengali." By 1964, being Dusty Springfield was a full-time job. Vicki Wickham says:

> Dusty wasn't typically '60s. She was a couple of years older than Cilla and Sandie Shaw, she was very well educated and very bright. She was also very glamorous and she loved Hollywood, and could analyze exactly what that meant. On top of that—she could talk and she had something to say. When you read Disc or Melody Maker she always had a bit more to say, it wasn't just the color of her shoes, it was something about Ireland or the world.

Dusty was sophisticated, Kiki Dee remembers: "She was glamorous. She always looked so stylish. Fabulous, all the time, not just on stage . . . She had the most beautiful hands. I always used to look at them—very delicate and small. Beautiful."

No rough-and-ready working-class icon, Dusty was a smoothly polished professional who was pursuing her career with an ever-increasing sense of perfectionism. If she was different in background to some of the other stars of the day, she was clearly part of what Jonathan Aitken later identified as the "talent class," a group of about two hundred young people who had broken through and become successful simply by their own merit. Aside from pop stars, Aitken also identified Vidal Sassoon (the East End Jewish boy turned celebrity hairdresser), Terence Stamp, David Bailey and Mary Quant. If some of these people, like the model Jean Shrimpton, later admitted to not enjoying the '60s as much as they were supposed to, it didn't seem that way at the time. Much of the fashion and liberal morals of the time still seemed to pass most of Britain by; it was the "talent class" that made London "swing."

With new bands dominating the charts, and more records being sold than even record companies could have imagined, or knew how to market, 1964 was both the high point of pop music and the most formative year of Dusty's career. It was the year when she would begin to record and release a stream of hits that would sustain her for almost a decade, and it was the year when she would forge and cement her relationships with three of the most fundamental influences in her life: Burt Bacharach, Motown and Madeline Bell.

Dusty had rejected a Bacharach song for her first solo single, and even admitted that some of them, like "This Empty Place," were beyond her range. Even so his complicated, intricate, melodies had appealed to her from the first time she heard "Don't Make Me Over," and she had recorded "Wishin' and Hopin'" and "Twenty Four Hours from Tulsa" on *A Girl Called Dusty*. Their eventual collaboration seemed inevitable. After launching "I Only Want To Be With You" Dusty crammed in a quick visit to New York, and met Bacharach for the first time at his apartment in Manhattan. Sandwiched between less glamorous appearances at the Essoldo in Sheffield and the Fairfield Halls in Croydon, Dusty's three-day trip in February 1964 consisted mainly of fending off pushy record promoters and PR men: "I didn't get a second to myself. The minute I got in my hotel room—pounce—business, agents, publishers," she said, as if she was rather enjoying the breathless whirl. Meeting Bacharach was an altogether more emotional experience. He began by playing her some other songs he thought would be right for her—including "I Just Don't Know What to Do with Myself." "I was falling off my stool in ecstasy," Dusty said. Bacharach played her many songs and she later admitted on his TV show that she had not been won over by any of them. At the time, however, she gallantly told the press that she left "thoroughly confused: for once I've got too much good material."

Welling up with tears at an emotional point in one track, Dusty ran into the bathroom and left with Bacharach's hairbrush in her bag instead of her own. There was something about the sensitivity of his music and personality that appealed to her deeply, and led others, including Pat Barnett, to think that if circumstances had been different they would have embarked on a romantic relationship. Later, when they met up again, Bacharach was married to Angie Dickinson, who became one of Dusty's great friends and supporters. "I couldn't do that to Angie," Dusty told Pat Barnett. "There was a strong vibe between them," Barnett says. "Dusty was so knowledge-able about music . . . They used to sit over the piano and talk about music all the time." In fact, Dusty told others that they had once slept together, although Bacharach's public comments on Dusty go only as far as acknowledging that "she was a nice lady."

Initially, Dusty claimed to be delighted by "I Just Don't Know What to Do with Myself," saying, "I fell in love with it at once—it had been recorded a couple of years earlier and hadn't gone anywhere, but that didn't worry me." The truth was more complicated. She hadn't loved it at once. It had taken her some time to come round to the idea of recording it, and characteristically, once she had recorded the song she began to have doubts again. It was "confused," she complained, and without anything to make it stand out. Her dislike of the song reached such a pitch that she tried to stop her recording manager from releasing it, saying, "I've gone right off it." Despite her reservations, the song shot to number three in the charts, and became emblematic of the '60s. Although it had previously been recorded by Tommy Hart in 1962, and was subsequently covered by other artists including Dionne Warwick, it was Dusty's reprisal of the third verse that made her version unique. Paul Howes wrote, "Her passionate and powerful delivery serves to accentuate the drama and despair."

Under Vic Billings's management, Dusty was following a carefully orchestrated plan for her recording career—two upbeat pop numbers followed by two ballads, and so on. Yet, already, it was Dusty's ability to connect with her audience through plaintive dramatic ballads that was making her into a memorable artist. Although she was undoubtedly pretty, she curiously said, "I tried to make myself as unsexy as possible," and it was indeed her appeal to some sense of loss and longing—rather than stirring up lust—that touched her fans. Dusty's melancholy resonated in millions of homes across the land, reaching out to lonely housewives and teenagers, somehow, in the words of Dusty fan and writer Laurence Cole, making them feel "less stranded."

To the outside world, Dusty appeared to be reveling in a life of wealth and glamor. "Living the life," as she put it. Her first single had earned her more than £300,000 (about $360,000) in today's money, and she brought in more from a solo appearance than The Springfields had between the three of them. Nor did Dusty have any problems spending her money, so much so that her accountant father, OB, mused to Doug Reece that he had no idea where her money went. Aside from the considerable professional costs of always making sure she toured with the best musicians, Dusty loved clothes and shopping, bought a big imported car, rented her own apartments, jetted to America and back—and vacationed in Hawaii and the Caribbean (often paying for her friends to go with her).

Yet Dusty remained dubious that she was ever truly enjoying herself. Later, she said that she recalled the circumstances of the 1960s very clearly, and would watch her old performances and ponder, "Was I happy, was I not happy?" The massive popularity of pop music meant that public attention on her was greater than ever before. As Dominic Sandbrook put it in *White Heat: A History of Britain in the Swinging Sixties*, "The enthusiasm of audiences, the interest of the press, and the general cultural cachet of pop music had never been more intense and would not perhaps ever be so again." Simon Bell, a backing singer and friend, would remark that later in her life, Dusty seemed unable to enjoy simple pleasures, like going to the pub with friends and having a laugh— it was as if she didn't know how to behave, or be at ease with herself. "She didn't know how to have a good time," Bell says.

Perhaps in the early days, however, things were different. "I think she did enjoy it," says Pat Barnett, "because in the very early years there wasn't too much pressure. It was all new, and it was exciting. Although she was always a perfectionist, and she'd always worry about whether she'd done things well enough." Vicki Wickham remembers driving up to gigs with Dusty before a performance, and having a giggle in the car. "I think at the very beginning she really did enjoy things," Wickham says. "She was not in any way antisocial," but she did not "hang out" either.

Most of us went to clubs, like Scotch of St. James, every single night, and she didn't. She came when there was someone she wanted to see. Then she would stay, and we would all stagger off in the early hours and go and eat breakfast in a hotel around the corner. But she was extremely shy. She hated walking into a room of people and having to deal with it.

Even then the dichotomy between Mary O'Brien and the increasingly famous Dusty Springfield was beginning to cause tension.

There were two Dustys. I really do think there was Mary O'Brien and Dusty Springfield. If she sat down to do an interview, she was Dusty—super bright, super intelligent, no messing. If she was walking into a room of people she didn't know then she became Mary O'Brien because she didn't know how to translate Dusty Springfield into that.

This question of Dusty v. Mary was often discussed by the people who knew her—with no consensus ever reached. "I don't think she saw herself as two people," says Pat Barnett, in contrast to Wickham.

I think she saw herself as having to put on an act for other people, with all the makeup that she had to put on—but she was still the same person underneath. She was herself when she was in the dressing room. It was only when she stepped out in front of the audience that she became the artist. So I don't think she saw herself as two people, I think she just realized she had to put on a Dusty personality when she was onstage, because that's what her fans expected.

Regardless of the extent to which Dusty and Mary were separate identities, Dusty admitted to experiencing a peculiar disembodied sensation when she appeared at a theater and saw the name "Dusty Springfield" up in lights—as if it was the name of a stranger.

The sensitive, intelligent, creative temperament that offered so much to her music also left her exhausted, terrorized by stage fright, and filled with self-doubt. Her first collapse in late 1963 was followed by others, including one in Tulsa, Oklahoma after her run at the Brooklyn Fox that left people questioning her emotional stability. "I believe Tulsa taught me a lesson," she said. "I don't think I'll ever work under the same pressure again . . . Some people said I had a nervous breakdown, but it wasn't that bad. I was just totally exhausted." Dusty had boarded a plane to the Caribbean numb and dazed, but attributed her state to being worn out by her own striving for perfection. It was something she insisted she could control, but would always struggle to do so. "She was a perfectionist," Vicki Wickham agrees, "and as she got older the perfectionist bit got harder to achieve. She always felt she hadn't quite got there."

Unlike other performers who had girlfriends, wives or husbands to support them, Dusty was officially still the "bachelor girl"— making her way on her own, seemingly with no one to fall back on. Her closest companion was a small teddy bear called Einstein, which she had found pinned to the corner of a shop window on Oxford Street. Dusty often made outfits for Einstein, who appeared in photo shoots with her—and she carried him around with her for the rest of her life. "Cilla had Bobby, Lulu had Maurice Gibb—they all had partners that they could go home to, but Dusty didn't have anybody, so she had to live a pretty private life," says Madeline Bell, who was to become a close collaborator and friend during these years. At the time, Jean Ryder remembers, "Dusty wasn't a family person, she didn't have a husband, she didn't even have a wife at that point and she didn't have any children, so she mixed mainly with the gay community."

The sense of being, at heart, solitary dogged Dusty throughout her life. "She craved love, and she never felt that she got it," says Pat Barnett. Yet Vicki Wickham remembers that Dusty was rarely alone in practice, and had quite a strong network of support: "Madeline was very supportive and helpful, and then later so was Norma Tanega." Wickham remembers that Dusty had at least "one or two serious relationships at the beginning that were good." She concedes, however, that none of the women she was involved with seemed to offer Dusty the support and validation she needed, and Dusty was far from easy to live with. 'She wanted to be loved, and she wanted to love—but she always messed it up. She was complicated because she didn't feel it was enough," Wickham says. "She was very jealous of other people's relationships, and she always felt that their relationships were better than hers."

It was at the raucous 1964 New Year's Eve party on *Ready Steady Go!* that Dusty wove her way across a crowded dance floor to introduce herself to Madeline Bell, then an up-and-coming, but still little-known, singer who had sometimes performed on the show, and managed to find her way into the green room. Bell had arrived from the US the previous year to star in Alex Bradford's gospel extravaganza *Black Nativity*, and Dusty—already a big star—enthused about Bell's performance: "Are you that singer I've heard about?" she asked, beguilingly.

Bell laughs and says, "She came to me first, and it was as if she had dropped out of the sky." Charming and friendly, Dusty continued. "She asked me if I did sessions," Bell says. "I didn't even know what she meant. Then she explained she needed backing vocals, and I said yes." Already in awe of Dusty's voice and reputation, Bell was further surprised when, at the end of the evening, Dusty insisted they swap telephone numbers. "She knew about music, she knew about soul music, she knew about Motown . . . and Motown had set the black community in America alight by this time. So for this little white girl to know all about Motown was like, wow—so I was impressed with that."

Although Bell never expected to hear from Dusty again, a

message was waiting for her later the next day when she got back to her bedsit in Ladbroke Grove. Dusty's recording manager, Johnny Franz, was offering her work as a backing singer. "I said yes. I needed the money, I would have done anything," Bell recalls. She had just got back from an interview at the International Cinema in Westbourne Grove where they had offered her a job as an usherette, working eleven hours a day, six days a week, paying the same amount per week as Johnny Franz was offering for a single three-hour session—six guineas (about $30). It seemed almost too good to be true. "It was the first session I ever did, and it was for Dusty."

With the exception of a couple of stars, there were few black singers in Britain at the time. "The blackest singers were Shirley Bassey and Cleo Laine," Bell says. "You didn't see many black people on television at that time. That was at a time when, when people like Little Richard and Ray Charles put out an album, it wouldn't have their face on the cover of the album."

Backing groups like the Ladybirds and the Breakaways were usually trained singers who could read music, but American imports such as Bell, and then P. P. Arnold and Doris Troy, had "the feel." Although they couldn't read music, they had an edge to their voices that Dusty believed could carry a song to new and exciting places. Soon Dusty began to work more with Bell (and then Lesley Duncan and Kay Garner, and Kiki Dee) and less with The Breakaways, who'd been with her since they first met on early episodes of *Ready Steady Go!* Jean Ryder, who was in The Breakaways, says:

> It was us for a few years, until she met Madeline. She was friends with Madeline, and she was much closer with Madeline than she was with us. We just worked with her. We weren't buddy-buddies, we didn't go out to dinner or go to parties with her or anything like that . . . We were on all of Dusty's

first work, and then she met Madeline Bell and she was abso-
lutely obsessed with Madeline—and so Madeline got our jobs
basically. She wanted Madeline with her, and on everything.

Slim and long limbed, Madeline Bell had grown up in East Orange, New Jersey, singing in the rival gospel choir to Dionne Warwick, her sister Dee Dee and their cousin Cissy Houston. The two choirs often competed against each other, but whenever Dee Dee and Cissy turned up, you knew you were going to lose, Bell says. The sound that Britain found so captivating was two a penny in New Jersey, and Bell would tell people who admired her voice that back in the US "you can find ten like me on any street corner."

In 1963 she left America, just as it began to confront the Civil Rights movement—and arrived in a Britain with a different, but just as entrenched, racism. The late 1950s had seen the rise of groups such as the White Defence League that organized popular public demonstrations against immigration and in favor of "Keeping Britain White." Just as race riots consumed US cities, London's Notting Hill riots in 1958 had exposed the deep seam of ugly discrimination at the heart of British culture.

With no money and few contacts, Madeline Bell often made the lonely trudge around the circuit of London bedsits in then-seedy areas like Ladbroke Grove, looking for somewhere to stay. "There really were the signs in the window that said 'No coloreds, no Irish and no dogs,'" she remembers. "I would ring up and they would say, 'Yes, the room is still available.' Then I would turn up, the landlady would open the door to me and say, 'Sorry, the room's just gone.'" Dusty had introduced Bell to Riss Chantelle, and Chantelle would drive Bell around, helping her look for a room. If Bell was turned away Chantelle would pop back to check, and would invariably discover that the room was mysteriously available to rent again—to a white person. "Britain was a very racist country, and it still is,"

Bell says.

A year after arriving in the country Bell needed to work and find a place to stay. Dusty offered both—as well as a deep friendship and a professional collaboration that would add much to both their careers. "Madeline was the best friend she ever had and she didn't realize it," Pat Barnett says. "Everybody had somebody but Dusty lived alone, she didn't have anybody," Madeline Bell says. "She was the biggest star and she didn't have anybody and people ask me, 'Well, you and Dusty used to live together?' Yeah, we used to live together and we used to sit up until four, five o'clock in the morning talking about our backgrounds and everything because she had nobody to go home and talk to."

Bell moved into Dusty's apartment, and estimates that Dusty must have been moved in and out of as many as thirty fully furnished, short-term apartments over the course of three years, including an aparment in Kensington Gore behind the Albert Hall. "We moved many times, we would stay in one place for three months and we would stay in serviced apartments." Dusty's restlessness could be temporarily allayed, but never for long.

> She was always quite happy to live in serviced flats because she was always like a transient person anyway, just come in and put the suitcases down and unpack them and then a couple of days later you've got to be on the road again so off you go again, so she didn't really need to be in one place, and also having a house and being alone meant that she would be coming home to an empty house.

So pleased was she not to be living alone, Dusty would later tell people she would wait with excitement to hear Bell's feet on the steps outside. Unlike Pat Barnett and Doug Reece, who always called her Dusty or "Dust," in private Bell would call Dusty by her real name. "When she was home and she closed the door she could be Mary," Bell says. "She liked that—Mary."

Sometimes Dusty would bring someone from a show back with her, and Bell remembers Ike and a very shy Tina Turner dropping in for some fried chicken. More often, Bell would cook dinner—"I was always the cook"—while Dusty would be working on her new songs, propping up some lyrics on top of her acoustic guitar because she was too short-sighted to see them otherwise, or learning a new language. Dusty lapped up stories about Bell's life in New Jersey, and they would talk about gospel and the origins of American music. "Me and Dusty used to sit and talk for hours," Bell says. "About gospel music, about what my background was and what it was like in America, and what the black churches were like—because she'd never experienced all of that."

Bell was surprised by Dusty's love of black music, but equally impressed by her knowledge of all kinds of music.

> The first time I ever heard "La Bamba," it was her singing it in Spanish, and I thought, "That's amazing, you can sing in Spanish?" And then on her TV series she'd do things like "If You Go Away," "Ne me quitte pas," in French. Wow! How did you do that? In those days nobody was doing that kind of thing. She was the only one that was doing that.

Dusty also talked about her own experiences and childhood. "I didn't know about convent schools, and she'd tell me stories about the nuns, who weren't the nicest people," Bell adds. "She always used to say that some of her emotional problems came from going to convent school, because they held you back so much in so many ways." One of those ways was Dusty's growing uncertainty over her sexuality, something she would also discuss with Bell.

By 1964 Dusty was already being forced into publicly commenting on her single status, and inventing a series of seemingly promising, but ultimately unfulfilled, romances with men. Most notably the press was invited to attend various set-ups with singer Eden Kane, who was also represented by Vic Billings. In carefully staged appearances, Kane was photographed waiting for her in her dressing room with a bunch of flowers and a kiss on the cheek, while Dusty would confess to reporters that she liked him very much, although it was "much too early to talk about marriage." Although Dusty always emphatically maintained that she would never agree to something so cynical just for publicity, Kane admitted in 2005 that their "romance" was entirely made up to throw the press off the scent.

"They hounded her because they wanted to know about her sexuality, it was always that," Bell says. "It wasn't like they were interested in her music, they wanted to know who she was sleeping with, and I guess that's another one of the reasons why she had to leave, eventually, because in those days you couldn't talk about your sex life unless you were straight, shall I just say that. She didn't know what she was at that time."

With friends like Vicki Wickham, Dusty could be open about her sexuality. "She was straightforward about it, except in public. It would have killed her career. She had become an icon that every taxi driver and shopkeeper loved. Had you told them that Dusty's gay, they would have gone 'Oh God!'" Dusty never talked in "gay slang" in her TV appearances, as was sometimes later reported. She would sometimes go to a gay club called Yours & Mine underneath a restaurant called El Sombrero on Kensington High Street with friends like Pepe Borza. Vicki Wickham and folk singer Julie Felix remember they visited the lesbian bar Gateways in Chelsea with a group of friends out of curiosity when it was immortalized in the cult 1968 film *The Killing of Sister George*. Gateways remained the only well-known location for London lesbians for years; its green door opened onto a narrow stairway that led down into a crowded basement bar and dance floor. At the time the lesbian scene was as restrictive as the heterosexual world, with butch women wearing men's suits and slicking back their hair, for their femme partners. Other women who visited Gateways at this time later reported that Dusty would turn up, sometimes out of hours, when the club was closed—although Wickham believes this lesbian urban myth is unfounded. Undoubtedly, however, Dusty witnessed this world, and remained confused, continuing to have casual liaisons with men as well as with women as she struggled to come to terms with her sexuality.

Rumors about her relationship and living arrangements with Madeline Bell upset Dusty, according to Pat Barnett:

> *I was walking down towards the front of the stage with Dust, and it was in the paper, and she started crying. She said, "Look, just because somebody's staying with me and she's female . . ." and it was hinting she was a lesbian, and she was in tears. And I said to her, "Don't worry about it. They're going to pick on you, and they'll pick on somebody else tomorrow."*

"The press had been insinuating it for years," Madeline Bell says.

> *I remember her doing an interview, I think it might have been in the* Ready Steady Go! *studios, and I was in the dressing room and Vicki Wickham was there and Dusty did this interview with this guy from the* News of the World, *and he wrote the nastiest piece about her. He said something like I was sitting there like her negro slave. And the way he wrote it, it just sounded so nasty. So really she couldn't talk to anybody, she had to keep her business to herself.*

Talking long into the night, Dusty could say how she really felt about all the things that worried her. "Late at night, after a gig, that's what it was like," Bell says. "But the rest of her life she had to concentrate fully on being Dusty, and that was a hard job." In the morning Bell's down-to-earth fresh-faced friend Mary would vanish again—and Dusty was back to being the woman who wouldn't go out without applying elaborate makeup, and spent hours of every day waiting for hair and nail appointments.

Bell remembers sitting with Dusty while she spent five or six hours getting her red hair bleached blonde. "They would be standing there with a hairdryer on cold as they were putting this stuff on, and she'd be in tears, floods of tears, she's going through all of this pain to be Dusty." Then they would rush to Darnell's for a long dress fitting "and then she'd have to go from there to start sorting out the music and rehearsing with the band. It was a 25-hour-a-day job for her."

Aside from personal support, Bell's influence soon started to shine through in Dusty's music. Bell began singing backup on all of Dusty's recordings and stage appearances, and Dusty returned the favor, singing backup on Bell's 1967 album *Bell's a Poppin'* under the name of Gladys Thong (a ruse she invented to avoid legal issues with her own record company). "I'm very strong willed and I do backing voices just for a laugh and because I enjoy it, so why shouldn't I?" Dusty told Penny Valentine in an interview for *Disc and Music Echo*. "It all started when I made some demo records for Doris Troy when she was here and then I started to sing on Madeline Bell, Lesley Duncan and Kiki Dee's records. I don't see why I shouldn't. They sing on mine and we're all friends."

Dusty had long been influenced by black American music, and she started to adopt some gospel intonations, like call and response, into her work. Vicki Wickham says:

> I fell in love with black music through Dusty. When she
> started going to America she brought back all these records
> from the Colony Record Shop, and we would go down to

> *Dave Godin's Soul City record shop off Cambridge Circus*
> *every Saturday and just take a stack of records home with*
> *us without even listening to them first. They had big holes in*
> *them because they were American and we'd have to put this*
> *transformer in the middle to make them play, and then we'd*
> *just sit and listen to thirty or forty records in one go. Her joy*
> *was listening to music and the voices that really affected her.*

Johnny Franz mused, "Dusty is such a record lover, you could give her one great new American disc and it would probably mean more to her than if you gave her a Rolls-Royce."

Like other British artists, Dusty covered songs that had been hits for black American singers. Unlike them, however, she was responsible for introducing Motown to the British public, acting as an unofficial promoter and ambassador. "It was through Dusty that Motown became what it was," says Madeline Bell. "Through her. When they came over to do their tour they called it the ghost tour because they were playing to mostly empty halls and then Dusty got onto Vicki Wickham and said, 'If you do a show with them I'll present it'—and that did it."

In 1963 Motown had sent over a delegation to set up a record deal with Oriole Records, a small London company that couldn't give the promotions needed to break into the UK charts. When Dave Godin wrote to Berry Gordy Jr. to explain why he thought Motown was not doing well in the UK, Gordy wrote back—offering, in a six-page telegram, to fly Godin to Detroit to find out how they could work together.

Godin accepted Gordy's offer and on his return, he decided to promote Motown as a sound and label in Britain, rather than choosing an individual artist who might, or might not, succeed. In 1964 Mary Wells's "My Guy" became the first Motown hit in the UK, followed by "Where Did Our Love Go?" by The Supremes, which reached number two in the charts after getting airplay on the new pirate station Radio Caroline. The single's success was quickly followed by "Baby Love," which shot to number one.

Within a year, in March 1965, the first Motown tour arrived in Britain—the Motown Revue, which was promoted by Dusty on a Rediffusion TV special called *The Sound of Motown*. Dave Godin remembered Dusty saying, "Package me with it, and my name will get it on." The TV special, taped on March 18 and screened in April, included The Supremes, Martha and the Vandellas, Smokey Robinson and the Miracles, and the Earl Van Dyke Six. Although The Supremes were by now the stars of Motown it was, of course, Martha Reeves who was Dusty's good friend. While Reeves seethed that Berry Gordy orchestrated the camera angles on the fast-paced nonstop music show to favor Diana Ross, she was the one who got to sing "Wishin' and Hopin'" with Dusty.

The closeness of the pair, who partied together and shopped on Bond Street, kindled a rumor that they were more than friends—something Reeves emphatically denied. When she could, Dusty drove around the country following the tour, and a Motown engineer found her fast asleep in Reeves's bed the morning after a late-night crying session, "with one of her legs stuck out from under the comforter, fishnet stockings and all." Dusty had simply cried herself to sleep, and Reeves mused that it was funny about how people's minds worked as there was no truth in the allegation.

With an unbeatable combination of artists including Diana Ross, Smokey Robinson and Stevie Wonder, the tour packed twenty-one shows into twenty-four days, but was rocked by a poor reception for accompanying artist Georgie Fame, from soul fans who derided him for not "being the real thing," and a musicians' strike led by the Earl Van Dyke Six. The turnout was generally lackluster in a country that was still to be fully exposed to black music—and the culture shock was mutual as Motown artists, including The Supremes' Mary Wilson, reeled at the bad hamburgers, drinks without ice and waxy British toilet paper. Vicki Wickham later admitted they had been "too ambitious" for a tour that included few artists with current hit records, in an era when having a charting hit really mattered, and Dusty told *Melody Maker* it was "too advanced." She added that Britain had a smaller black community than the US and, aside from The Supremes and Martha and the Vandellas, "the majority of the acts weren't sufficiently well known." Without Dusty's intervention, they would have been even less well known, with Martha Reeves admitting, "Dusty had a lot to do with our recognition. She touted us."

Playing to empty halls was not something that artists enjoyed but "the small crowd played well to the snobbery of we serious Motown fans," soul fan Adam White wrote. "This was 'our' music, and they were 'our' artists and the fact that the majority of British concert goers didn't recognize the uniqueness of this sound only reinforced our innate sense of superiority." Above all, Dusty remained an enraptured fan, admitting that she "absolutely idolized" Reeves, and even called her dog Motown—delighting when the tour returned home and Reeves sent her a bejeweled dog collar as a thank-you gift. She could reasonably claim some modest credit for Motown's success, saying, "I think I unofficially helped push Motown . . . because I made people listen to it."

Dave Godin remembered the electric atmosphere on the first night of the tour at London's Astoria Theatre in Finsbury Park. "Every soul fan in London had turned out to pack that place," he told Lucy O'Brien, adding, "I can't describe the air of celebration." Dusty was there too, of course, sitting in the stalls, watching breathlessly—happy not to be the center of attention, and turning down autographs. "Any other time," she told the few fans who recognized her, "but not tonight." Dusty was the one who really got the music. "She was in awe of us," Martha Reeves said, "and we were in awe of her."

8

DEFINITELY DUSTY

"Dusty was the first Diva I ever met."
KIKI DEE

Dusty could be difficult, they said. Dusty was a diva. Yet, on a cold night in 1965, Dusty Springfield was outside, shoveling snow outside Club Fiesta! in Stockton-on-Tees, as biting winds and a blizzard swept across the bleak industrial northern England town.

With the area's heavy manufacturing, and the sprawling ICI chemical factory in nearby Billingham, even regulars like Jon Allan remarked, "There couldn't have been a more unlikely venue for a luxury cabaret club in the whole world." The Lipthorpe brothers had opened the Fiesta in mid-1965 with the intention of rivaling top London venues like Talk of the Town or Manchester's Golden Garter. The Fiesta, with its concrete curtained front and distinctive neon sign, served dinner and cabaret to patrons who had been drawn in from across the northeast. Adding to the allure of top talent (Cliff Richard, Shirley Bassey and Roy Orbison also played there), scantily clad "Fiesta Fawns," wearing fishnet stockings, deer ears and stiff white collars, served drinks and cigarettes to men downing pints while their wives ate chicken-in-a-basket.

A few weeks earlier Dusty had been singing "I Just Don't Know What to Do with Myself" in front of the Queen at the Royal Variety Performance, something she was irked not to have been invited to do in previous years. "I was very hurt by being left out in '64," she said, blaming unnamed "powers that be" for dropping her from the bill on an "I hate Dusty" pretext. Now she was back on the road, mixing the ridiculously glamorous with the utterly mundane, and giving pleasure, as she rather patronizingly put it, to working-class women with "swollen ankles" eating scampi and chips, enjoying their one treat of the week.

When press photographer Ian Wright arrived to get shots of the evening for the local paper, he was amazed to discover Dusty out in the snow "spreading salt, encouraging the troops, occasionally stopping to sign autographs, nipping into the club to purchase a tray of 'hot toddies' to keep up everyone's spirits." At one stage a stray dog appeared and followed Dusty inside. "Dusty immediately nicknamed the collie 'Orf,' short for orphan. We did a photo story about Orf in the morning edition; alas, no one came forward to claim her so she remained at the club all her life—well looked after by the staff."

Onstage, Dusty's act included "I Only Want to Be with You," "I Just Don't Know What To Do With Myself" and "Wishin' and Hopin'" as well as "Mockingbird" with Doug Reece, "My Coloring Book" and "Dancing in the Street." After the show, Wright slipped backstage and saw Dusty, in her element, welcoming people in and out of her dressing room, and tippling on sweet Mateus Rosé wine, which was then very popular because of the design of the bottle. Like the life and soul of the party, Dusty amused everyone: "She kept everyone in stitches changing wigs, which were beautifully coiffed and displayed on Styrofoam heads with labels—Cilla Black, Shirley Bassey, Sandie Shaw and Lulu. Dusty tried each wig on while doing spot-on impersonations of each of their namesakes." That week, Dusty was photographed onstage at the height of her powers, wearing a long blue sequinned gown, her arms outstretched and her face open in an expression of something akin to surprise and joy.

"Mary seems more sophisticated now," her mother Kay wistfully told a journalist from *NME*. "It might be an affectation, though. And she's got more responsibility. When she was with The Springfields she could lean on the two boys. She comes home when she can, you know, and unwinds. She's a home lover—fireside and buttered toast type. But there isn't much time." While Dusty's father, OB, butted in to draw attention to a new record by The Seekers, the new band Tom was managing, Kay continued, "She phones me from just about everywhere when she's away. She rang up one night and said, 'Daddy and you must come to America with me.' And we did. It was marvelous. I get anxious about her sometimes but she says, 'Mum, don't worry about me—it only makes me worried too,' so I try not to." Quietly her mother concluded, "Mary always wanted to be famous. She says it all boils down to an inferiority complex. She insists she's not beautiful, but talent will out, and that's the important thing."

All of Dusty's friends were well aware that she suffered from dreadful insecurity about her appearance, something that would only get worse. She never thought she looked right, and had already undergone her first nose job at the London Clinic—calling Riss Chantelle repeatedly, begging her to come and visit. Later, when she came offstage, Dusty's Australian hairdresser John Adams remembers, she would rip her wig off in the dressing room and cry "I look like Burt Lancaster!" with her face twisted up in anguish. If her jokes about her appearance could sometimes sound amusing, her sense of self-disgust was real. Dusty had some of the same demons that plagued Marilyn Monroe, according to Kiki Dee: "Dusty didn't feel herself that people adored her, and they did, they loved the way she looked, and yet she didn't feel that inside. It makes it even worse in a way because even if you are getting all this adoration it doesn't feel real to you."

The previous twelve months had proved to be a microcosm of Dusty's life and career. After meeting Madeline Bell at the *Ready Steady Go!* New Year's Eve party, Dusty had departed for the San Remo Song Festival in Italy, where she sang "Di fronte all'amore" and "Tu che ne sai?," but was eliminated in the semifinals after a full-out rehearsal had drained her voice, leaving her hoarse and strained for the performance itself—something that was to become a regular feature of her career. Instead she watched from the wings while her rivals Kiki Dee and Petula Clark took center stage. "Kiki has remarkable voice control, for someone her age," Dusty remarked. It was the first time that Dusty and Kiki had spent time together. "I felt that she always had respect for me," Dee says. "I don't think she was that interested in me. She was very much interested in herself and her career and people of her own age. She was always very nice to me, but we didn't hang out, that wouldn't have happened." On that trip, Dee remembers, Dusty had a backstage tantrum that involved hurling a vase down the hallway due to an upset with the management.

Dusty's outbursts could be wild and were unpredictable: Pat Barnett had dreaded telling Dusty that she had ruined her favorite dress in an ironing accident before the same trip, but Dusty had been remarkably calm about it, and had simply chosen another outfit. Although she was eliminated in the competition, the trip turned out to be crucial for Dusty's career—listening in the audience she heard an Italian ballad, "Io che non vivo senza te," and returned to London determined to turn it into a hit. Dusty asked Vicki Wickham to hastily compose some lyrics, which she did with the help of The Yardbirds' manager Simon Napier-Bell. After rejecting the premise of "You Love Me" as too sloppy, they settled on "You Don't Have to Say You Love Me" instead, and Wickham showed them to Dusty, who agreed that they were not the greatest lyrics in the world, but would have to do.

"'t's commercial, and I've been crazy about it since I heard it first. It's good old schmaltz," Dusty told *Melody Maker* when the song came out in 1966. A ballad "has to take me by the scruff of the neck," she later added, "which is how I found 'You Don't Have to Say You Love Me,' when I heard it in Italian. My Italian is not good, but I'm deeply impressed when an audience stands up to applaud the instrumental, which they did in San Remo. That's how I recognize songs. It's not exactly difficult. It's as if someone's run a train through your stomach."

For the rest of 1965 she toured across Britain, first playing in a three-week package tour with the Searchers and the Zombies, and then alone in cabaret, doing a week at a time on the rota of northern clubs including Newcastle's La Dolce Vita, Mr. Smith's in Manchester and in Jarrow, a tough shipbuilding outpost on the banks of the Tyne, Club Franchi, owned by a family that had a lucrative sideline in fish and chip shops.

"I have no super major nostalgia for it," Dusty recalled in 1995. "We're all nostalgic about what we listened to, but if you were actually doing it, being the singer, traveling, getting on the bus outside Madame Tussaud's at eight in the morning with your beehive done perfectly . . . It wasn't that much fun, to tell you the truth."

The year was also punctuated by episodes of temperament, and nervous collapse. In March Dusty had taken herself, Madeline Bell, Martha Reeves, her brother Tom and Pepe Borza to Rio de Janeiro for Mardi Gras, dancing, watching drag queens and enjoying the heat for what she later called "the five craziest days of my life." Picking up the bill everywhere she went, Dusty and the girls samba-danced their way across the city and had their photos taken at scenic look-out spots wearing gold lamé trousers, and headscarves to protect their hair from the wind. Late in the proceedings, Dusty trod on a broken bottle, which cut deeply into her foot, injuring her badly. "They sewed it without any anaesthetic," Dusty said; "they see a lot of broken bodies in Carnival and they were not impressed by this white woman treading on a broken bottle, then screaming the place down." Dusty hobbled back to Britain and undertook her engagements, including the *Sound of Motown* show and the *NME* Poll Winners' Concert at Wembley, with some difficulty, while Martha Reeves recalled that the incident was not entirely accidental: "The reason for the stomping on the broken bottle was never explained to me. However, it was after a heated argument."

In February Dusty had released "Your Hurtin' Kind of Love," which she claimed to have developed a "pretty strong loathing for," perhaps because the song was her first flop as a solo artist, reaching only thirty-nine in the charts. In May the pressure was on with her next release, "In the Middle of Nowhere," the first song to feature Madeline Bell, Lesley Duncan and Doris Troy as backing singers. Two flops in a row would spell disaster, but the song did relatively well, climbing to number five in the charts. "She usually knew what she wanted," Madeline Bell says. "When she did 'In the Middle of Nowhere' or 'Little by Little' those cover demos would come over from America finished. All she had to do was get an arranger."

Although Bell had never sung a session before, she had good musical ears, "The session was usually three hours long, and we could do three or maybe four tracks in that. It didn't take long for us to understand what she was looking for." Dusty would sing in the studio with the musicians and the backing singers, and then record her final vocals again alone. Despite the different sound, Dusty claimed that "In the Middle of Nowhere" was one of her worst ever records, although she had not felt that way when one of the writers, Bea Verdi, had played it for her on a ragtime piano at a New York publishing house.

By the summer 1965, Dusty was exhausted and emotionally drained, collapsing in New York before being ushered onto a plane to the Virgin Islands, numb to her surroundings—neither knowing nor caring where she was heading. After ten days on the beach a bored and restless Dusty returned to the US and embarked on a Wild West road trip across Arizona with Pepe Borza. "We ran out of [gas] and it took fifteen hours, even in a Thunderbird," Dusty said.

The distraction appeared to do her good. When she returned to the UK, the release of "Some of Your Lovin'" in late September 1965 provided her with a rare moment of contentment and satisfaction. Although the song only reached number eight in the chart, it fatefully led to her deal with Atlantic Records. "I was so ecstatically proud of it," Dusty said.

"Some of Your Lovin'" was a Goffin/King number Dusty had recorded in June with Madeline Bell, Lesley Duncan and Kiki Dee on backing. Carole King had pressed the demo into Dusty's hand in New York. It was originally intended as an album track for *Ev'rything's Coming Up Dusty*, but its potential was immediately apparent and it was released as a single. "I think I've already done my next single, by mistake," Dusty told Penny Valentine for *Disc Weekly*. "I'm very pleased with it indeed, which is really saying something for me." She added that she thought it was a "really, really great song," and the only song she ever made that she took home and played fourteen times in a row. Unlike some of her previous recordings Dusty's voice was pushed right to the front to maximize her sultry seductive sound.

"The one thing she was really good at was choosing material," Vicki Wickham says. "She really chose great writers and great songs, and even when she was doing covers, the covers became Dusty's. The one exception to that was Carole King. She did copy Carole King, and if you listen to the demos they're very similar." Indeed, Dusty admitted that she slavishly followed King's style of singing on "Some of Your Lovin'."

If *A Girl Called Dusty* had been a blast of uninhibited young pop, *Ev'rything's Coming Up Dusty*, released in October 1965, moved into a more adult category. Gone was the denim-clad fresh-faced girl with the blonde bob; in her place there was a mature woman with hair pinned up, flawless makeup and a high-necked gown. The opening track, "Won't Be Long" (a hit for Aretha Franklin in 1960), has a strong gospel feel, complete with tambourine. "Oh No! Not My Baby" was recorded twice, first as the final recording with the Breakaways, and then again with Madeline Bell and Doris Troy on backing vocals. Dusty believed the second combination was better, forcing her up to hit the high notes. "Doris Tory, Mad and I worked on the same mic," she said. "It ended up as the Madeline Bell Show, not her fault." While her own favorite track on the album, "I Had a Talk with My Man," was a "lovely song," she said, the immense variety of music and tempos reflected the diversity of Dusty's musical interests. Tom played piano on "La Bamba," while Dusty herself conducted the orchestra through "Who Can I Turn To?," which she wanted to have an unusual Latin beat.

"Live It Up," a favorite of Doug Reece, has a very different sound—a gritty energy and exuberance that came from a series of recordings Dusty made in 1964 in New York. Shelby Singleton, who had organized The Springfields' recordings in Nashville, produced the sessions and pushed Dusty's vocals out front. In total, eight songs were recorded in New York, with four later released as the "Dusty in New York" EP. It was the start of Dusty's long friendship with sound engineer and then producer Brooks Arthur, who says:

> *Dusty and I, we just clicked. We didn't yack much, we didn't say much to each other except she always asked me what I thought and I would try to defer it to Shelby and Shelby would say "Tell her what you feel, tell her what you think." Once she tore into a song and claimed it as her own, the vocals were undeniable and the audience would love her forever.*

When she walked into the studio, Dusty was already rock 'n' roll royalty, Arthur adds. "Her hair was gorgeous and she had such a beautiful face. She had elegance and grace and reeked of being a superstar; a real singer, the real deal." She was friendly with the musicians but disliked those who were too touchy-feely or tried to hug her. She was ready to get to work. Arthur recalls:

> *She'd be out there for a live vocal. We would get a few takes down and see maybe we could capture some magic in one of them, maybe edit a few of the takes together, or go for one from top to bottom that can be called a great take. Shelby would always say "There's your record!"*

Dusty would stay into the night, after the session finished, to work on her vocals with Arthur, Singleton and Jerry Kennedy. "We'd either attempt to redo her vocal or attempt to punch in and punch out on a preexisting vocal that was live. Shelby was a proponent of that live thing," Arthur says. He adds that

Dusty, like Barbra Streisand, became "overly caring," but then Arthur himself was overly caring too—"as long as it didn't end up sounding artificial. As long as it kept her beautiful sound and her beautiful soul."

Above all, Arthur remembers his blossoming friendship with Dusty. "We just had a groove going there in those '60s sessions. And somehow or other, because we got a groove going, when we would see each other, either in the studio again or even at a restaurant or whatever, we were always like two old friends." That friendship was to be tested to the limits a decade later when Arthur produced Dusty on her ill-fated, but hauntingly beautiful, album *Elements*, also known as *Longing*. In 1964, though, all was still relatively rosy, and Dusty reveled in the freedom and cooperation of working in an American studio as compared to the restrictions she faced back at home.

Not only did Dusty look more mature on *Ev'rything's Coming Up Dusty*, she was more determinedly grown up and in control of its creation too. Recording with Dusty was an eye opener for both Kiki Dee and Madeline Bell. It was also an exercise in patience and willpower. Dusty would often sing one line, or even one word, and then stop.

When she sang "You Don't Have to Say You Love Me" she literally did it line by line because she wanted it to be perfect, and it was. She would sing "You don't have to say you love me, just be close at hand," stop. She'd listen to that. If it sounded all right we'd carry on. If not then they'd run the tape back and she'd wait for that bit and she'd sing it again. "When I said I needed . . ."—if it wasn't on that, "need," on the right beat, you'd have to stop and go back and do it again. Line by line. She would do a recording like that because she was so unsure of how good she was.

In addition, British musicians were not used to being told what to do by a female artist—one who was exacting, and demanding the very best from them. Bell recalls that in those days recording engineers at studios like EMI still wore white coats like lab technicians and worked a board which musicians and singers were barred from ever touching. Sessions were strictly limited to three hours by union rules and at the end of each session a woman appeared with a plate of biscuits and a pot of tea. In the US the atmosphere in the studio was far more open and collaborative, but in Britain musicians had little time for a woman singer who wanted them to play differently but didn't know the technical terms to describe what she wanted. On "Some of Your Lovin'" Dusty wanted a muddy piano sound, with the notes rolling into each other. "They were going 'It's not clear, it's not clear,' and I went 'I don't want it to be clear. Take all the treble off, it's got to be like that . . . keep the pedal down, let the notes roll into each other.'"

The result was a recording that Dusty described as "light years ahead of its time," and one that secured her a later deal with Atlantic Records after she played it to Ahmet Ertegun, who'd dropped in for tea with Goldie and the Gingerbreads, an all-female rock group who were renting a large apartment in the building where Dusty and Madeline Bell lived in Bayswater. Ertegun was known for having fantastic ears when it came to artists and material, and he had established Atlantic as an independent R&B studio, taking on the record industry giants. Now, however, Atlantic was trying to find an audience with young white record buyers—and Dusty's sound was perfect. She remembered that he told her, "'If you ever get free of your obligations elsewhere, come to Atlantic.' So I did."

Dusty was invariably pushing and pushing to get the sound she wanted, leading to what Johnny Franz called "foot-stomping sessions," as she told *Mojo* in 1995:

The magic of my situation with Johnny Franz was that he allowed me the freedom to follow my enthusiasm. He'd sit in the control room while I'd go out and scowl at the musicians. It was very difficult for them because they'd never heard this stuff before. I'm asking somebody with a stand-up bass to play Motown bass lines, and it was a shock. The ones who thought I was a cow I didn't work with again. The ones who wanted to learn with me, they had the greatest time.

In truth, Dusty had produced both of her first albums herself, something she never took credit for.

I never took the producer's credit for two reasons. For one, he [Franz] deserved it and I was grateful. And then there was the calculating part of me that thought it looked too slick for me to produce and sing. Because women didn't do that. And there remains in the British audience, though less so, that attitude of "Don't get too slick on us. Don't be too smart or we won't love you." And I wanted to be loved.

When one musician called her "a bitch in the studio," Dusty shot back, with some bitterness, that there were a lot of men who had called her names behind her back, but were happy to live off the money they earned from her:

Men have been good to me. But I shouldn't feel they've been good to me. They should have just bloody well listened. But in those days it was quite something to listen to a woman who had a musical mind. You sang the song. You sang it fast and cheaply. And they might take you out for a meal. I worked with some bastards, and some nice guys who saw that I knew

what I was doing. A few of them went away and said what a
cow I was, having made a great deal of money off me.

"She was one of the first female artists, at a very chauvinistic time, who knew what she wanted and went for it," says Kiki Dee, who worked on those sessions. "She knew what she wanted from the artists and musicians. She was a bit of a perfectionist—which was new to me as I was doing everything I was asked to do. To see someone like that was quite an education."

Not many artists attempted to exert such creative control, and fewer still got away with it. "I had kind of the opposite experience, coming in so young and being with a lot of older people and kind of trying to get them to hear what I said and/or believe in what I felt instinctively, but I always had to back down," Lulu remembers. "If you're a female singer you won't get a musician's respect because you can cut it. Even working with musicians who respect you, you've got to fight harder to get what you want than a man. But it was all down to Dusty and it was her responsibility, and she took it on."

British musicians suffered from "a singular lack of 'feel' for what I can only describe as 'funk,'" Dusty told *Melody Maker* in 1968. "We can produce the most marvelous big, fat sounds, but we seem incapable of producing the sort of loose, uninhibited sort of funk that, say, Motown gets. But I don't expect we can ever achieve it, because it comes naturally to them. My trouble is that I want Detroit moving to London."

Dusty's tireless search for perfection was further hindered because, as we have seen, she often couldn't communicate what she wanted. Jean Ryder says:

She gave the musicians a very hard time, and the session
musicians in England are the best session musicians in the

world. She wasn't a trained musician, she hadn't gone to music college or anything like this, and so she didn't how to articulate musically to the musicians what she wanted or how she wanted it to sound. So she would go over to a guitar player for instance and say, "Have you heard this record?," and she'd name some obscure American record that she'd heard, and she'd say, "You know the guitar player on that goes tick-a-ting-ta-ting-tick-a-ting-ta-ting," and the guy would say, "Well, is this what you'd want?" and he'd try to play it, and she'd go, "No, no, that's not what I want, that's not what I want," and she would get all sort of uptight . . . She was very passionate about her music, very passionate about what she wanted, but she didn't have the means of communicating with the musicians on a musical basis and so she would get up their noses, and the musicians used to think, "Oh God, another Dusty Springfield session," which was a shame because they were good and she was good.

Johnny Franz often sat up all night at Dusty's recording sessions, going through take after take. "I will say this. If Dusty had just made an absolutely sensational record, and she felt that by trying again she could get it just 1 percent better . . . then try again she would," he told *NME* in 1966. "She is such a perfectionist that sometimes she has been misunderstood by people who don't know her well. I have heard it said that she can be difficult, but what can you expect when she loves her music so much?" He added that she also spent a long time with Madeline Bell and Lesley Duncan getting the backing sound she was looking for: "Dusty sessions are quite hard work. She is pretty serious in the studio, and it's a good thing."

Dusty even rebelled against the sound of the studio, complaining that Philips had "such a dead sound" and was similar to recording in a padded cell. She often resorted to recording in the hallways, hanging over a stairwell in the case of "You Don't Have to Say You Love Me," or even—to the bemusement of the cleaners—in the ladies' toilets.

The resulting sound on *Ev'rything's Coming Up Dusty* caused a sensation, selling £5,000 (roughly $6,000) worth of records per day and taking the album to number six in the charts. Reviews proclaimed that Dusty had earned her place at the top of the league of women singers, while the lavish album sleeve was made up of a twelve-page booklet of color and black and white photos of Dusty—something no other band or singer was gifted with at the time. While Dusty giggled over the idea of the album cover, she was immensely pleased and proud to see the efforts of a work that was truly of her own making.

Others in the industry, however, had also been taking note of how the process had unfolded, and the seeds of Dusty's reputation as a recording artist were sown. "Cilla had Bobby to tell her what to do, and Lulu and Sandie had their managers, but Dusty wouldn't do what she was told because she figured she knew what was best for her—and she was right," says Madeline Bell. "She always said, 'I won't get very far in this country, because I won't do what I'm told.'"

Her live appearances were beautiful but sometimes equally fraught, with Dusty constantly striving for perfection onstage as in the studio. "The notes had to be correct, the approach had to be right, the dynamics should be there—light and heavy, loud and soft—but it had to have feel. If all these things were there with a good balance on the band and she could be heard over the band, she was great to work with," Doug Reece says. "She had really good ears, she could hear any mistakes that may have been made by the band. She knew how it should sound for her and how it should feel. If it wasn't right she'd let you know. I always stood to her left onstage and I knew if something wasn't right I would get a look or nod if I had not already picked it up." Just good enough was never good enough for Dusty.

"When she was onstage she had to be Dusty—the princess. But I saw her freak out a couple of times as well," says Madeline Bell. At one club Dusty was disturbed by builders working on a construction site in the roof: "She really was frustrated, and so she got Pat and Doug to get some bags of flour, and she went up into the construction site and started throwing these bags of flour. That was the only way she could get rid of her anger."

Pat Barnett often went quietly about her business in Dusty's dressing room, watching as her boss got more and more upset.

> She was always terribly nervous before anything she did. All her front used to go red, and I never used to make a sound, I'd quietly do whatever I had to do, and one day I was doing the silver she was going to wear—so I'd bent down and it was lucky because she couldn't find the other shoe she wanted. She threw something over her shoulder, one of the other shoes, and it just missed me and I went, "What was that for?" I thought she was throwing a shoe at me. She went, "Oh my God, did I hit you?" I said no, but only because I was bending down. But she used to get very het up before every single performance. Once she stepped out onstage she'd be like another person: serene, the artist. In the dressing room sometimes she could be a lunatic.

Dusty was now frequently being asked by the press to defend her outbursts, and her food- and crockery-throwing compulsion: "Well, I haven't thrown any here yet!" she told an American journalist in November 1965. "And I only do it under extreme stress and only in my own place and I always clean up the mess."

Her practical jokes, which often sounded more extreme in print than they were in reality, were also good fodder for the newspapers. "Dusty and her group of London-based friends have quite a time playing practical jokes on each other," US reporter Louise Criscione wrote.

> There was the time Dusty had cans of [gasoline] sent to a friend's house and the time she opened her purse to find it filled with soap powder just wet enough to make a huge mess and total ruin! "And whenever I put on weight," said the slim-figured Dusty, "they send me dresses which are about this big," continued Dusty indicating about a size twenty-four dress. No one is immune from Dusty's jokes and the Shangri-Las found that out when they went to put on their boots one morning only to find them filled with anchovies!

Dusty's quirkiness could be hilarious, or disturbing—depending upon your point of view. While close friends like Pat Barnett, Doug Reece and Vicki Wickham adored her quick wit and sense of fun, her oddball humor was not to everyone's taste. One weekend she stayed in Brighton with Riss Chantelle's sister, who was supposed to be teaching her how to swim. She had a big old house, with five bedrooms, and late at night after everyone had gone to sleep, Dusty crept out and trailed a stream of toilet paper up and down the hallways and stairs, until it carpeted the house. Riss remembers that her sister woke up the next morning and was bemused to find her home decorated in this way—complaining that she found the episode weird rather than hilarious.

In addition, Dusty was quick to vent her rage, but rarely backed down or apologized, preferring instead to let things quiet down and then carry on as though nothing had happened. "She never said she was sorry," Pat Barnett recalls. In forty years they only argued twice, but Barnett still remembers the fight that erupted when Dusty blamed her for failing to get her London garage to bring her car to the front of her building for a swift departure. As usual, Dusty was running late and had little time to get to her engagement for the night. The garage had not listened to Barnett's instructions, and Dusty's car was not ready – leading Dusty to fire off an intemperate telegram to Barnett, accusing her of making Dusty late. "When I got it, for once in my life I got really annoyed," Barnett says. "Normally I could say 'She doesn't mean it,' but this in writing—I thought, 'How dare she!'"

Barnett rang Vic Billings and said, "If she doesn't apologize I'm coming home, she's had it, I'm coming home, she can do it on her own." Enraged, she then proceeded to tear up the telegram into tiny pieces, and dump them in front of the makeup room mirror.

When Dusty arrived at the club, the two eyed each other coldly. "She came in very late and she didn't go into the dressing room, she didn't even look at me, she walked straight past me, went straight down and got onstage and started rehearsing, which she's never done before. She couldn't face me," Barnett remembers.

Dusty went on to do her act, and then sat down in the dressing room afterward. When Barnett went in she saw that Dusty had wordlessly swept up the pieces of the telegram and put them in the garbage. "I went in and she didn't say anything, she didn't even speak to me, and I started unpacking her stuff. I said to her, 'You might have asked me whether I rang the garage.' Casually Dusty replied, 'Oh, don't worry about it.'" Barnett said that she did worry about it, and that she was ready to leave on the spot, adding, "You know I have never forgotten to do anything as important as that, and that telegram really upset me." Dusty said, "Oh, well, you know what I'm like." Barnett adds, "She couldn't say sorry, she just couldn't say the word 'sorry.'" Then Dusty asked her, "You're not really going home, are you?" Somewhat mollified,

Barnett replied, "No."

When they argued for a second time, Barnett said, "I know you can't say sorry." Dusty admitted that the argument was her fault. "I said, 'Yes, it was your fault,'" Barnett remembers. Then Dusty rolled her eyes and said, "Oh all right, I'm sorry!" Later Barnett walked outside with one of the men from the tour who was amazed by Dusty's admission, remarking that "she's never said that before to anybody!"

Dusty's normal way of smoothing over disagreements was to buy presents. "She'd buy them a pen with their name engraved on it if she'd upset the band leader, or something like that," Pat Barnett says. But she wouldn't apologize.

Yet despite such outbursts and tantrums, Dusty's childlike vulnerability, and genuine warmth, meant that her frustrations were quickly forgiven and forgotten. There were fun times, lots of laughter, and few people were ready to give up on her—certainly not at the height of her career.

When Dusty invited herself and Madeline on a vacation to Cornwall with Doug Reece and Pat Barnett (who were then an item), Doug locked Dusty in the car to prevent her from causing a catastrophe putting up the tent. At work, Barnett remembers Dusty collapsing in hysterical laughter when a grand piano rolled off the stage at one of the clubs they were playing, and she was often struck down by helpless laughter if she found something funny. Sometimes Dusty and Madeline would go to Alexandra Palace to watch Pat speed skating. Madeline was a fairly decent skater, but Dusty was not. "Dusty fell over and she got a big cheer," Barnett says, but she tried anyway, and turned up on another occasion to give out the prizes.

As a group they were full of youthful curiosity, holding a séance at Dusty's apartment which terrified them by ushering in evil spirits, and—on occasion—smoking dope. One night when Dusty and The Echoes had the evening off the week of Christmas, Dusty asked if anyone had any grass. Someone rustled some up and the band started smoking, so that by the time Dusty and Pat came down from their rooms everyone was laughing uproariously. Pat says:

> Dusty had a puff and I had a puff. It didn't do anything to me, but after a while Dusty started to see the funny side of things that weren't funny at all. They'd look at a cup and go, "Look at that, isn't that funny?" And of course it wasn't funny at all. They were all rolling around the room, and Dusty started to get giggly. I couldn't inhale so it did nothing to me. I went to bed in high dudgeon because I couldn't get high on it. But Dusty never touched it again after that, funnily enough.

If Dusty was drinking more, she was still only dabbling at the edges of drug use, and never smoked cigarettes at all. "I had weird times with Dusty, and I had great times with Dusty," Barnett says. Although set apart by her magnetic talent and increasing success, and the pressures associated with them, Dusty could still be young and easy with her few true friends.

9

YOU DON'T HAVE TO SAY YOU LOVE ME

Elusive, unpredictable and hard to pin down, Dusty had a "peculiar quality of individuality," mused *Teen Trends* magazine in January 1966, one that combined the shocking contrasts of the '60s with the Hollywood glamor of old. "I hate work," she told the journalist, "but I love singing," before going on to crush any discussion of her private life by adding rather severely, "I am not fun-loving," and then shrugging and saying, "I like parties of course." As ever, when the question of romance reared its head, Dusty deftly weaved a tale of double-speak: "I suppose some people manage to have a successful career and marriage too . . . I'm sure I couldn't," she sighed, before quickly adding, "but I'll probably try." Apparently unable to fathom her out, *Teen Trends* wistfully concluded, "This chick is full of surprises."

Despite her clipped British tones and middle-class inhibitions, perhaps she was more "Harlow, Lombard, Shearer, Dietrich and Garbo" than a Lulu or Cilla Black, the magazine imagined—a comparison that Dusty pondered too. As more strands of her life and career became interwoven with America, Dusty was struck by a growing unease that she was too big for Britain—or, if not "too big," then at the least too complicated, too mysterious and too restless. Madeline Bell says:

> *She fell out of love with the UK. She paid her dues, she did all the clubs up north, you had to do that—but the sound people didn't agree with her taste in music and what she wanted sound-wise, like she always wanted to hear more bass, she wanted to hear more drums. Oh, the sound man at the BBC didn't like the idea of that. So she wouldn't fit in with the powers that be, because she wouldn't do what she was told.*

The subject of "America" reared its head as early as 1968, Doug Reece remembers, although she was not to make a move to California until 1972, by which time both her career and her life were in a far stickier situation. "She called me up one day and asked me if I wanted to go with her to the Jensen Interceptor factory in Birmingham,' Reece says. The Jensen Interceptor was the kind of stylish, fast sports car Dusty loved and the company had invited her for a red-carpet tour of the premises complete with tea and the chance to handpick her own model. At the end of their day out, Dusty asked the man at Jensen, "Can I get it delivered to America?" It was the first time Reece had heard her seriously discuss a move, and as they made their way home, Dusty asked him if he would go with her as her musical director.

Reece had no desire to move to America, and had already got his heart set on moving to another country he had visited when touring with Dusty—Australia. Even so, the conversation did not surprise him. From her first album, made up solely of American songs, through her championing of Motown and success with Burt

Bacharach, Dusty was heavily influenced by the music and sounds that US artists could achieve. Her great, and mutually creative, friendship with Madeline Bell was well known, and in 1966 she had fallen in love, and moved in, with another American singer and artist, Norma Tanega.

Tanega had grown up in a Filipino-American family in California, and was in Britain to promote her one hit single—"Walkin' My Cat Named Dog," so named because she lived in apartment building that banned dogs. Although she had made her way to New York, played folk songs and took part in the popular political activism of the time, Tanega was unfamiliar with both show business and British trade unions, and was therefore surprised when she stepped out onto the set of *Thank Your Lucky Stars*, which was being filmed in a Manchester studio, to find that all the lights had suddenly been turned off. Meanwhile a bubbly, vivacious blonde was standing on some scaffolding rehearsing her song, going over and over it until she believed she was somewhere nearer to perfection. "What's going on?" Tanega asked her. The woman informed her that the lights had been shut down as nothing interfered with the union rules protecting the sanctity of the Great British tea break. The blonde was funny, charming, warm and intelligent. With a smile, Tanega admitted, "How could you not love her?"

Although she returned to America, Tanega kept in touch with Dusty through a series of long, intriguing, phone calls. Eventually Dusty flew to New York so that they could meet again in person—leading to an awkward reunion in a hotel room. Both looked shyly at each other, perhaps realizing that they were in fact little more than strangers, until Dusty said, "I've come all this way across the ocean to see you—the least you could do is come across the floor to see me!" Soon after, Tanega agreed to relocate to London, moving into Dusty's carriage house in Ennismore Gardens, which was the last in the series of homes she had shared with Madeline

Bell.

By now Dusty was at the peak of her career. With a two-year string of hits behind her, she began the year with the pop-sounding "Little by Little," written by the composers of "In the Middle of Nowhere," and much in the same vein, serving as a bright and bouncy follow-up to "Some of Your Lovin'." In April 1966 Dusty finally achieved her first number one single, reaching a wide audience that went well beyond Mods and teenagers with "You Don't Have to Say You Love Me." It had been more than a year since she had first heard the Italian version at the San Remo song festival, and both Dusty and Vicki Wickham agreed that the new English lyrics (written by Wickham and Simon Napier-Bell in the back of a taxi) left much to be desired. Despite Dusty plaintively singing for someone to give her some quick sex, with or without love, the ballad was unstoppably popular, with its surge of strings and instantly recognizable key change turning it into her emblem for the rest of her career—one she would have to sing in every performance, even when she could no longer hit the high notes.

Yet it was another song, released in July of that year, that encapsulated her haunting and fragile life, and sent shivers down the spines of her fans. When Madeline Bell first heard "Goin' Back" she burst into tears:

> *My favorite track that she recorded was "Goin' Back" . . . We were doing Dusty's backing vocals, and during a rehearsal this piece came up and when we heard it, me, Lesley Duncan and Kay Garner, all burst into tears because the arrangement was just, ah! We'd never heard anything like it. And that was something else for a little pop singer to do something like that.*

The Goffin/King song had made Dusty cry, too, the first time she performed it, on Tarbuck at the Prince of Walesz—a factor which convinced her to release it as a single, even though some questioned the wisdom of following up the no-holds-barred "You Don't Have to Say You Love Me" with such a restrained, adult-sounding, number. "I remember hearing the string arrangement . . . and I remember bursting into tears because it was so pretty. Anything that fills me that way, I can really get into singing it," Dusty said.

As ever, the recording and release of "Goin' Back" was surrounded by drama and confusion. On the night of recording, Dusty and Johnny Franz cowered in the Stanhope Place studio while thunder and lightning raged overhead. There had been some stormy disagreements over the release too, with some confusion over whether Goldie and the Gingerbreads (Dusty's old housemates from Westbourne Terrace) would release the single first, with Carole King eventually denying them permission after they changed the lyrics. "When Goldie nearly did it first, I nearly committed suicide!" Dusty dramatically told *Melody Maker*. Although the song only reached number seven in the charts, and was never released as a single in the US, Carole King said that Dusty was the only performer ever to make it worthwhile, to which Dusty replied, "What could be better than that?" "Goin' Back" proved to be her masterpiece. "She sang with so much emotion," Madeline Bell says. "She used to say, 'You've got to think about what you're singing, so that your body will express what's going on in your mind if you're thinking about what you're singing,' so that's why I still try to do that as well."

With Norma Tanega now encouraging her to settle down, save some money and even consider buying her own home, it seemed that Dusty was becoming more established both personally and professionally. In the early summer of 1966 the BBC offered Dusty her first solo TV series, a series of six half-hour programs simply titled *Dusty*, which she recorded with Doug Reece as her musical director and a 32-piece orchestra led by Johnny Pearson. Backing singer Jean Ryder remembers the rehearsals in Shepherd's Bush and Dusty's commitment to them, as well as her sense of still keeping herself slightly apart.

> *When we used to work on TV series with her we used to see her every single week, and we'd be sitting in the stalls in Shepherd's Bush Empire where we did a lot of the recordings and chatting in between rehearsals . . . We used to pop out before the show and have a meal in the local Italian restaurant but she would stay inside the theater getting her hair done and her makeup and all that sort of stuff, so basically it was a work relationship.*

As ever, Ryder remembers, Dusty was intent on doing the best job that she could:

> *She was a perfectionist, and I think this is where some people got her wrong because they thought that she was just a pain in the backside because she was picky. I don't think it was so much that. I think it was because she was such a perfectionist she wanted it to be the best, so she did nitpick over everything, but that's okay, it's her job and it was her career on the line. Her name is out front, they advertise the Dusty Springfield television show, so if it's not up to scratch it's reflecting on her.*

Dusty chose the music for the programs herself, picking songs she couldn't record but admired. The programs included Dusty's renditions of Mary Wells's "You Lost the Sweetest Boy" and the Four Tops' "Something about You," and featured Dudley Moore,

Woody Allen, and jazz singers the Four Freshmen as guest stars. "She was on TV, and that reached a huge audience of people who wouldn't have bought her album. There were only three pop shows a week, and they had a huge impact," says Elvis Costello, who later wrote a song for Dusty which she recorded on the White Heat album. "She was the bridge between English and American music—and she had great guests."

The series pulled in an audience of nine and a half million viewers and exposed the country, not only to the full range of Dusty's musical talents, but also to her shy, quirky and sweet personality, which shone out through her nervous jokes and breathy introductions as being young and innocently unaffected.

Other performers who met her at this time were equally disarmed by the mixture of her talent and shy temperament. "When I finally met her it was really lovely," Lulu says, "because she wasn't disappointing as a person. She was not all-important. You can't help it when you're in this business, but Dusty had none of that—and that was a joy." Although Dusty was older and more experienced, she told Lulu that she found her courageous.

> There was a really sweet respect for one another; a recognition of something in each other that's beyond words. I wasn't really close to her, and I know a lot of people were, but I felt that somehow like she was a soul sister. I felt something with her that I can't say about any other female singer in this country.

Now that Dusty was firmly established as a star she took urgent steps to remedy what she perceived to be her lack of success in America, breaking with Philips there and signing with Atlantic. Dusty had long been dissatisfied with Philips's efforts on her behalf in the US, complaining, "I have no real quarrel with the company here but in the US they have done virtually nothing to promote me or my records." In protest Dusty undertook a three-hour strike unless Philips released her from the US arm of her contract, which they were eventually forced to do despite Irving Green, President of Philips US, flying to London to try and resolve the dispute with Vic Billings. Happily Dusty signed with Atlantic for £30,000 (about $36,000)—then a vast sum—and immediately released "You Don't Have to Say You Love Me" in the US, which shot to number four in the charts. Dusty had got her way but it was the beginning of a lifetime of wrangling with record labels, and few deals would be so advantageous to her in the future.

What Dusty rightly believed was an exercise in wrestling control over the destiny of her own career and her music, others labeled "difficult"—and a series of incidents in 1966 reinforced the notion that she was becoming temperamental and unpredict-able. In September Dusty returned in high spirits from a Spanish summer holiday with Tom, Pepe Borza and Vic Billings, which had included flying Madeline Bell's bikini bottoms from a flagpole, and walked into a controversy about throwing a cheese tart at Stanley Drake, the assistant manager of the revolving restaurant at the top of London's newly opened Post Office Tower. Then a trendy, futuristic venue, Dusty was in the restaurant accepting her *Melody Maker* award for Top British Singer when she saw Drake being rude to one of the waiters. Always on the side of the underdog—and against pomposity—Dusty launched the tart across the room, but it missed its target. For good measure she took an extra tart in hand and made sure to squash it firmly into the manager's palm when leaving. "The little waiter was doing everything that he could," Dusty said. "I hate waiters being pushed around." When questioned later, Drake diplomatically replied, "Miss Springfield's a charming lady," but the press had a field day with another example of Dusty's eccentric behavior.

Less amusing for all concerned was the legal case concerning an accident that occurred when Dusty had been driving her sports car through central London, late at night, in dark glasses. Ida Metzger, sixty-three, was crossing Berkeley Square with her shopping when Dusty knocked her down and then emerged from her car, crying and virtually hysterical with shock. "I have no doubt that she was driving too fast," the judge remarked to the *Evening Standard*, "and I don't suppose her ability to keep a proper lookout was enhanced by wearing dark glasses." The judge was equally unimpressed by Dusty's nonappearance at her own court case, at which she was ordered to pay £1,900 ($2,300) in compensation, a considerable amount of money then, amounting to about two weeks' earnings for Dusty. When pressed for a response, an unrepentant-sounding Dusty complained that everyone talked about the damage she'd inflicted upon Ida Metzger, but not about the damage the tin cans from Ida Metzger's shopping had done to Dusty's car. In truth, Dusty was not in court because she had flown to New York, and was engaged in another, even more memorable, battle.

Basin Street East was one of the most prestigious clubs in New York City. Not only had it hosted many of Dusty's heroes, but rivals like Dionne Warwick were also frequently in the audience, checking out the acts. In short, it was the kind of venue that would only heighten Dusty's already considerable nerves and stage fright. Since her first nervous collapse two years earlier, Dusty had pulled out of a series of appearances and shows, stating nervous and physical illnesses. "There would be times when she really would say, 'I have the flu,' and we all would say to her that it wasn't the flu, it was nerves, she was nervous about doing something. She would pull out of things as much as she could," says Vicki Wickham.

She could not pull out of performing at Basin Street East, however, despite a deeply unpleasant run-in with jazz drummer Buddy

Rich. Rich and his band were booked to support Dusty, but when she arrived—two weeks in advance of her November 23 start date—she discovered that Rich refused to allow her any time to rehearse with them, and then disparaged her onstage. She told *NME*:

> *A four-letter word is what I would use to describe Mr. Buddy Rich. Buddy Rich refused to let his band rehearse with me until the afternoon before the show! I had two hours to work out fourteen new arrangements. I could have cried. I can't understand the man . . . I even heard him tell his band not to put too much effort into playing for me, in case they tired themselves out.*

Dusty's set included "Sunny," "Kansas City," "England Swings," "God Bless the Child," "You Don't Have to Say You Love Me" and a Bacharach medley. On opening night, however, a Mexican quintet performed first, followed by Rich, who then invited his friends to come up onstage and tell some jokes. Two and a half hours later Rich finally announced Dusty by saying, "She's supposed to be a great singer, but I've seen better." Onstage, Dusty retorted, "We have three sexes in England: male, female and Buddy Rich." Rich said he had to be restrained by Tony Bennett from punching her in the mouth. "It was like that for three weeks," he added, "and then it really got bad."

The culmination of the bad feeling between them led, according to Dusty, to Rich saying, "You fucking broad, who do you think you fucking are, bitch?!" Dusty responded by slapping Rich across the head, knocking his hairpiece sideways and delivering a deeper humiliation than if she had merely floored him. "She took a swing at me," Rich told the *Milwaukee Sentinel* in January 1967. "She missed. If she'd ever connected it would have been the late Dusty

Springfield. Joe Morgan, the press agent, picked her up bodily, pinned her arms to her side and threw her out."

Both the media and the band were firmly on Dusty's side, with American newspapers berating his inexcusable rudeness, saying, "The spotlight should have been on the British star, Dusty Spring-field," while *NME* fumed, "Through no fault of her own . . . Britain's top girl singer was thrown right into a complete fiasco that was an insult to her, both as a lady and as an entertainer." At the end of the run, Rich's band presented Dusty with a pair of boxing gloves, claiming she had done what they longed to. Their note read, "You were brave enough to do what we couldn't."

It was an uncomfortable situation for Dusty and one she should never have been subjected to. Perhaps one of the most over-looked benefits of the trip, however, was that for the first and only occasion in her life she resorted to bolstering her confidence by taking voice coaching. Without training, Dusty often struggled to maintain her voice, whereas lesser performers and singers—which was almost everyone else—could sing on forever and ever.

Dusty returned to England feeling bruised by her experience in New York, only to plunge into the kind of entertainment she dreaded—pantomime. All British singers and light entertainers of the time, including Cliff Richard and Lulu, were obliged to serve out their time on Christmas shows, but the pantomime/cabaret circuit was one that Dusty was increasingly feeling restricted by. "They said, 'If you do the pantomime you can do this,' and 'this' happened to be my first Talk of the Town season, which I knew I really *needed* for my career," Dusty told Penny Valentine. In an interview with the US magazine *After Dark* in 1978 she said:

> I sensed there wasn't any further to go, and I didn't want to
> end up playing summer variety shows at seaside resorts or

> *doing pantomime . . . In* Cinderella, *for instance, guys play the Ugly Sisters, and some sweet young thing—a female—is Cinderella, while another girl plays Prince Charming in a butch get-up, slapping her thigh a lot and saying things like "What ho, me hearties!" Frankly, I didn't care to be typecast in either role.*

With some wrangling, Dusty eventually took a spot singing in a cameo role at the end of *Merry King Cole* at the Liverpool Empire. The proviso was that she did not take part in the show itself, sang her own songs (as well as "Yellow Submarine') and wore a long white gown rather than appearing in costume. It was a sort of "mini-concert," she consoled herself, telling people, "I just do my act at the end."

Dusty was usually far from scornful about popular culture, or financial gain. She had begun the year by delighting residents of the London district of Bethnal Green by singing her way up a terraced street in an ad cheerily promoting Mother's Pride bread, and she continued to play the circuit of northern clubs. Nonetheless, she was aware of the fact that in 1966 she had achieved more hit records than any other artist, and increasingly wanted to stretch herself musically and artistically. To put it simply, she did not want to enter her thirties playing Puss-in-Boots.

10

WHERE AM I GOING?

Late in the evening of a June day in 1968 a car pulled up at Vogue House in Hanover Square and Dusty Springfield emerged. Still at her professional peak, Dusty had triumphed in her first season at Talk of the Town the previous year, seized control of her career in an acrimonious split from her manager Vic Billings, and was about to plunge into her second season at Talk of the Town—which, unbeknownst to her, would break box office records. The following day she would release one of her biggest hits of the decade and, soon after, she would depart for Memphis to record an album that would ensure her status as a soul legend but prove to be the artistic high water mark in her turbulent career.

On that cool evening in the summer of 1968, the world was in turmoil, and Dusty was in turmoil too. The peaceful hopes of the Prague Spring were turning sour, while the previous month a million students had rioted through the streets of Paris. A few streets away from Vogue House, antiwar protestors were regularly protesting outside the American embassy, while the assassination of Bobby Kennedy seemed to have snuffed out any flicker of light left after the murder of Martin Luther King Jr. Dusty—never one to be drawn on political matters like Vietnam in any public interview—later admitted that over that summer she was "crying at least once a day," and the pressure was mounting. Most likely she was crying for herself: Could she manage her own career, and make the necessary transition into her thirties? Was she out of touch with the antiwar "summer of love" ethos that was transforming pop music? Could she sing soul in the same studio as Aretha? Would she really be able to settle down and share her home, and life, with her girlfriend?

"I'm sure I've worked as hard [in previous years] as I have this year but it wasn't so pressurized," Dusty told Penny Valentine in *Disc and Music Echo*. "The past few months have been very hard. To say I cry once a day sounds soppy but it can be more—it's just the strain. You have to have a release. Half of it is self-inflicted. I get in a ridiculous panic over things that always get done eventually. It's just when I look at what must be done I think 'Oh, there's no *time*,' and flap like mad."

Talk of the Town had requested huge images of Dusty to advertise her second season, and photographer Peter Rand had been waiting for her to appear at his studio in Vogue House all day. "She was supposed to turn up about 5:30—but she didn't," Rand remembers. "This person kept calling to say that she would be there. She turned up at 10:45. Security were going mad, but the studio manager got dispensation and a special crew to stay on." Dusty eventually turned up with Norma Tanega, who Rand was surprised to see was dressed in a hound's-tooth three-piece suit and a black bootlace tie. As soon as she arrived, Dusty announced that she was hungry and wanted hamburgers. As there weren't many burger joints around Hanover Square, Tanega was dispatched to the Dorchester Hotel and returned much later with a box of burgers. "The best I've ever had," Rand says. "The Dorchester made them up specially for her, and sent champagne."

After they'd eaten the session began. "It was the most wonderful session—we finished about dawn. It was the most amazing shoot, and she really worked very hard, she worked terribly hard. My assistant and I didn't even have time to feel exhausted or tired until we left, and then we collapsed."

Dusty had brought her entire wardrobe with her. "All various things she was going to be wearing in the shoot, frilly things, and one was covered in huge glass baubles. I asked her to sit down—there was a huge crunching sound and she started roaring with laughter because she'd broken these glass baubles on her bum," Rand says. "She was so alive . . . She certainly wasn't down when we were photographing her—she was fantastic. We talked about the music scene, and where she was going, you know. What tours she had coming up, things like that."

The final result included an unforgettable image that seems to reveal all of Dusty's inner anguish. "She said to me that she thought that was her favorite picture of all time," Rand says. Wearing a short gown with flares underneath, Dusty presses her fingers to her face, staring out with eyes that are vulnerable and haunted. "Straight with the hands. Very soft . . . I can't put my finger on it," Rand says. "She was really crazy, I mean she was so effervescent. She was a very, very sexy girl. That's why those pictures are so strange, she comes over looking . . ." his voice trails off. "She said I caught something that nobody else had done before. It was in the middle of the night, and we'd been having such an uproarious time of it until then . . ."

Much to Rand's delight, Dusty agreed with all of his image choices, and then sent him tickets to Talk of the Town as a thank-you. "We got a whole batch of tickets and a special table right at the front and guess what? I didn't go. Apparently she was furious.

I think I sent something to her to apologize but I never heard from her again . . ." But Rand's photographic instincts proved to be spot on. Dusty's last album, *Where Am I Going?*, released ten months earlier, reflected the same sense of agitation and uncertainty conveyed in the image: Dusty was a woman at a crossroads.

In 1967 she had released three singles, none of which had provided the big hit she needed. "I'll Try Anything" in February reached number thirteen in the charts and was followed by "Give Me Time" in May, which made it to number twenty-four, while in September she released "What's It Gonna Be"—an underrated number that failed to chart but was to have a longer life on the northern soul circuit. She also sang the theme song to the film *The Sweet Ride*, released the following year. The clash between Dusty's reliance on hit singles and her overall direction as an artist was becoming more apparent. However, the day after Dusty's photo session with Peter Rand, "I Close My Eyes and Count to Ten" was released in the UK, shooting to number four and giving Dusty the boost she needed after a year-long absence from the charts. Written by Clive Westlake, it was the kind of big gutsy ballad that would become synonymous with Dusty—yet, as with many of her hits, she nearly didn't record it at all.

"She didn't regard me as an important songwriter," Westlake told the *Dusty Springfield Bulletin*—despite the fact that he had been involved with three other songs, and was in the process of finishing "All I See Is You." Nonetheless, when Vic Billings asked if Westlake had anything else in the bag, he listened to a few bars of "I Close My Eyes and Count to Ten" and said, "Finish it—for Dusty." Billings had originally been toying with the idea of giving the song to Kiki Dee, who was staying with his management – unlike Dusty. After hearing a demo that uniquely included a sixty-piece orchestra, Dusty claimed ownership over it, however, calling Westlake to say, "I want to record this song, please don't give it to someone else."

Admitting to Keith Altham at *NME* that her previous single had been "a flop," she added that hit singles were still the mainstay of her career. "It's very good for my ego. I certainly have not got to the stage where I can do without hit records. I can exist without them but I would rather not!" Was the increasing length of time between singles because of the difficulty of getting good material, Altham probed? The gap had certainly annoyed her record company—and her fans, who complained that she was neglecting them and spending more time traveling abroad. "It really is enormously difficult," Dusty replied. "And I waited a long time for this song—I was so lucky to get it." As to whether she was neglecting her fans, an irritated Dusty shot back that she was the one being neglected—by those who might supply her with better material for songs.

Although she was relieved to be back in familiar territory in the higher reaches of the singles chart, Dusty was aware, and disappointed, that her last album had been a relatively poor-selling mixture of styles and sounds, and that critics were suggesting her attempts to go with the new style hadn't quite come off. "Pop has changed, and so has she. Now it's mainly quiet and gentle, Flower Power and so on; but Dusty's impact seems to wilt as she becomes more muted," wrote one critic in response to her second BBC television series that year.

Successful appearances at venues such as Talk of the Town were pushing her further into the cabaret world of performers like Eartha Kitt and the idea of being a "rich man's entertainer"—singing for her supper. "I'm moving into the cabaret bag," she complained to Penny Valentine, "but cabaret isn't for me." The problem was that Dusty was unsure what direction she should take, adding that she felt like she was "groping and wandering," with a distinctive voice she didn't like listening to. Returning to the theme of an earlier interview she'd given to the London *Evening News*, where she'd proclaimed that she certainly hoped she wouldn't still be singing when she was forty-seven—"Who wants to be singing at forty-seven? By then I hope I'll have a settled mind"—Dusty told Penny Valentine that she dreaded becoming an aging teenybopper: "If I have to go on *Top of the Pops* again, waving my arms about, I'll go potty."

Speaking to *Melody Maker* she tried to couch it in more diplomatic terms than she sometimes felt:

> *In Britain, one can only go so far. I'll probably do more cabaret. The ideal thing seems to be to model myself internationally in the same way that Petula Clark has done—walking a very clever tightrope between various countries. I'd like to work both here and in the States regularly, with occasional appearances on the Continent. I'm very happy because the age group of my fans runs from five-year-olds to seventy-year-olds.*

Managing to walk along such a tightrope, however, would require a clearer head and calmer thinking than Dusty often possessed.

For Jean Ryder, many of the contradictions in Dusty's life and personality were summed up on a trip they took to a concert in Berlin in March 1969. Ryder had always liked Dusty, and was particularly touched when Dusty and Tom sent her a dozen red roses after she gave birth to her first baby. On this occasion Dusty booked Ryder and two other singers for the Berlin concert, and they set off from Heathrow with the band and various others. Ryder recalls:

> *As we took off there was an almighty bang and the undercarriage wouldn't go up into the plane because the tire had burst on takeoff, so all the rubber from the tire was all mangled in the undercarriage. The plane was shuddering, and immediately your heart goes into your stomach.*

The plane circled the control tower a few times and the pilot confirmed that the undercarriage was stuck, so the plane could neither fly nor land.

> *We were all sitting there obviously terrified. We couldn't fly out to sea to jettison any fuel because we couldn't get any height. We were literally flying almost at the level of the top floors of apartment blocks we were flying so low, and they had to clear the airspace around Heathrow and nothing could land.*

While they circled and circled, trying to burn off fuel, Dusty's agent, Dick Katz, who was sitting next to her, began to write a farewell letter to his wife in case the plane crashed. Dusty, however, remained unmoved by events. She had already started taking pills, which were to become a very big and destructive force in her life, and sat happily stoned while the plane circled round and round. Ryder says:

> *Dusty put her headphones on and God only knows what she was doing, she was popping pills of some description, and she had her headphones on and she was singing, and in the end Dick Katz bashed her on the arm and said, "Shut up! Shut up! Can't you take this seriously?" He was so scared, and she was like, "What?"*

Eventually the plane executed an emergency landing and the passengers disembarked on emergency chutes. Back in the terminal, Dusty drank some spirits, which Ryder noticed did not react well with her pills:

> *God only knows whether the stiff whisky or brandy didn't mix with Dusty's tranquillizers, but by the time we got back on another plane and got to Berlin she was stoned out of*

*her brain! So, we got to the concert and she was all over
the place, and the strange thing is when we got there we
had very little time to do any rehearsal, a sound check or
anything because the concert was about to start. People
were beginning to come in to this massive great big stadium
in Berlin and we were on stage trying to get a sound check.
So apparently out front it wasn't very good and the audience
started booing, so we didn't finish the set.*

Ryder also remembers the trip because it was one of the few times
she had an insight into Dusty's personal life. Norma Tanega had
accompanied Dusty to the airport to see her off.

*They were hugging each other and it was all "Oh, I'll miss
you!" and all this sort of thing, and then, when we got to
Berlin, Dusty had the hots for our drummer, a handsome
young guy called Chris Karan, and he kept saying to us,
"Don't leave me on my own, she's coming on to me all
the time, don't leave me with her!" So, we just accepted
whatever she is, it's her business.*

Dusty's flirtation with the drummer may have come from a combination of boredom, her zany sense of humor and too much to
drink. She would have relationships with other women during
these years with Tanega, but she was settled with her and had
moved into a house in Aubrey Walk, between Kensington and
Notting Hill. Getting Dusty to commit to buy a house was not
easy, but Tanega was anxious that Dusty invest some of her money
rather than just spending it. Eventually, Dusty sat down and wrote
a shopping list that began with milk and ended with a house.
After a year's renovation, overseen by Tanega, the house was ready
to move into, with a large living space and kitchen on the ground

floor, an epic sound system, Dusty's enormous bedroom on the first floor and a large music room on the top.

Vicki Wickham thought the stylish, but simply furnished, house was "magnificent—I'd never seen so much carpet in my life—everything was carpeted! It was very modern. She loved colors—purple, pinks, really bright colors, both to wear and for her home. You'd walk in and it was really colorful. She had very good taste."

While Dusty had left matters like dealing with the builders to Tanega, she did love shopping, and often bought big. In one excursion an enthusiastic Dusty trailed a reporter and a large entourage through a department store, teasing a bemused shop assistant while she bounced up and down happily on the biggest bed in the store and announced that she would be back to buy it (she did). An egg chair that she bought in Harrods was so enormous that Pat Barnett, Doug Reece and two deliverymen had to demolish the door frame in one of Dusty's apartments to get it in. Once it was subsequently installed in Aubrey Walk it hung suspended from the ceiling, and visiting friends would twirl in it, listening to music or enjoying one of Dusty's parties.

Dusty and Norma often entertained at Aubrey Walk and their parties, unsurprisingly, often culminated in food fights. The tales of Dusty's parties stretch back to the early days when Martha and the Vandellas fought each other with French loaves, and people skidded across the floor on sardines. Dusty would disappear and word would spread: "Dusty's in the kitchen," which meant the food fighting would soon begin.

Often OB and Kay were in attendance, as well as some of the women from the international tennis circuit when they were in town (Dusty was particularly good friends with Billie Jean King and Rosie Casals). The combination of people and events at Dusty's parties was sometimes fun but sometimes odd, according to Riss Chantelle. "I used to look round and think, *This is not right. Some of it is, some of it isn't.*" Pat Barnett remembers an encounter with Doris Troy in Aubrey Walk:

> *I never got accosted by a lesbian ever. Once Doris tried, but she was absolutely stoned out of her mind . . . I had this little gypsy-type dress on, and Doris was really a big lady. As I got to the stairs, Doris came out and she went "Oh, Pat!" and she came up—and then to my horror she went flip, and flipped my bust out of this little dress. Madeline Bell was watching, and almost helpless with laughter. She grappled Troy, telling her, "Doris, get off, she's straight!" I put myself back in my dress and carried on. Two minutes later Doris Troy was flat out on the floor.*

Much later Simon Bell told Dusty that Troy had made a pass at him, in exchange for her mentoring his career, and Dusty exclaimed, "She did exactly the same thing to me too!"

Madeline Bell says that in fact she rarely went to Aubrey Walk after Dusty and Norma Tanega got together—and their more distant friendship was something Dusty told hairdresser John Adams she regretted. "Their relationship seemed to sort of sum it all up and Dusty could never, ever find that again in anyone else," Adams says. Bell had supported Dusty on her first and second TV series, and in the first season at Talk of the Town in May 1967, where Dusty sang a collection of her hits including "You Don't Have to Say You Love Me," "La Bamba" and "Live It Up," but by 1968 she was busy with her own career, and stopped featuring as one of Dusty's backing singers. By then Dusty and Norma Tanega were inseparable, and Dusty appeared to be infatuated.

John Adams had met them both in the autumn of 1967 when Dusty brought Tanega with her on a three-week engagement to the Chequers Club in Sydney. Despite an initial hiccup when Dusty realized she didn't have a bass player, and flew in Doug Reece to rectify the situation, the trip went well and Dusty asked Adams to take over as her hairdresser back in London. When Adams arrived, Dusty was still in her apartment in Ennismore Gardens and generously invited him to sleep on the couch until he found somewhere to live, but Adams ended up feeling awkward and unwelcome when Dusty and Tanega disappeared into the bedroom and didn't emerge for three days. "She stayed in bed sometimes for a few days, she just wouldn't surface," Adams says. "Her daily routine was like, if I can be lazy today I'll be lazy. With something that she was doing, she worked hard on it, but if she could be lazy, she'd be lazy."

In Dusty's very private world, Tanega was playing an increasing important role in both her life and career. Vicki Wickham believed Tanega was a very positive and stabilizing influence on Dusty: "They were a great couple. They were really good together," she says. "They both loved the music. It was much more settled, and Norma would go everywhere with her. I think it was a good time, until Dusty messed it up!" But others amongst Dusty's old friends, a tight-knit inner circle including Doug Reece and Pat Barnett, were not so sure. Riss Chantelle remembers meeting Tanega at a television program that Dusty was preparing for. Dusty was rehearsing a song, and Chantelle remembers Tanega leaning over and criticizing her. She says:

> I must admit I didn't like her. Dusty did something wrong and Norma Tanega bent over the top and said, "You can do that better than that, you know," and all the interference under the sun, and I thought, "What is she doing? Nothing to do with her really." And Dusty looked very shy and very embarrassed and did it again. I thought, "Well, bully for you, Dusty, it's all wrong, you should have told her to either shut up or get out, because it's what you were doing." And I didn't like her from that minute.

If Dusty knew her own mind in the studio, and wasn't afraid to express it, Chantelle adds that she was always personally influenced by the people around her. "Dusty got in with the wrong people. She would have been perfectly all right had she not gone in with those people. She was easily led in that way."

"I saw her [Tanega] as being part of the problem," John Adams says. "Norma was a very heavy sort of person. She was quite intimidating." Dusty in some way liked being dominated by the women she was with, Adams believes, and she was addicted to emotional upheaval. "The more drama in her life, the more she created," Adams says, adding:

> *I can't tell you how many times I got that phone call at three in the morning—"Get over here, Cat's trying to kill me!" [Cat was Norma's pet name for Dusty] or "John, come quick, Norma's trying to kill me!" And I'd go over and the bath was full of water and one of them is holding the other one underneath—and she loved it, she thrived on it.*

If Tanega appeared to dislike Adams as much as he disliked her, she had her reasons—namely that he was Dusty's go-between in facilitating her relationships with other women. It was during this time, shortly after she had met Tanega, that Dusty also began a relationship with American folk singer Julie Felix, and Adams was responsible for arranging times when they could be together. "Dusty needed a bit of fun to keep her going," Adams says.

Felix, like Tanega a Californian, but of Mexican and Native American descent, had been performing "I Can't Touch the Sun" on *Ready Steady Go!* in 1966 when Vicki Wickham invited her to dinner afterwards with a group of friends including Dusty. They began talking, and Felix felt a strong and immediate connection to Dusty, who invited her back to her flat afterward to listen to music. Dusty was still living in a rented apartment in Kensington and Tanega was away in America at the time, while Felix was living with her female partner in a somewhat open relationship. While she wouldn't go as far as to say that she and Dusty fell in love, Felix says, "We were infatuated with each other," and she could appreciate Dusty's brilliant, tempestuous personality and talent.

"Just after she had recorded 'I Close My Eyes and Count to Ten' she told me the lyric made her think of me," Felix says. "I was very touched by her words." She still considers Dusty to be "the best female singer to come out of this country" and one who taught her much about musicianship. "I was a folk singer, but I wasn't a musician back then," Felix says. Dusty could listen to Felix's music and pinpoint a wrong note, or a place where she was out of tune. "I remember once I had come back from a recording and Dusty was listening to it, and she said, 'Who is the bass player?'" Felix told her she didn't know. "Dusty was astonished and appalled— she said, 'How can you not know who the bass player is?'" Dusty then went on to analyze what the bass had been doing, and how she thought it could have been done differently. Dusty appeared on Felix's BBC TV series, and Felix returned the favor, appearing on Dusty's 1968 series *It Must Be Dusty*.

Norma Tanega may have guessed at Dusty's relationship with Julie Felix as, whenever Felix rang the house, Tanega would never let her speak to Dusty on the phone. "I tried to get Norma to like me more, by recording one of her songs on my TV show, and she was very pleased about that," Felix says. Dusty told Felix to use the pseudonym "Miss Brown" if she ever wanted to leave a message for her anywhere.

During their encounters in London, and on one occasion in Germany, Dusty was either intense or mentally absent—away in a dream, thinking her own thoughts. There was rarely a calm in-between state. "She talked about her emotions a lot," Felix says, "and she would get mad at me sometimes—she could throw things! She loved drama, and she could be exciting and funny and sweet." Without her makeup she looked vulnerable and childlike, with soft red hair. Felix believed it wasn't so much that Dusty craved love and never got it, but more that she wanted to feel safe—and never did. At the time Felix was less experienced than Dusty both in music and in love. "I wouldn't say she was protective towards me," Felix says, "but sometimes she wanted to control me." Ultimately Felix believes that she was "too soft" for Dusty. "I melt. She liked women who could be dominant, and take control of her."

Being gay women in the public eye was a strain for both of them, Felix believes. She was "terrified" of people finding out, partly because the music and entertainment industry was deeply homophobic and sexist, and partly because being a lesbian was considered shocking and awful by the public at large. Dusty, Felix saw, had the added problem of a very large fan base who would have deserted her. When they attended an event together with John Adams and some other friends, Felix was surprised when Dusty pulled her aside and said, "Don't get too close to John tonight, I want people to think he's with me."

Sometimes, Felix noticed, Dusty would get incredibly upset, as if under the influence of some kind of medication. Dusty was already taking Mandrax, a popular "downer" in the 1960s and 1970s that was especially dangerous in combination with booze. "At night she'd have a few Mandrax and a few bottles of vodka and life got totally upside down, and that's what created a lot of those problems," John Adams says. When she became really hysterical, Adams or one of her friends would call for help. "Dusty had a great doctor, and he would come over and give her a shot and calm her down."

Mandrax may have had an even more profound influence on Dusty's life. Doctors now know that it sends people with bipolar disorder into accelerated cycles, leading to more uncontrolled behavior and episodes of psychosis. Such a link was not known at the time, however, and psychiatrists and doctors were far from understanding the condition.

When Dusty was sober she was her normal, somewhat high-strung, self, but when she did drink it was to excess—another possible symptom of a bipolar condition. Often things would turn nasty. Adams remembers seeing Dusty appear more than once at a session or rehearsal with a black eye that had to be carefully disguised, while other friends noticed that she had started harming herself by cutting her arms with a knife.

Pat Barnett noticed that when Dusty was vulnerable there were plenty of people around to feed off her fame—and spend her money. "Lots of people took advantage of Dust, especially where money was concerned," Barnett says. "Oh boy, the money she's been swindled out of is nobody's business. That's why she never had money." Now that Dusty was managing her own affairs and finances, money was a particular concern. Dusty had always recorded her spending on a tape machine and sent it off to an accountant, but Vic Billings had been a constant presence—dealing with the administrative headaches and the decisions that Dusty was unfamiliar with making. Now she had to juggle the full-time job of being Dusty Springfield with managing her own business details. Although she had a lawyer and business manager in the States who stopped her being "conned," there were a million other matters to attend to.

"Now I'm worried by petty things I wasn't before," Dusty told Penny Valentine in *Disc and Music Echo*. "Like bills and stupidity— five people ringing me from the BBC one after the other asking exactly the same thing. I like to only have to answer to myself for what I do but I find the financial side a strain. Of course I want to make money—but I don't like those pieces of paper they keep throwing at me!'

Dusty's decision to split with Vic Billings had followed a long and acrimonious series of arguments, usually mediated by friends such as Doug Reece, who says:

> *There were moments where she had terrible arguments with Vic. I think Norma and Vic had conflicts because I think Vic would say "I want to do so and so"—and sometimes your partner can influence the way you think about things, and sometimes it wasn't always the right thoughts. So there would be a conflict, and a lot of times I was in the middle.*

Dusty and Billings would reach an agreement, about a performance or something he wanted her to do, and then she would return the next day having changed her mind—her friends believed, due to the influence of Norma Tanega. Reece would try and smooth things over, listening to Dusty shouting, "I've had enough of him, I want a new manager," while Billings would tell him "She's a real bitch" and complain about the way she was doing things. In addition, Dusty was convinced that the only way forward professionally was in America, and that Billings did not have the experience and contacts to help her make it there.

For five years Vic Billings had steered Dusty to the heights of her career, and kept her more or less on track. In parting, Dusty agreed to pay him £20,000 ($25,000) in lieu of two years' work, and signed a contract with Atlantic to release her work in the US, while she would continue to work with Philips in the UK. To the dismay of almost everyone who knew her, Dusty's relationship with Billings was over. "That was a bad mistake," Riss Chantelle says, "but you can't tell people, people do what they want to do."

Her estrangement from Billings had been having an effect on Dusty, and those around her, all year. After recording a second successful TV series with the BBC in 1967 that included guest stars Warren Mitchell, Mel Tormé, Tom Jones and Scott Walker, Dusty decided to film her third series in 1968 with ATV, at the Hippodrome in Golders Green, north London. Using a different orchestra led by Jack Parnell, *It Must Be Dusty* featured guest appearances from her brother Tom, Donovan, Georgie Fame, and most memorably Jimi Hendrix, with a duet of "Mockingbird." Despite the caliber of the shows and the guests, however, Dusty felt the programs had not included the same innovative spark as her BBC series, and bristled at criticism that she was failing to break new ground. "And quite right too," Dusty told Keith Altham of *NME* when he raised this criticism with her.

> *I didn't produce it and all I can say is that I tried my best and channeled as much energy into it as the previous series . . . There was a total lack of imagination about the whole series and although I don't like to bring politics into it—the other two series were with another company [BBC]—and I hope to be doing the next series back with the old firm. I'll never work for the other one again, I'll tell you that!*

John Adams and his friend the Australian singer Judy Stone remembered that the series began badly, with Dusty having a fight with the producer. Adams says:

> *Dusty was rehearsing and I think at the end of the rehearsal something had gone wrong—I think it was that she couldn't hear herself. She wanted the amplifier in front of her turned up so loud she could hear herself, but of course back in those days you'd get a lot of feedback and so it was very difficult. Anyway, she had this very expensive microphone in her hand and she whacked the producer across the head*

with it so hard that she smashed the microphone, because
she just wasn't getting what she wanted.

Such behavior was a revelation to Stone, who normally liked and admired Dusty tremendously. "I was absolutely amazed," she says. "I've never seen anything like that, but I can understand where she was coming from. She's going to appear on television in front of millions of people and if it is not correct you're not going to be very happy about it and you tend to lose your patience."

On the day before the last show Dusty asked Adams if he'd organized the final-night party. Not realizing that was expected of him, Adams ran out and quickly put something together at the restaurant across the street, including some jugs of sangria made with vodka, red wine and apples. As the evening progressed someone picked a bit of fruit out of the punch and threw it at Adams—who bent down, picked it up off the floor and threw it back. Dusty took this as a personal insult. "She'd had quite a few drinks at this stage and she stood up and was hysterical," Adams says, describing how Dusty shouted at him:

> *"How dare you upstage me, throwing food is my thing!"*
> *And with that she picked up this big bowl of red punch, of*
> *course she had white blonde hair, and she put it over her*
> *own head. Well, I thought it was the funniest thing I'd ever*
> *seen in my life and was hysterical, and the more I laughed*
> *the angrier she got. So I got out of there and went home very*
> *quickly. She was very, very angry.*

Fortunately the traumas associated with *It Must Be Dusty* were largely forgotten a few months later when Dusty did a series of concerts at Talk of the Town. The unusual set mixed her classics with a Peggy Lee medley, a "golden oldies" medley and a scene where she appeared dressed as Shirley Temple, complete with ringlets, and sang "On the Good Ship Lollipop" (she'd first thought of doing Carmen Miranda but abandoned the idea when she considered the logistics of moving around the stage with a stack of fruit on her head, and a dress slit to her waist).

Dusty's normal publicist was Keith Goodwin. He had been working with Dusty from the days of The Springfields and knew the stresses of shepherding her through a big public occasion. At the time of the Talk of the Town show he had booked a vacation in France which he refused to cancel, telling his assistant Mike Gill, "She won't do anything anyway, and it will be a huge pain." By 1968 there were many journalists Dusty disliked and would not give interviews to (probably with good reason) and many photo calls she turned up late for. Publicists, and even her hairdresser John Adams, also had to accommodate the fact that Dusty's dissatisfaction with her appearance had grown over the years, and she now insisted on being photographed from only one side. This also meant she could only be booked into the left-hand side on an aeroplane so that no one would see her from the wrong profile.

As a young newcomer to the business, Mike Gill had his work cut out for him, but despite all warnings to the contrary, he managed to get Dusty to turn up—charm personified—for a Monday morning photo shoot wearing her Shirley Temple polka dot dress, red tap shoes and white ankle socks. When the opening night of the show was a triumph, and London was buzzing about Dusty's sell-out season, the photo appeared full length on the front page of every tabloid, earning Dusty's delight. On a more personal level, Dusty's parents watched her performance with Penny Valentine, and told her that their daughter was the best they'd ever seen her—giving Dusty a rare moment of the approval and recognition she craved.

Yet, despite the enormous success at the Talk of the Town, perhaps the pinnacle of her live career, there was something poignant about a performance by a grown woman dressed up as a little girl. Many of her friends believed that Dusty was indeed a little girl inside. She was certainly trapped by her own mask, one that appeared only more restrictive and unreal over time. "I feel like two separate people," she reflected after one performance. "I was coming here tonight and I saw my name up in lights. People say 'It must give you a kick seeing your name up there,' but it doesn't. It doesn't give me a thrill. Not because I'm ungrateful . . . it just seems like a separate person."

Judy Stone often visited the house at Aubrey Walk after a performance, or when John Adams was pottering around fixing things, doing odd jobs or laying tiles. As well as Einstein, Dusty's teddy bear, Stone noticed that "the notepads were all Charlie Brown and Peanuts and Snoopy. In that way she had that little-girl-type love of things." Even though she was still a relative unknown in London, Stone still felt an irrepressible urge to look after Dusty. In particular, she admired Dusty's huge dressing room, and loved watching her put her makeup on and begin the metamorphosis. One night, after she had been drinking a few glasses of champagne, Dusty confided in Stone, who recalls:

> I'll never forget when she actually looked at me and said, "Who do I look like?" And I said, "You look like Dusty Springfield," and then in front of me, which I was quite amazed about, she started peeling off her eyelashes and the makeup and then her wig and then said to me, "Now who do I look like?"

Stone replied that she still looked like Dusty. "And she said, 'No I don't, I look like Burt Lancaster.' Apparently she had a thing about looking like Burt Lancaster, and that threw me a little bit, because I thought she must be very upset about something." Stone felt sad and confused, while Dusty, without saying much more, drifted off into a troubled sleep fueled by Mandrax and drink.

11

DUSTY IN MEMPHIS

Dusty landed in "Soulsville" in September 1968 ready to record the album of her career. The enormous success of Atlantic Records, and its offshoot Stax, had helped turned the sleepy, rundown, Southern city of Memphis into a musical moneyspinner, worth an estimated thirty million dollars a year. From the jazz of Beale Street to the rock 'n' roll of Sun Records and Graceland, Memphis meant music—so much so that at one point even the Memphis-based Holiday Inn chain decided to a launch its own record label.

Stax had stiff competition, not least from their local rivals Hi Records, who worked with Al Green and Tina Turner, but Atlantic was riding high that year, with twenty-three gold discs and a massive upsurge in profits. The small band of musicians and producers working at the unprepossessing American studios had developed a new way of recording, layering sound upon sound, that had made soul artists—like the new and mighty Aretha Franklin—as great a force as the Motown hit machine in Detroit. The sound was "hotter than a pistol," but cleverly packaged for crossover to a white audience—and it spoke to America's need to hear something real.

Dusty arrived at the end of the angry, troubled summer of "Reetha" and "Respect," as the media had proclaimed it, making the still-shy Franklin their emblem. In March, *Time* magazine had written that "schools were desegregated, black people voted, and the police had never faced a serious charge of brutality," yet still "Memphis simmered on the rim of racial rampage"—and this was before Martin Luther King Jr. was assassinated coming out of his motel room in the city two weeks after the article appeared. While *Time* may have underestimated the racism that black people in Memphis faced, there was no doubt that one of its musical strengths was the ongoing collaboration between musicians of all races. This mixture of white and black should have appealed to Dusty, and was one of the reasons why she chose to record in Memphis, rather than Atlantic's first choice for her, the Muscle Shoals studio in Alabama, which she deemed too "countrified."

Moving to Atlantic as her US partner was a brave new start for Dusty. The label had been set up in 1947 by New York jazz aficionado Herb Abramson and the 24-year-old son of the Turkish ambassador to the United States, Ahmet Ertegun—drawing together the jazz and R&B passions of its founders in seat-of-the-pants recordings hastily convened when money allowed (the first ten thousand dollars to establish the company was a loan from Ertegun's dentist). Luckily Ertegun and Abramson met the brilliant young recording engineer Tommy Dowd in their first year of operation, and Dowd would anchor all of Atlantic's output for more than twenty-five years. According to the music writer Peter Guralnick, Dowd gave Atlantic a "clarity of pitch, trueness of recording, and engineering balance" without compare to other independents. He was a "broader engineer than any of us," says Dan Penn, a guitarist who ended up at American Studios in Memphis after working for Muscle Shoals. "We were mono men when he was two track. We were two track when he was eight track."

Ertegun was responsible for signing Dusty, and Dowd would work closely with her in the studio—but at the helm of her output was Atlantic's vice-president, Jerry Wexler, whose style of work would have immense consequences for Dusty and her album. After hearing what they were doing with Otis Redding, Wexler had gone to Memphis to meet Stax in 1965. Founded as Satellite Records by Estelle Stewart Axton and her brother Jim Stewart, the company had joined forces with producer "Chips" Moman and changed its name to Stax in 1961, garnering huge success with artists such as Redding, Percy Sledge and Sam and Dave. In Memphis, Wexler was "blown away" by what he found and was introduced to a new way of recording that involved putting a session together one step at a time—"rhythm section, horns, the whole thing," according to sideman Jim Dickinson. "Memphis was a real departure," Wexler said, "because Memphis was a return to head arrangements, to the set rhythm section, away from the arranger. It was a symbiosis between the producer and the rhythm section, and it was really something new."

It would prove to be really something new for Dusty too, who was now used to coming into the studio after the track had been laid down, and adding her vocal on top. Memphis did not work that way, at least not at American Studios, where the musicians liked to work with the singer, sometimes taking a few days to get to "a lick," a sense of direction. And Memphis had attitude too—Peter Guralnick recounts how, when reporter Stanley Booth questioned Dan Penn at American Studios in 1968, he asked what was behind Memphis's sudden success: "'It ain't Memphis,' Penn said, 'it's the South.' 'Well, what is it about the South?' 'People down here don't let nobody tell them what to do.'"

Dusty would not be alone in finding the transition to a different style of recording difficult—Petula Clark was reportedly in tears for the first days of her Memphis sessions, and Lulu says she experienced similar difficulties:

I found them very difficult too. I mean, to have Jerry Wexler,
Tom Dowd and Arif Mardin produce your album . . . I had
bought all the records they'd ever made, and Jerry was a god.
But I don't think they knew what to do with me, and the only
big hit I got out of it was a song that I took with me.

For Dusty, however, Aretha Franklin's recent success at the studios
also added an extra layer of pressure, at least in her mind. Franklin
had also arrived at Atlantic needing a new sense of direction. Like
Dusty she was a music veteran, with more than a dozen years in
gospel behind her, but it had been five years since her last R&B
hit and her recent recordings were "a peculiar mix of show tunes
and schmaltz," according to Guralnick. Everyone was watching
Wexler, and Aretha, in the spring of 1967, "and not without scep-
ticism, for this was not her first chance at stardom, and not the
first time that great claims had been made for her." Yet, working
together, great things had been revealed—the real Aretha, soaring
on inspired vocals that transformed "Respect" from a song about
conjugal rights into a cry for freedom everywhere. In the autumn
of 1968 the question was—could Wexler do that with Dusty?

The first signs were not promising. Before Dusty arrived in
Memphis she had spent time at Wexler's house in Great Neck, New
York listening to demos of what Wexler believed were wonderful
song choices. Hours passed, with Dusty rejecting each demo in
turn until the pile of records was waist deep, and more than eighty
potential hits lay rejected on the floor. She did not like any of
them, and Wexler was briefly at a loss about what to do next. But
after Dusty left, Wexler took his time and pulled together fifteen or
so of what he believed were the best songs from the pile, and later
played them again to her, not mentioning that she had previously
heard them. Dusty loved all of them. Wexler now had his material
for *Dusty in Memphis*.

American Studios was tucked away behind a restaurant in a bad part of town, not far from the city's other illustrious studio—Sun Records. Rats ran rampant in the roof, with one once falling dead from the rafters onto an alarmed Elvis Presley—but, defying her surroundings, Dusty still arrived every day looking like a "magazine lady," according to Tom Dowd. With her blonde beehive, and John Adams in tow to maintain it, Dusty looked like the epitome of a white Southern madam. But unlike all the other matrons, cruising around town in their convertibles, when Dusty opened her mouth she either spoke in beautiful, clipped, English tones—or sang with better intonation than any other soul star in the business.

Those musicians who were keen to hear that voice in action were soon disappointed, however—for Dusty didn't sing. At first, Wexler recalled, Dusty would flit about the studio, saying things like "Aren't all these boys good at playing!" while he would tell her, in exasperation, "Dusty, we need you at the microphone!" Dusty explained:

> I wasn't used to singing to a sparse rhythm track. I prefer to sing last, after the strings have been written, because I get moved by a string line or an oboe solo and it will bring things out of me. It was the opposite of the normal thing, which is to say: the singer's the important thing, let's surround her.

Always prone to nerves and intense insecurity, Dusty was overwhelmed with Wexler's style of recording, and the idea that so many soul legends had stood in the same spot, and possibly given a better performance than she could. In truth, few could rival Dusty's amazing voice, yet even though musician Bobby Emmons said that Dusty's groove was "as black as the next," she believed that every musician in the 827 Thomas Street Band rhythm section would be comparing her unfavorably. "I hated it because I couldn't be Aretha Franklin. If only people like Jerry Wexler could realize what a deflating thing it is to say "Otis Redding stood there" or "That's where Aretha sang." Whatever you do, it's not going to be good enough. Added to the natural critic in me, it was a paralyzing experience," Dusty later told Mojo.

So strong was the shadow of Aretha that it played on her mind endlessly. When she returned from Memphis, she complained to Penny Valentine, "People like Aretha Franklin can sing forever because they've had church or operatic training. I can be in the middle of my act and realize I'm not breathing properly, but I'm so intent in getting over to the audience I forget about it.'

In the studio the tension was growing: Dusty seemed unable to produce any vocals. "One time she shoved an ashtray at me in the control room," said Jerry Wexler. "She had a terrible argument with Tom Dowd and called him a prima donna," something that made Wexler very angry indeed: "There's only one prima donna in the room at the moment!" he yelled back. Dowd laughed off the incident, but later told Lucy O'Brien that Dusty was a "tough, tough, tough taskmaster on her own vocals" who would drive them all to the limit in her search for perfection.

For once, Dusty couldn't complain that she had little input into the creative process, Wexler's whole set-up was designed to give the artist full interaction with the musicians. Nor was Dowd a play-by-numbers engineer—instead he had spent a great deal of time studying Dusty's range, and appreciated her for the great jazz artist she was. "I recognized in her a deep jazz root," he told Lucy O'Brien. "When she told me that Blossom Dearie was one of her heroines, I realized that she had obscure avant-garde genius as her goal . . . It disturbed her that she was popular for less." Yet none of this prevented Dusty from wondering, "What am I doing on this label?" and she later told the BBC she was consumed with the question of "Why are they recording me?"

John Adams was responsible for explaining the problem to the studio. "It came to the point where Dusty couldn't sing, she just had no voice, so the idea was to tell Atlantic that it was because she felt so humbled . . . intimidated by being in the studio."

Adams now admits, however, that this was far from the whole story. Adding to her feelings of being intimidated, Dusty had arrived in town carrying a large amount of personal baggage. A few weeks earlier she had been staying in a bungalow at the Beverly Hills Hotel with Norma Tanega when John Adams introduced her to a friend of his called Sandy. The two hit it off, and when she found out that Tanega was not accompanying her to Memphis, Dusty suggested that Adams invite Sandy along.

"Dusty was sort of taken by Sandy," Adams says. "She said, 'You know your friend Sandy, do you think she'd like to come to Memphis?' And I said, 'I'm sure she'd love to.' She said, 'Well, will you organize it?'" Adams agreed, and Sandy flew in, meeting Dusty in the top-floor suite of the Holiday Inn Rivermont.

Adams already knew that Dusty had enjoyed the odd dalliance, and more. Not only did he arrange for her meetings with Julie Felix, he had once had to smuggle a drenched Dusty in through a hotel reception in Australia when another girl she "had a thing with" had argued with her and thrown her into a fountain. "Dusty actually liked a bit of being pushed around, because theirs was quite a fight-based relationship as well. And this girl picked her up and threw her in the Alamein Fountain one night."

Dusty's brief, substance-fueled, liaison with Sandy in Memphis was turning out to be equally tempestuous, according to Adams. "I had a phone call at about four in the morning from the hotel manager saying, 'Sir, could you come down and see us please?'" Adams remembers. When he protested that it was the early hours, the manager said, "'Yeah, well—I've got a television in my swimming pool.' One of them had picked up the television and thrown it at the other one, then it had gone out, and down fourteen floors into the swimming pool."

In addition, Norma Tanega kept ringing the hotel, convinced that something was going on:

"I think Norma was onto the fact that Dusty had something going on there. So there'd be fights about absolutely nothing. It came to the point where Dusty couldn't sing, she just had no voice." Adams says that he was responsible for explaining the problem to the record company.

> *I was the one that had to go to Atlantic and say that Dusty's not been able to sing, and the reason that she can't sing is because she's so intimidated by this whole thing of all these black musicians and being in the studio where Aretha had recorded, etc. etc. That was the thing we came up with when she couldn't sing, but it wasn't the case. . . . In actual fact she was partying too hard every night with Sandy and staying off the phone from Norma . . . She just had lost her voice totally from too much alcohol and everything else.*

So Dusty left Memphis with a rhythm track laid down but no vocals. A few weeks later she reconvened in New York with Jerry Wexler, who had added horns and a backing track from the Sweet Inspirations, led by Cissy Houston. Dusty went into the booth, laid aside all the troubles she'd encountered in Tennessee, cranked up the volume to ear-splitting level, and produced the most beautiful work of her career.

Arif Mardin, who arranged the strings and woodwind for *Dusty in Memphis*, said that whatever difficulties they had encountered, and however many late nights they had spent getting it right, sometimes sleeping on the studio floor, the project had an unmistakable "aura" about it, "like a blessing from above." The song "In the Land of Make Believe" was as complicated and delicate as a Ravel string quartet, he added.

Critics were torn as to which song was the highlight. Was it the Goffin/King number "I Can't Make It Alone," with Dusty sounding low and chilling on "There's something in my soul . . ." or the fragile rendition of Randy Newman's "I Don't Want to Hear It Anymore"? What about her defiant interpretation of "Windmills of My Mind" where she threw out the cyclical intention of the writers, and steered the song with her own interpretation (she hated the lyrics, but admitted she'd done her best work on the vocals)? Or was the best song "Breakfast in Bed," written by Muscle Shoals guitarist Eddie Hinton and Donnie Fritts, who were ecstatic at Dusty's sexy, haunting delivery? Dusty's own favorite was "Just One Smile," her second song on the album by Randy Newman and a former top ten hit for Gene Pitney in 1966.

To hear just how well the combination of Dusty and Jerry Wexler worked it was only necessary to compare Dusty's version of "Don't Forget About Me," recorded a year earlier in London, with the Memphis track. While the London version slides along nicely, making for a pleasant forgettable song, Wexler's Memphis recording begins with a startling guitar intro, before bringing in Dusty's husky, emotional vocals and Memphis horns—building to a thrilling climax.

Reviewers loved it: Bill Buckley in *Blues & Soul* cooed that "rarely in recording does everything come together so magnificently." Yet *Dusty in Memphis* did not sell. In the UK the album struggled into *Record Retailer*'s chart of top fifteen albums, and slowly made its way into the American top 100. "Everybody loved it except the damn public," Wexler said, frustrated about a masterpiece that epitomized an almost perfect album that encourages a listener to drop the stylus onto the first track, and not stop until the end of the final song on the other side.

"Windmills of My Mind" was a US hit single, but only "Son of a Preacher Man" made it in Britain, and even that took its time to make its way up the UK singles chart. Dusty was angry with Wexler and Atlantic for not allowing her to recut some of her vocals on "Son of a Preacher Man" and her reaction to the relative commercial failure of the album was surprise, dismay—and then dismissal. Her great work of art was a "rather overrated classic" she said, sniffily, in the 1990s, as if she was still burned by the events of the summer of 1968.

> I was someone who had come from thundering drums and Phil Spector, and I didn't understand sparseness. I wanted to fill every space. I didn't understand that the sparseness gave it an atmosphere. When I got free of that I finally liked it, but it took me a long time. I wouldn't play it for a year.

However, Vicki Wickham remembers a rather different reaction:

> Once she'd got over not recording it in Memphis and recording the vocals in New York, and it was finished, she loved the album—she really did. I was in London, and she played me "Son of a Preacher Man" over the phone three times asking me what I thought—I thought it was great. It was. But then, of course, commercially it didn't do well, and nobody liked it. Funnily enough, in retrospect when we would talk about it much later on, she would acknowledge that it was a really good album and that she really liked it.

Even if Dusty reached an uneasy truce with *Dusty in Memphis*, she was never truly at peace with it. When Aretha Franklin later recorded "Son of a Preacher Man" herself, Dusty took to copying Aretha's different, and many thought inferior, phrasing. It was a song that Aretha had originally turned down, because of its religious connotations, and that Dusty had so defiantly made her own. Dusty told Mojo:

> *"Son of a Preacher Man" was just not good enough. Aretha had been offered it but didn't record it until after I had, and to this day I listen to her phrasing and go "Goddamit! That's the way I should have done it: 'The only one who could ever reach me' instead of 'The only one who could ev-er reach me.'" Now, if I do it onstage I'll copy her phrasing! It was a matter of ego, too: if I can't be as good as Aretha then I'm not gonna do it at all.*

"I didn't like 'Son of a Preacher Man,'" Dusty admitted in an unpublished interview for *Rolling Stone* in 1973. "I knew it was a hit song, but I didn't like the record; I liked the other side, 'Just a Little Lovin'.'"

The recording of *Dusty in Memphis* concluded in much the same way that it began, John Adams remembered—in chaos. Dusty refused an invitation to a private dinner with Jerry Wexler as she'd been arguing with Norma Tanega on the phone, and she sent Adams in her place, while a grand-finale party on the top floor of the Holiday Inn further soured proceedings when someone stole money and plane tickets from Adams's room, forcing Dusty to buy replacements herself. She returned to England and appeared on TV with a black eye and a nasty gash on her forehead that she claimed—implausibly—were the result of "falling out of a tree in Tennessee."

Dusty had "never hit a wrong note" on *Dusty in Memphis*, Jerry Wexler concluded, and the final product demonstrated that she was the very "incarnation of white soul." Ultimately, however, the album marked a sea change in Dusty's career. The process had been torturous, and the result was commercially unsatisfactory—yet the music was a dream. Dusty had created something fragile, beautiful and complicated, and in it lay her triumph and the elements of her downfall.

12

A BRAND NEW ME

"What I've just said could put the final seal to my doom," Dusty cheerily announced as she climbed out of Ray Connolly's car and signed off what became the most infamous interview of her career. For once, she was not exaggerating. It was September 1970 and things had not been going well. In private Dusty was fighting more with Norma Tanega, who was on the verge of deciding to leave and go back to America for good, and her public life seemed equally tenuous for, as the article pointed out, "she's thirty and hasn't really had a big hit record for some quite considerable time."

Dusty was in fact thirty-one, and had decided to use the opportunity of an interview with Ray Connolly of the *Evening Standard* to open her heart about her sexuality, her lapsed Catholicism and her ongoing relevance to the music business. She had been dancing around more personal issues for some time, discussing her personality traits in print with Penny Valentine and taking part in a profile in *The Observer* by Marcelle Bernstein in 1968.

Bernstein spent several days with Dusty; she sat with her in a darkened hotel room in Darwen, Lancashire, where Dusty spent all day before a performance making clothes for Einstein, then she listened to Dusty warming up for the show with the tape from her coach saying "Keep it dark Dusty, keep it dark," and met her several times in her last London apartment before she moved into Aubrey Walk where, Bernstein noted, an unfinished portrait of Dusty by Norma Tanega hung on the wall, and Tanega told her, "All the toys and orange things belong to Dusty."

The issue of how to describe Tanega was never discussed, and Bernstein opted for "flatmate" while describing the closeness of the relationship and the prominence of the double bed. Tanega was quite "brash" and "Californian," Bernstein remembers, and came on to her one day while they were alone in the living room.

> *We were waiting for Dusty—someone was always waiting for Dusty. They had an egg chair hanging from the ceiling and I was sitting in it. Norma came across to me and stood right up close, couldn't have been closer, her legs either side of mine, so I couldn't get up. She was holding onto both sides of the chair at about my head height. She was swinging it forward and back and watching me very intently. It was almost like a challenge. In those days I had long blonde hair and pretty legs. This extended moment seemed to me to go on for a very long time. But that is all it was. If she said anything, I don't remember. It was more of a testing of the waters.*

Tanega was the "carer" of the couple. "She was the looking-after one, she really was very protective," Bernstein noticed. Dusty, by contrast, seemed almost asexual to Bernstein, who never picked up the slightest sense of frisson from her in any of their conversations. Bernstein thought Dusty was "an adorable woman, and so shy," who even bought her a present from Habitat at the conclusion of their time together. Yet she was also intensely self-critical, and a perfectionist about her work who couldn't bear to be alone and bit her nails with anxiety. Onstage, she transformed herself, like a little girl dressing up, into an electric performer who seemed to grow taller and slimmer and exude a magnetic presence:

> She was alive on the stage, but you also felt she was terrified of it, terrified of failure . . . She was like somebody going into a lion's cage. She was on edge all the time she was doing it. I always felt worried for her, perhaps because she felt worried for herself . . . There was a fragility there, and she fought it.

Dusty was intelligent and could have been anything, Bernstein thought. There were no books lying around, but Dusty had a huge and eclectic collection of music, ranging from Aaron Copland to Bach. Yet despite her obvious drive and ambition, she seemed to have maneuvered herself into a place where she was no longer comfortable. While some entertainers seemed utterly relaxed and confident, "she was never like that," Bernstein says. "There was always this feeling of reaching with her."

Bernstein's excellent profile described Dusty's world and the contradictions of her personality, but Dusty said little directly about her personal life, leaving it to Tanega to comment that she couldn't bear to "see someone who inhibits herself so much." After holding forth a little about her views on marriage, Dusty strayed only so far towards suggesting the truth, saying that she felt more "masculine" in her relationships as she was invariably the bread winner.

With Ray Connolly, however, she appeared sick of the charade. Perhaps it was the prospect of talking to a journalist she'd never met before that pushed Dusty into revealing far more than she ever had done before. After describing Dusty in slightly unflattering terms—plump, with a "pretty, lumpy little face" a big shiny grey filling in her tooth, and hair the "color of dried leaves," Connolly recorded Dusty's doubts that her current record, "How Can I Be Sure," would be a hit in Britain—a kick in the teeth for the record company in whose building she was conducting her round of press interviews—with Dusty musing that "the last few records have gone wrong. And I'm always a bit surprised to sell records anyway." To drive the point home she added that unless she found another direction to go in she'd have to be a "cabaret type of entertainer. Whether or not I could be defeated into accepting that type of existence I don't know."

From the outset Dusty seemed determined to lead the interview into uncharted waters, first peering at Connolly through a pink Perspex ruler and telling him she loved pink and purple because they are "erotic colors" and that she had "very erotic tastes." When Connolly failed to take the bait, Dusty used his question about her "little vices" to announce that, in addition to not cutting her toe nails, "I'm promiscuous. Not often, but when I am, I really am."

She used to go to church to confess such impure thoughts, she said, but not any more since she had renounced her faith—a fact that she admitted her mother might be unhappy to read about in the newspaper. As it happens Connolly was a Catholic too, and they discussed the concept of mortal sin for a while. Then, hesitating for only a second longer, Dusty plunged into what she really wanted to say.

Connolly remembers Dusty interrupting what had until then been a jolly conversation, by saying, "Go on—ask me." When Connolly said, "What?" Dusty replied, "You know . . ." Connolly says he was unsure what to say next as "in 1970 you didn't ask the nation's favorite girl next door that sort of question . . . but she wanted it out, so I must have mumbled something about 'girls.'"

This gave Dusty the opening she was looking for. "There's one thing that's always annoyed me," she says, "and I'm going to get into something nasty here . . . But I've got to say it, because so many other people say I'm bent [gay], and I've heard it so many times that I've almost learned to accept it." After denying the rumors that she went to gay clubs, and stating that she "couldn't stand to be thought of as a big butch lady," Dusty admitted she wasn't troubled when girls ran after her—which they often did—and that "I know that I'm as perfectly capable of being swayed by a girl as by a boy." Only a few nights earlier, she said, she was watching someone on television say he "swings either way." Why was such a declaration acceptable for him, but not for her, she asked? "I, being a pop singer, shouldn't even admit that I might think that way. But if the occasion arose I don't see why I shouldn't."

Connolly says that at this point he was thinking, "How do I get this into the paper? I liked her quite a lot, I was a big fan, and in those days girls in her situation didn't come out and talk about being gay or bisexual—no one did . . ."

To muddy things up a little more, in true Dusty fashion, she said she shared her home most of the time with Norma Tanega, but also told Connolly that she was not involved with anyone at that time, and implied that she was still weighing up whether or not to have children, although "there's something which stops me from just reproducing" (Despite once alluding to herbiological clock ticking in a drunken fumble, none of Dusty's friends believe she ever seriously considered having children. Sue Cameron says, "She wasn't even that interested in her friends' children."). Connolly then took Dusty home, happily chatting as he drove passed Hyde Park and dropped her at Aubrey Walk, where Dusty said, "Well, I won't ask you in, Norma's waiting for me."

When the interview was published it caused surprisingly few ructions as Connolly had agreed with his features editor to bury the paragraph about her sexuality in the middle of the story, which was blandly headlined "Dusty at 30." No one wanted to be the one who "outed" Dusty and ruined her career—even if Dusty had dared them to do it. Mike Gill, Dusty's press agent, said he read the piece and viewed it as her "usual bit of mischief" that didn't cause phones to ring off the hook with astonishment. Dusty rang Connolly's house and told his wife that she was fine about all of it apart from the sentence where Connolly said she looked older than thirty—which he subsequently removed. He says:

> She didn't like the bit about me saying she looked more than thirty. I was twenty-eight and she did look older than me . . . the stars all did. They seemed older because of what they'd been through . . . If you're onstage from twenty it does age you, you have a worldly wise feel.

Only later did journalists seize upon the significance of what Dusty had said that day—and not only about her attraction to women. Read in retrospect, the interview offers many clues to Dusty's state of mind. Most tellingly, she ended by plaintively saying that, with or without children, she had to find more in her life than music: "There has to be something more than what I do. There just has to be something more for me."

The desire to be a star never left Dusty, but by 1970 it seemed that the tide was temporarily ebbing. Although she had branched out in a new, more mature, musical direction, Dusty still craved hit singles and Lulu and Diana Ross were beating her to the top spots in the *NME* Readers' Poll, where she had reigned triumphant only a few years before.

"There is a point when you think it is going to go on forever. But of course for most people it doesn't," Vicki Wickham says. "She chose great songs and kept having hits, but you know that you are only as good as your last hit and you know that you must be sure you get the right next one." Looking back, Wickham says, Dusty had reached the critical juncture in her career. "I think *Memphis* probably was a red line—what had come before it was great and that was the culmination. If you listen to the other albums after that, there are some great tracks, but also some that you think "I'm not sure why they are there.""

For the follow-up to *Dusty in Memphis*, Dusty returned to New York in the spring of 1969 to record a further series of tracks with Jerry Wexler. Booked in for ten days at Groove Sound Studios, Wexler once again pushed Dusty to gritty heights, yet thoughts of an album were abandoned without explanation, and ultimately only three songs were finished, including the very Southern-sounding "Willie and Laura Mae Jones," Goffin/King's "That Old Sweet Roll (Hi-De-Ho)" and "To Love Somebody," which Barry and Maurice Gibb had originally written for Otis Redding. While "Willie and Laura Mae Jones" and "That Old Sweet Roll (Hi-De-Ho)" were released as US singles and then on the *See All Her Faces* album, all traces of "To Love Somebody" appear to have been lost, apart from a live studio recording belatedly included on *Dusty: The Complete BBC Sessions.*

With her work in Memphis yet to receive the critical acclaim it deserved, Dusty was unsure she wanted to work with Wexler again, and tried her luck elsewhere, finally settling on recording her second Atlantic album with Kenny Gamble and Leon Huff at the Sigma Sound studios in Philadelphia a few months later in September 1969. Tommy Dowd recalled that Dusty had not been "enthralled" with the material Wexler had offered her, while Arif Mardin added, "I don't think she realized *Dusty in Memphis* was going to be a classic . . . Next time she didn't want to work with the same musicians in the same town."

Whatever was going on in her personal life, Dusty invariably had her finger on the musical pulse and "Philly soul" was about to emerge as the hot sound of the 1970s. With its unique mix of black R&B and Italian strings and orchestration, Philadelphia had its own smooth, jazzy sound that was to overtake Motown midway through the decade. "We had really lush arrangements, and we utilized a lot of classical instruments, and we concentrated mainly on songs," Gamble says. "We concentrated on how to write a great song that would be tailor made for the artist."

Unfortunately Dusty was slightly ahead of her time, arriving to record Gamble and Huff's first album just before they had fine-tuned their work into the hit-making machine that would create classics such as "If You Don't Know Me by Now" for Harold Melvin and the Blue Notes and "Love Train" for the O'Jays—as well as Billy Paul's Grammy-winning "Me and Mrs. Jones."

Huff, an R&B session pianist, had written "Live It Up," which Dusty had recorded in New York in 1964, while Kenny Gamble was a songwriter and Philly native who had already produced the hit single "Expressway to Your Heart" for the Soul Survivors and "I'm Gonna Make You Love Me" for Dee Dee Warwick. Together, it was envisaged that Gamble and Huff would write all ten tracks for Dusty's new album, giving it a unique flavor and consistency. "We enjoyed writing for Dusty because she was so different to the male artists they were used to working with. We had different kinds of songs with her, we had a couple of songs that were almost like country songs," Kenny Gamble says. In the end they were involved in all ten tracks, but several were covers—including the title track, "A Brand New Me," which had originally been a B-side for Jerry Butler.

Gamble recalls:

> We were just getting started really, and Jerry Wexler asked us to record Archie Bell and the Drells, Wilson Pickett, the Sweet Inspirations and Dusty Springfield. So we did

a couple of albums on Archie Bell, we did an album on
Wilson Pickett, and both of them were very successful. And
we enjoyed working with the Sweet Inspirations. And then
there was Dusty Springfield—and boy, that was a treat.

With the travails of Memphis still smarting, Dusty made much of how much she enjoyed her new "melodic R&B" sound and working with the musicians, especially drummer Earl Young, who was later to become renowned for his disco-drumming style with The Trammps. "The rhythm section are the best I've worked with," Dusty said, adding that they played tight, "and very loud, which I like." Dusty was in Philadelphia for more than a month, with Norma Tanega at her side in the studio every day. "We never had any difficulty with Dusty," Kenny Gamble says. "She was very cooperative, and she was always on time, and we made her laugh. We had fun when we were recording her." The Dusty who Gamble remembers was "soft and gentle,' and they treated her with "kid gloves," not only because she was sweet, but also because she connected to Gamble and Huff's way of working, rehearsing songs repeatedly with artists until they were right.

She enjoyed it because we rehearsed so much—we didn't
even do all the songs that we rehearsed; we did the ones
that we thought she sounded best on, and she helped us
decide. She said, "I really like this one, I really like that one,"
and she really rehearsed. That was the key to our way of
recording.

Out of the sessions, however, the only hit song was "Brand New Me," which would turn out to be Dusty's last US top forty entry for seventeen years, and which failed to chart in the UK at all. In Britain, Gamble & Huff's album, released towards the end of

1970, was retitled *From Dusty with Love* and reached number thirty-five in the album charts. Critics liked Dusty's new sound, Rob Hoerburger saying it was as if she was "a couple of drinks past midnight, shoes off, hair undone, makeup smudged."

Kenny Gamble says:

> *I thought the company could have promoted it better, because it hit both markets. It hit the rhythm and blues market here and the pop market. So you got a good spread on it in that it was a crossover album. I thought that we had more singles in it than just "Brand New Me."*

Gamble's greatest regret was that Atlantic failed to release more singles, and that he didn't have the chance to work with Dusty again: "The girl was in a class all by herself, and I think the album we did with her was one of her best." The album's relatively modest success showed that her fans were less sure, though, betraying the fact that, while having one songwriting team provided a consistency of sound, it failed to deliver any memorable stand-out hits of the kind that Burt Bacharach and Carole King had contributed to Dusty's career. Speaking to Ben Fong-Torres for an unpublished interview in 1973, Dusty admitted the result was less than she'd hoped for:

> *I was disappointed. While I was making it, I was entranced, because I loved the musicians and the way they played. But the end result wasn't really exciting . . . I was trying things that really weren't in me. For example, there's a song called "Let's Get Together" or something [actually "Let's Get Together Soon"]. It needed a much more loose singer. When Kenny sang it, teaching it to me, he sounded terrific, natural. I had to think about it a lot, and it sounded like*

*it. I loved them very much, but the kind of music they
like takes a lot of improvisation, and I'm not that kind of
singer. Basically I'm a melodic singer; it's hard for me to
ad lib.*

Nor was Dusty's plan to work with two different record companies, simultaneously releasing material on both sides of the Atlantic, as successful as she'd hoped. Each company was reluctant to release or promote the other's material—tearing Dusty's career in two separate directions.

Despite the demands associated with making *Dusty in Memphis* and *A Brand New Me*, Dusty found time to swap the recording studio for the television studio. After a successful *Show Of The Week* television special of the 1968 Talk of the Town show, Dusty returned to the BBC in the summer of 1969 to record her final series, *Decidedly Dusty*. With Madeline Bell re-joining Kay Garner and Lesley Duncan as backing singers, the series featured guest appearances by Spike Milligan, Danny La Rue, the Bee Gees and Dusty's old favorite, Shari Lewis. But it received a mixed reception when it was screened that autumn: the format seemed tired, reviewers complained, and Dusty agreed that she was now equally uninspired by it.

Dusty was beginning to seem weary of her career, and weary of herself. John Adams remembers a journalist asking Dusty what her favorite color was, and being both amused and worried when she answered "Vodka." Others were taking note too, a *Daily Express* reporter recording that Dusty had three bottles of champagne and a bottle of vodka in her dressing room at the Batley Variety Club. "I'm having a down day," Dusty told him, "I seem to be having more of those lately." Vicki Wickham confirms, "She was doing a lot of drugs and drinking so it was harder and harder to record, harder and harder to get a deal. I think when you start drinking, you presumably wake up not feeling so great, and it alters your judgement on things."

Dusty's judgement regarding her career, many felt, was indeed beginning to go wonky. "She didn't want to tour, and there were a lot of package tours in those days. She had done a couple with the Searchers and others, and she didn't want to," Wickham says. "So she was doing her own concerts and there was a strain because when you are doing your own thing, it's on you." Going solo, Dusty faced not only the physical and emotional strain of carrying the show, but also a financial burden. Dusty's costs were always high, in part because she was a perfectionist who demanded the highest standards and best musicians, and when her 1969 US tour sold poorly she was left £12,000 ($15,000) out of pocket—a very large sum. In Britain there were only three or four venues lucrative enough to make financial sense, and Dusty reckoned she had, at best, three good months a year of work in the UK. Her thoughts turned again to America as the place where, she believed, the answer lay. "She had reached the stage in England where she had done everything she could," Wickham says. For Dusty, America "was a whole new continent."

Pat Rhodes believes that motivation to move to the US was also driven by Norma Tanega. "Dusty always wanted to go to America, she loved America. She wanted to go, and Norma was the person who was saying she could do it." As Dusty's relationship with Tanega unraveled, the situation became more pointed. Tanega could not stay in Britain indefinitely and, moreover, her life had been consumed by Dusty's career since their first meeting. "Dusty devoured me," Tanega once said. As the arguments between them became more frequent, and more unpleasant, Tanega was also exploring her own art and music again. When Tanega had a brief affair during one of Dusty's absences, the subsequent rows were so intense, according to Penny Valentine, that Tom Springfield sent Tanega a note saying, "Since you two are arguing all the time don't you think it would be better if you went back to America?"

Before her departure, Tanega was a guest at Pat Barnett's wedding in the summer of 1970. "Norma showed herself up tremendously," Barnett says. Dusty had flown in from the US to attend, and bought a low-key off-the-rack dress so as not to outshine the bride. When the car pulled up at Aubrey Walk, Dusty was, of course, still getting ready, and Tanega answered the door. Seeing that it was an ordinary saloon car rather than the limousine that Dusty had ordered, Tanega sent it away. "Dusty was explicit—'We mustn't be late,' and Norma sent it away—she wanted to arrive in a limo, that's what it was," Barnett says. When Dusty discovered that Tanega had sent the car back, she "went berserk at Norma. She said, 'I'll go in a Mini, as long as I get there on time.'" They eventually arrived half an hour late, with the registrar holding back the ceremony for a final five minutes before threatening to abandon the wedding altogether. Barnett says:

> *Dusty was furious with Norma over that, and I think that was possibly where she suddenly realized that it was Norma that really cared what car she arrived in. Dusty didn't. She'd booked a limo to arrive in because it was my wedding, but she really didn't care about it being a limo as long as she got there. And I think that's when she realized that she was always searching for the right person, and she never found them.*

Despite the ugly fights, however, Tanega's departure for California signified a crisis for Dusty. Her career had stalled, and she had been abandoned by her lover—even if many of their problems had been caused by Dusty's need for drink and drama. With little on offer in Britain, apart from further tours of northern clubs and the dreaded "panto," Dusty flew back and forth to the US, meeting potential managers.

In New York, Dusty had undertaken to do a series of recordings with writer/producer Jeff Barry. Barry had been responsible for some of the biggest pop hits of the 1960s, including "Be My Baby" for the Ronettes and "Chapel of Love" for the Dixie Cups; he had worked with Phil Spector on "River Deep, Mountain High," for Ike and Tina Turner and had produced the Monkees. In 1969 Jerry Wexler and Ahmet Ertegun had approached Barry and asked him if he wanted to work with Atlantic. "I told them there were only two Atlantic acts I wanted to work with," Barry says, "One was already working with another producer, and the other was Dusty Springfield." Wexler put them in touch via a phone call to London, and Dusty expressed her enthusiasm too.

Pulling together a series of songs specifically commissioned from writers including Neil Brian Goldberg, Gil Slavin, Ned Albright and Mike and Steve Soles, Barry started recording in his tiny New York studio. "Dusty arrived for her first day, and I was working on the head arrangements on the first song," Barry says. "I looked into the control room and I could see Dusty with a somber look on her face and her arms folded." Quickly he moved on to the second song, but when he looked again Dusty was still equally serious, and seemingly unhappy.

By now Barry had heard all the rumors about working with Dusty, and was starting to get alarmed. "After I'd committed to work with her, people said, 'Oh my God, Jeff, she's so difficult, she takes over sessions . . . I don't know if you know what you've got yourself into.'" He stopped recording, and ushered Dusty into his office down the hall, asking her what was wrong. "I love what you're doing," Dusty replied. "That expression is me not having to worry about what's going on. But it's my life, and if I don't like a session I will certainly come out and do what I can."

After that, Barry remembers, their work together was "totally relaxed," with Dusty recording the highest note she'd ever hit. The two became friends and socialized together, with Dusty taking Barry to watch Rosie Casals play tennis in London. Dusty was sweet and funny and feminine, Barry thought, without any hint of "diva-ship" or any sense of the problems he'd heard so much about—except for an occasional cloud of depression. For Barry it was one of his happiest sessions. "When I talk about great artists I've worked with it's usually two—Dusty Springfield and Johnny Mathis . . . they were just great singers," and Dusty sounded upbeat too, telling the press that she was very happy with the work: "The album is completed . . . It's all out of my hands now . . . It's certainly as strong as my English LP, in fact it's a lot stronger."

As work began on the final mix-down, however, Dusty and Atlantic began haggling over the renegotiation of her contract. With no end in sight, Atlantic pulled the album from the schedule —while most Dusty fans remained in the dark that a third Atlantic album was even under way. In the end Atlantic released two singles from the thirteen tracks that had been recorded, "Haunted" and "I Believe in You," and then dropped plans for the album altogether. Although the songs had been slated to appear on *See All Her Faces* they remained unreleased until 1980 in the UK, and rumors abounded about what had happened to Dusty's "lost" Atlantic album. Tapes of the recordings were destroyed in a warehouse fire, and the majority of the songs only came to light when Barry revealed, decades later, that he had kept his own session tapes.

See All Her Faces also included Dusty's final recording in Britain for many years, signifying the end of her journey with Stanhope Place Studios and Johnny Franz that had catapulted her to stardom and carried her through the remarkable years of her career in the 1960s. Out of a set-up that she had often found frustrating, Dusty had produced an outstanding string of hit records, and demonstrated a depth of talent and artistic development rarely matched. But with little promotion from Dusty, *See All Her Faces* struggled—making it a sad finale.

Dusty had already sold her house in Aubrey Walk and moved to America permanently in early 1972. The sense that she had closed one door and opened another was heightened when a return performance at Talk of the Town ended in disaster. The club had been the scene of some of her greatest triumphs, but on the greatly anticipated opening night of December 4, 1972, Dusty was nowhere to be seen. An impatient audience, including Rod Stewart and Elton John, clapped impatiently and whistled until Dusty appeared, forty-five minutes late, claiming she could hardly sing due to laryngitis. A doctor had been summoned backstage to spray her throat with cortisone, rendering it numb. After much encouragement from the audience, Dusty struggled through a few songs and apologized, saying, "There are many songs I'd like to sing but I can't because it would be an embarrassment to you, and me."

The following day Dusty submitted a doctor's note saying she had to have three days of complete rest, at which point Talk of the Town fired her, and brought in Bruce Forsyth for the remainder of the four-week run. Now down by approximately £10,000 ($12,000), Dusty and her US management issued a lawsuit, with a statement saying, "As far as we're concerned she will never play Talk of the Town again," which sadly turned out to be true.

Still, if Dusty was distraught, she was taking pains to hide it. When photographed on a London street Dusty was smiling, and looking sanguine. The image symbolized Dusty's new attitude: she was done with Britain, and consumed with her new life, and love, in LA. "She saw America as the Garden of Eden," Vicki Wickham says. "It was going to be absolutely great, she was going to do all the things she wanted to. And of course it wasn't."

13

BEVERLY HILLS BEIGE

"America was her death and destruction," Pat Barnett says, and yet nothing could have seemed further from the truth for Dusty on the opening night of her set at the West Side Room of the Century Plaza Hotel in Los Angeles in May 1972.

The Century Plaza was a sweeping nineteen-floor hotel on Avenue of the Stars that held society galas where Andy Williams and Bob Hope entertained Ronald Reagan, and where President Nixon had hosted a state dinner in honor of the moon landings. Dusty's show was a serious attempt by her American management to position her as the kind of high-profile artist who would rake in the takings night after night, doing the hotel cabaret circuit in cities across the country. Not rock 'n' roll enough for Whisky a Go Go, and not funky enough for The Troubadour, Dusty would sing above the clatter of plates and cutlery as middle managers and their wives enjoyed an evening out.

For those who knew Dusty this clearly spelled doom, but hopes were still high as she opened at the Century Plaza, and her new manager, the chubby and cheerful Howard Portugais at ICM, nervously waited in the audience for her to appear onstage. *Hollywood Reporter* columnist Sue Cameron was also waiting in the audience. Cameron had written about everyone in the entertainment industry, and played drums with Frank Zappa for fun. She had met Dusty three years earlier, backstage on the TV show *Shivery*, and been unmoved. "When we met at *Shivery* she didn't interest me," Cameron says. "We were in a hallway. She was going to the stage to rehearse and she was all alone, and we looked at each other and said hello, and we shook hands and kept on walking."

Back at the Century Plaza, Dusty appeared onstage and sang a medley of her hits, as well as "Ain't No Sunshine Since You've Been Gone" and "Up on the Roof," closing with "Higher and Higher." While Nat Freedland from *Billboard* sniffed that Dusty's voice no longer "cut through the walls of sound that we are used to on her records," he conceded that she did at least sound "mellow voiced and relaxed." Out in the audience, Cameron was blown away by what she'd heard: "Talent is what gets me, because what I saw that night I'd never seen another singer do."

Cameron rushed off to the opening-night party, hoping for an interview, but was annoyed when a nervous Dusty failed to appear. After waiting for forty minutes, Cameron left: "She completely blew her opening night party; by the time she got down there almost nobody was there." When Dusty did finally appear, according to Freedland, she seemed uncertain about her performance and complained about poor acoustics in the hall, covering up her inherent shyness and insecurity with a series of amusing "flaky stories."

Knowing how important it was to keep the press onside, Portugais immediately called Cameron and arranged for a one-on-one interview soon after. When Cameron turned up in the hotel suite after the show she spent an awkward few minutes chatting with Tom Springfield, conductor Marvin Laird and Portugais, who was praying that Dusty wouldn't stand up an interview twice. "I had no thoughts of anything other than 'I just am crazy about this talent,'" Cameron says. Dusty finally emerged from the bedroom wearing a hostess gown similar to those worn by 1940s movie stars, and "swished around" chatting about music. Cameron recalls:

> One by one everybody left the room because they could see that we were really getting along. I didn't notice that she was drinking but I finally realized that maybe three quarters of her way through the interview she was slurring her words, let's just say she was warm and fuzzy, and she started talking about the Troubles in Ireland. She was so passionate about that, it upset her terribly, and she started to cry over the war—and I'd never seen that. All of a sudden I saw this passionate, alive, talented person, and I put my arms around her to comfort her and that was it—I never left her side.

Dusty was living in an apartment on Hilgard Avenue in Westwood. Recently converted from UCLA student dorms, the apartments were mustard yellow, and were an altogether strange choice for a major recording artist. Although Dusty had spent most of her twenties moving between equally uninspiring serviced apartments in London, the choice seemed to reflect the fact that her new management was unsure of exactly what to do with her, or where to put her. Fred Perry, her lighting director, had also decided to make the move to LA, but Doug Reece was now married and living in Australia, and Pat Barnett had decided to stay in London because she was pregnant. Barnett says:

> There was nothing organized over there. She asked me could

I go but I'd just got pregnant with my son, and I couldn't leave. I didn't know what to expect over there. We didn't know whether she would make it, and she couldn't afford to pay my husband as well. So it was not meant to be. But I often think "If I'd gone, would it have been different?"

Without her established support network Dusty was now dependent on Howard Portugais, who also represented Dory Previn, Andy Williams and Randy Newman and, increasingly in all other areas of her life, on Sue Cameron. When they met, Dusty had been in the final throes of an affair with a tennis player—a relationship born of her long interest in women's tennis, and one that explained her rather curious appearance at some low-key tournaments. Soon after the night at the Century Plaza, however, Dusty and Cameron began to spend most of their free time together and Dusty called up the tennis player and broke off their relationship. Cameron would become Dusty's lover for the next few years, and a part of her life forever. "I was attracted to her because she was so alive," Cameron says. "I'd never seen that kind of passion and commitment. I just fell like a ton of bricks—and I love her today as much as I loved her at that moment."

Dusty quickly moved out of the Hilgard apartment and rented a house a few blocks from Cameron in trendy, gay-friendly, West Hollywood—although they soon gave up on the pretence of having separate residences, and moved in together. Cameron says:

One day we were talking about swimming pools and I said, "Oh, I love to swim." That's all I said, and two days later she said, "There's something I want to show you." She drove me to a house and she had the keys, and she said, "This is yours, I just bought it."

Impulsively, Dusty had bought a two-storey modern house on Dona Teresa Drive, at the back of Laurel Canyon looking down over the San Fernando Valley, complete with a swimming pool in the backyard. "I didn't need a house," Cameron says. "Dusty loved to love people, and she was unfailingly generous."

Just as she had been the face of the '60s, but not really a part of the '60s scene, the same was true of Dusty's LA life. Laurel Canyon was at the heart of the music scene, it was where Joni Mitchell, Graham Nash and Carole King played songs to each other in rickety cottages high in the hills and it was where Neil Young had slept in a hearse by the side of the road when he first arrived in 1966. Yet, by comparison, Dusty's house seemed more like a suburban dream. Tucked away on a quiet street, the modestly sized Dona Teresa house had a vaulted ceiling in the living room and a large sound system, but the only other movie star touches were Dusty's enormous bed, draped in curtains and positioned to look out over the lights of the valley, and a bowling alley which was installed along the full length of the top floor. "The carpets were lime green, and the bedroom was bright yellow. I hated those colors but Dusty loved them," Cameron says. She elected to keep her own bedroom, decorated more sedately, complete with homely touches and possessions.

Most of the time they lived a cosy compatible life. "It was very domestic," Cameron says. Dusty would iron all Cameron's shirts and clothes (she had been an expert ironer since her schooldays, and she was a pretty good cleaner too) and they would cook dinner together and watch TV. "It wasn't a crazy life. It was strange, but it wasn't a crazy life. It was only when 'Dusty' appeared that it got nuts."

Every evening, when Cameron got home from work, they would dance together. "We would waltz in the kitchen; when we lived together we waltzed together every night before dinner." Dusty and Cameron's songs were "You Are Everything" and "You'll Never Know."

> *We picked "You'll Never Know" as our song, because we were watching an old Alice Faye movie and she came on singing "You'll Never Know" and we just looked at one another and got up and started waltzing. And so our codename for "I love you" was "Alice Faye"—we said it for years.*

However, living with someone who worked a day job, and was every bit as ambitious about their career as she was about hers, was a revelation to Dusty. "She desperately needed to be the star," Cameron says. "When she picked me she had real trouble with that, because we were more or less equal." Cameron was as likely to be going off to interview a famous movie star as Dusty was to be cutting a record, "and she never had anyone in her life who would do that, they'd be there doing the dishes." She adds, "I wasn't going to stop anything I was doing for her, no matter what, and I didn't . . . I was very ambitious and I worked hard for my career and that's what I was going to do."

When they went out, people were as likely to know Cameron as they were to recognize Dusty, who had yet to achieve the same celebrity status in the US as she had in Britain. "I would take her to parties sometimes because I needed to cover certain things, but she didn't like it," Cameron says.

> *She was famous because of being known as "Dusty—from England." But because I had this very famous column, I was the one that was invited to parties and if I brought her along it was a nice accompaniment. She was not used to that. She was the star, and it was very, very difficult for her to handle*

me and my success . . . So she met her match and that is why
I always intrigued her.

They had many good times. Cameron loved to drive Dusty's Jensen Interceptor—"it was like driving a bullet"—and laughed when Dusty told her that her own Cadillac was for old ladies. They celebrated Christmas and Thanksgiving twice, once in their own home where Dusty cooked, and once with Cameron's family down in Newport Beach where Cameron would watch in amazement as Dusty charmed her mother and they all sang around the piano. One Christmas Eve they ran out of gas in a bad part of town, and Dusty persuaded her to stay overnight in a sleazy motel with a chair propped up against the door to keep out intruders. "I was terrified and she was laughing the whole time . . . When I was with her it was an adventure."

Adventurous or not, in moving to Los Angeles, Dusty had found the kind of settled relationship that she craved.

> *About six months into our relationship, Dusty said, "I'm taking you somewhere." It turns out we went to Grauman's Chinese Theatre, where they have the footprints of people. Alice Faye has her footprints in the front, and we stood in Alice Faye's footprints and she asked me to marry her and she gave me a ring. It was very sweet, and it was way before anybody would ever do anything like that.*

As well as giving her a secure domestic base, Cameron also began to accompany Dusty to professional meetings—and was generally considered to be a calm and steadying influence. Dusty, by contrast, showed little interest in what Cameron did for a living. "There was really never any discussion of my work. I was devoted to her work, and I don't ever remember her being interested in mine," Cameron says, but she was still happy to come home at the end of the day and talk through whatever issues had arisen with Dusty's career.

Cameron "was a very stabilizing kind of a force in Dusty's world, at least from my point of view," the songwriter and producer Dennis Lambert says. "She was a very calm person, very thoughtful, very articulate—as was Dusty on the surface, but Dusty also had the inner potential to implode." Lambert was engaged on Dusty's first piece of work after the Century Plaza and a series of hotel engagements in other cities, the ABC Dunhill album, *Cameo*. In the summer of 1972 Dusty and Cameron began regularly meeting with Lambert and Brian Potter, hanging out at the company building on Beverly Boulevard and talking through what she liked musically, and where she saw herself going.

"She was a pop artist with R&B undertones, and she was a singles oriented artist," Lambert says. "Although she sold albums to her fans, most of her success was dependent on getting on the radio with singles." Yet, just as Gamble and Huff had, Lambert hoped to achieve an album with the same unique, consistent sound as *Dusty in Memphis*.

The album that would become *Cameo* "felt connected musically and song-wise, since we did it all in one place with a band we regularly worked with, including me on keyboards. It was a very intimate affair, and if it was that good, that tight, that accessible and qualitatively recorded, we'd be in great shape. That was our vision." Lambert and Potter carefully balanced playing Dusty their own material, which they were careful not to push at the expense of other songs. Lambert says:

> If she didn't like something that we wrote, that was the end of it. Fortunately she was very responsive to what we brought to her. There were certainly things that she said, "No, I don't hear that," but I believe that the majority of

the things that we custom-wrote for her got recorded. We probably brought ten or twelve songs we loved, and she chose three or four of those.

"Every single recording was a calculated choice," Sue Cameron says. "She would sit down with the demo and on a big yellow sheet mark everything that she was going to sing and then go in and record it exactly the way her notes were. There were accents, funny signs on words. I didn't know what the code was."

With Joni Mitchell's success and Carole King's *Tapestry* album, it was clearly the era of the female singer-songwriter. Although Dusty was no songwriter, Lambert and Potter believed her voice and style fitted well with the changing times. Lambert says:

I had followed her very closely through her recording career, and knew all her work really well. So when we had the opportunity to sign her to ABC Dunhill in the early '70s, I volunteered to say we would love to get involved and write songs for her, find her great music, meet with her, make sure that everybody is on the same page and we get along.

Although it was only a couple of years since her most recent hits, Lambert remembers that in the industry Dusty's career seemed "very cold, and not on a roll and not an automatic by any stretch on radio." Yet Lambert and Potter had achieved similar success reviving the career of the Four Tops (and would go on to do the same with other artists, including the Commodores after Lionel Richie's departure). "So it didn't bother me that an artist had not had any recent or current success," Lambert adds. "We were very high on the fact that she was just a timeless artist with an incredible voice, a recognizable style—and there began what for me was one of the highlights of my career to this day. Working with her was joyous, and we expected that we were going to have great success with that record."

Dusty seemed optimistic too, calling Lambert and Potter a "hit factory" who really knew how to write great songs. She added ominously, "I may be their first mistake, but I'm praying I'm not." After agreeing the material, recording began—and it quickly became apparent that Dusty's dissatisfaction with her own performance and ruthless self-criticism had only strengthened. "She would be in total character on mic," Lambert remembers. "I mean we got the whole deal, the hands, the whole Dusty thing, that made her so special and so unique." Yet, for Dusty at least, it wasn't working. "She was very hard on herself. She wasn't rude to us, she had a gentle, creative soul—but she was really tough on herself. And it didn't seem that she liked any of her performances, not one." Although Lambert says he tried to calm Dusty into believing her performances were, in fact, very good, "she was really almost out of control with personal disgust with her performances, to the point where she would pick up an ashtray and throw it."

Sue Cameron remembers that Lambert and Potter were recording the Four Tops at the same time, and that Dusty would overlap with them when she started late in the evening—which was always her favorite time to sing. Yet Cameron noticed that Dusty was also drinking more, and that it was affecting her while she worked. "One night she simply couldn't sing anymore. Not that she lost her voice, she had a voice, but nothing was on key and she just fell down on the floor." Unsure what to do, Cameron picked Dusty up and drove her to a rehab center in Long Beach. "I was so angry," Cameron says. "I did not have an understanding of the alcoholic problem; to me I just saw this great artist who couldn't sing on key who fell on the floor in the middle of a session in front of everybody." In another session, late at night, Cameron emptied the studio, apart from the young female engineer and herself, and said to Dusty, "Just sing, I'll produce—you just sing it." It seemed to be the only way of getting through the track, although the song did not make it onto *Cameo*, but was passed on to Dusty's next album with Brooks Arthur instead.

With the torturous recording process finally finished, ABC released two singles from *Cameo*—"Who Gets Your Love?" and "Mama's Little Girl," which was swapped with its B-side, "Learn to Say Goodbye," the theme to the 1972 TV movie *Say Goodbye, Maggie Cole*. Neither made much impression.

Cameo's lackluster performance provoked much discussion about whether it had suffered from the wrong singles choices, a poor cover or lack of promotion. Although fans criticized the album for being "formulaic" and "plastic," it undoubtedly reflected the sound of the early 1970s, and critics loved Dusty's breezy vocals. In *Rolling Stone* Peter Moran said he could not have imagined "such a superior and involving piece of work," adding, "Her smoky, intimate voice has been singing in my living room for weeks now, and I'm not tired yet." Furthermore, he drew attention to the intended synchronicity between Dusty and her songs:

> *I can't say that I've ever heard a better match of material to singer/persona. Dusty is a mature woman, one who's been around, who's upfront about her experiences. She strikes a balance between the sensibilities of Joni Mitchell and Loretta Lynn. The songs seem to be her own; the integrity is striking.*

Billboard called "Learn to Say Goodbye" "one of the most touching beautiful songs of the year, or any year." Despite such praise, the song spent only three weeks in the US chart, getting no higher than 118. "Who Gets Your Love" also spent three weeks in the US chart, but only managed to reach number 121. Dusty had recorded "I Just Wanna Be There" by the same writers as the song she would really have loved to have recorded—"Ain't No Mountain High Enough" but that, and standout songs like the super-smooth version of "Tupelo Honey," went unremarked on.

"We were very disappointed, I am to this day," Dennis Lambert says. "'Mama's Little Girl' wasn't the first single, and it should have been." Opinion was divided, he recalled: "Some people loved 'Breakin' Up a Happy Home,' 'Mama's Little Girl'; others liked 'Easy Evil.' The label was very committed, they spent money and they took the record out into the marketplace with every intention of delivering a huge hit album and hit singles, and it just fell flat."

Fans also complained about the cover, which featured a rather crude drawing of Dusty set on a cameo brooch—and which had originally been intended to work on a blue felt background but was eventually downgraded to a less successful ordinary card rendition. Dusty did little in the way of promotion, and blamed both the record company and herself, saying, "I wasn't proud of the sounds coming out of my throat," and complaining that ABC had not even bothered to discover what key she sang in (something that seems unlikely given Lambert and Potter's extensive research and conversations with her). Despite her misgivings, the problem did not lie with Dusty's voice, which was as smooth and fluent and faultless as ever, even if constrained by the easy-listening sound of the time.

"They were very successful pop song writers," Sue Cameron says of Lambert and Potter, "but they were too white. She liked some of the songs, she didn't like all of them." The album was "beige," Dusty concluded, a derogatory term that she eventually applied to much of Los Angeles in the 1970s. Rather than the black America that had stirred her soul, and the freedom that had emerged from the revolution of the 1960s, California was embracing a culture as white and tasteless as Wonderbread—and Dusty hated it.

Every morning she woke up with a small cloud of depression sitting over her head which only lifted when she was onstage. To make matters worse, and even though she was now far away from the prying eyes of the prurient British press, Dusty could still not come to terms with her sexuality. Sue Cameron says, "She hated being gay. She hated everything about it, and it destroyed her. When you drink you want to bury something and that's what she was trying to bury, she hated it every day of her life for as long as she lived, which is a terrible shame."

And if Dusty had hoped that LA would be more tolerant and open than London, the reverse was true. Hollywood was even more "closeted," Dusty later told *Gay News*. "There is a very strong antigay feeling in Hollywood, which is extraordinary in an industry which is 75 percent gay." You could sit around a dinner table with eight other gay people, and no one would admit it—being gay was career poison.

When Dusty returned to the UK at the end of 1972 for her ill-fated Talk of the Town appearance, a few shows in Manchester and Batley and two concerts in late January 1973 at the London Palladium (which she later admitted she had been too stoned to remember), she asked Cameron to fly over and join her for Christmas. It was Cameron's first experience of a family event with the O'Briens, and she was taken aback by what she saw.

First Dusty took Cameron to a Christmas party at her brother Tom's house. "Those infamous Christmas parties," Cameron says, where people would arrive early in the evening and drink all night. "Always at one point during the party Pepe Borza would dress up as Dusty and sing or lip-synch to 'All I See Is You' and 'You Don't Have to Say You Love Me' in front of Dusty's parents—and Dusty loved it." Although Pepe was a good impersonator, Cameron found this a strange way to celebrate Christmas, especially when her own background was more conservative. "Eventually we would all pass out, and the only one who remained standing or sitting upright was her mother. At six o'clock in the morning I walked to the living room, and there she was. I'd never seen anything like this kind of behavior." Despite appearances to the contrary, however, the O'Briens were much like Cameron's own family in that "there were no feelings and no emotions and nothing was ever discussed."

On Christmas Eve, Cameron decided she wanted to go to Brompton Oratory to hear the choir, but Dusty at first refused to go with her and started to cry, saying, "If I walk into that church the ceiling is going to fall on me, I'm going to be dead because I'm such a sinner." "She was serious," Cameron says. "That deep feeling of shame lasted throughout her entire life." Eventually Cameron persuaded her to enter the church and sit in one of the back rows, and Dusty began to pray. "She prayed all the time. She was very religious inside and didn't act like it outside, but religion was the formation of her entire life. Either fighting against it, or being afraid of it, or following it explicitly. Religion was the key."

Dusty's conflict over her Catholicism was thrown into further relief a few days later when they impulsively decided to fly to Rome for dinner on New Year's Eve. Cameron was immensely excited by the idea of her first trip to Europe, although that soon gave way to a more familiar and wearying scenario. After checking into the Excelsior Hotel they ate at Doney's on the Via Veneto— Cameron remembers:

> *After dinner she was, of course, really drunk and I was very unhappy and we ended up back in a hotel room with her passed out on a bed and me sitting there just going, "I don't know what to do with my life, this is just crazy, but I love her so much, surely this can be fixed." I had that conversation a million times with myself.*

The next morning, however, Dusty woke her before sunrise and said, "I want to take you somewhere." They jumped in a taxi and drove across town to the Vatican where they found a staircase that opened up onto a balcony looking out over St. Peter's and the whole of Rome. Dusty and Sue stepped out together onto the balcony to see the view on the first day of the New Year. "The sun came up and she turned to me and she kissed me and she said, 'I love you so much.' That was the greatest moment of my life," Cameron says.

> I realized later that she was saying F-you to religion—"I love this girl." Now that's very dramatic. If a Catholic girl wants to say she loves another girl where is the riskiest place you can do it? That is the biggest statement against the church, and I didn't realize until many years later what courage that took.

Looking back on that freezing, unforgettable, New Year's morning with Dusty, Cameron concludes: "That was probably the most significant thing that she'd ever done to fight for who she really was."

14

LONGING

"I live with an emptiness in some part of my heart that I never completed her thought," Brooks Arthur says. Arthur had fallen in love with Dusty's talent as the sound engineer working with Shelby Singleton on the 1964 New York recordings like "Live It Up." A decade later he was a well-known producer working with artists including Janis Ian and the young Bruce Springsteen, and when he met Dusty's new managers Howard Portugais and Alan Bernard at a recording at Carnegie Hall they persuaded him to hook up again with his old friend.

Brooks Arthur met Dusty and Sue Cameron at their house on Dona Teresa Drive, and told them he had a vision for her:

> I rebuilt the bridge that was started here in the '60s and we moved it into the '70s, and then all the things that might have been lacking in Dusty's New York days, when I recorded her with Shelby, I more than made up for it by tailoring the tracks so that she can breathe and sing

223

*and have the ebb and flow. The result would be a Dusty
Springfield that you just want to put the needle on and then
go to paradise. We got halfway there.*

The failure of *Cameo*, Dusty's inability to settle into California
life, and her growing dependence on drink and drugs meant that
by 1974 she was far from any kind of personal heaven. Her house
had a "fantastic view, a big pool, all the gadgets," Dusty recalled
later. "It was sort of nouveau riche. The trouble was that I was not
nouvelle, and not very riche. I staggered around that house for a
while, trying to convince myself that I really belonged. But every
time I looked at the burned-up hillside, I felt terribly alien."

A party thrown by her friend Elton John in the summer of 1973
seemed to signify all that was going wrong with her life. Elton
was celebrating the launch of Rocket Records with a big event in
LA, and two of Dusty's friends, Lee Everett and Penny Valentine,
had flown out to stay for two weeks to go to the party and, in
Valentine's case, cover the launch. Once settled into the house they
proceeded to get very drunk and silly, laughing at old jokes, and
playing pranks like stealing the bottom half of a mannequin from
outside a shop. When Dusty forbade Everett to put chicken bones
from a KFC takeout into the garbage in case their cats chewed and
choked on them, Everett resorted to throwing the bones into the
swimming pool. Soon all manner of other items and furniture got
thrown in the pool too, driving Sue Cameron so "ballistic" that
she moved into a hotel for two weeks. "We threw a chair off the
top deck," Everett says. At the end of the fortnight Dusty held a
surreal poolside meeting with an agent who could hardly believe
his eyes as he nervously stared at the vast mass of debris floating
in the dirty water.

Valentine noticed that Dusty seemed to get drunk and depressed
more quickly, and sometimes had nasty accidents that left blood

on the poolside table. Everett remembers how much her friend missed England, saying she couldn't make friends with people in California because "they're all Americans." When Cameron had returned home at the end of the first day of their stay to find them all drunk and lying about, Everett complained that Cameron glared at her, "stiff" with disapproval and disappointment. Cameron *was* disappointed: she longed for the easy-going, happy, brilliant Dusty who sometimes met her on a good day, and the intrusion of these friends who seemed to bring out the most wayward side of Dusty was not easy to cope with. She recalls:

> *I began to notice that it was kind of excessive drinking. When we went out I'd be a little worried about being embarrassed. But it escalated. It escalated early on and all my friends said, "You've got to leave, this is a person who scares you, this is dangerous." And they were right—but I said, "I'm not leaving her."*

Undoubtedly, beneath Dusty's apparent merriment that summer, the launch of Rocket Records was playing on her mind. She had met with Elton in a bungalow of the Beverley Hills Hotel and they had agreed to record together but, somewhere in the details, something had gone wrong—and the offer had been withdrawn. While Elton admired and adored Dusty, perhaps his more cool-headed business partners had taken note of the growing rumors that she was too much trouble to work with. Now Dusty's old rival, Kiki Dee, would be taking center stage with Elton— it was finally her turn.

"It was a fluke that I got on it [Rocket Records]. It was through John Reid," Kiki Dee says. "She should have been the one, everybody adored her and knew her greatness." Showing enormous grace, Dusty wrote to Dee to express her good wishes, but inside it hurt. Her letter read: "All the very best with Rocket, you always did have a bloody great voice." Only later did Dee find out that Dusty was going through a heck of a bad time. "It wasn't like it was a time to be naturally generous—when things are going well it is much easier. That was a time when she was having some tough personal issues and her career wasn't going that great. Really, she should have been on that label."

"Don't Go Breaking My Heart" was written for Dusty, according to Sue Cameron. "He did that for Dusty, and she was just too sick to record it and too unreliable, and Elton didn't want to wait and so he had Kiki Dee do it. That really upset Dusty. But it was her fault, and Elton didn't do it to hurt her." When it was released in June 1976, "Don't Go Breaking My Heart" was the first UK number one for both Elton and Kiki Dee, and stayed at the top of the charts for six weeks. In the US it topped the *Billboard* Hot 100 for four weeks. The song's phenomenal success could easily have relaunched Dusty's career and sustained her financially for years.

At the party itself, Dusty jumped up onstage and sang backup with Elton, Kiki Dee, Lee Everett and Vicki Wickham's partner, Nona Hendryx from Labelle. Everett had blacked up her face and Hendryx had "whited up" hers. In the photos everyone is laughing and having a great time, and with her hair hanging straight and natural, Dusty looks young and fresh—like someone who should have the world at her feet.

In truth, "I felt I was obsolete with a feeling of uselessness and depression," Dusty remembered. In an interview with Peter Evans in LA she said, "My thinking musically was here only I lost confidence in myself. I lost the ability to voice my opinions. I started thinking that maybe my views were amateur and empty. After all, I kept telling myself, 'This is Hollywood!'" Cameron would try to coax Dusty to go out more, and make friends—but inside Dusty was as shy and insecure as ever. It was easier to slope around at home wearing her favorite tracksuit. Dusty could have socialized with any number of Hollywood stars, but the idea terrified her. Cameron says:

> Dusty didn't let anybody in unless they were less than her. So she was very shy with Ann-Margret, very shy with Angie Dickinson. I introduced her to many people who were famous then, including Debbie Reynolds, and everybody on television in the '70s. She didn't associate with any of them. She didn't make any attempt to be friends with them, she was alone. It was too glamorous for her, it was too much for her.

Later, Dusty remembered how she had tried, and failed, to become a lady who lunched, "doing the things that Beverly Hills women do." It all involved fixing your makeup, going to lunch, drinking too much, experimenting with drugs, shopping, making appointments and expanding your social circle, she said. "And I really hated it. It became so incredibly boring after a while." She added, "I began looking at these women and thinking, 'Christ . . . what a load of bullshitters.' I realized their lives didn't add up to anything.'

What Dusty possessed that set her apart from everyone she met, of course, was her unique talent and voice—but, for one reason or another (her excuses were numerous), she was often reluctant to work, or take up the opportunities that came her way. Cameron remembers:

> I'd come home from work and Cass Elliot would be sitting outside by the pool. She was there a lot. Melissa Manchester came over to play a demo that she really wanted Dusty to sing, it was "Midnight Blue." She told Melissa no. Melissa leaves the house, I went, "Are you crazy?" I didn't know until later that she was

offered "Killing Me Softly" before Roberta Flack.

(Cameron was even more incredulous when Dusty later turned down the chance to record "Nobody Does It Better" for *The Spy Who Loved Me* in 1977. "The Bond people waited forever for her to get it together to record it, they couldn't wait any longer, they gave it to Carly Simon. I went through the roof. I was so mad at her for drinking and causing that. It made me crazy.")

It seemed a miracle when Dusty said she was ready to go back to the recording studio, this time with her old friend Brooks Arthur. Arthur had built his own workshop in Blauvelt, New York, named the 914 Studio after one of the New York area codes. Dusty arrived in the summer of 1974 and, after finding a house to rent, she settled in ready to begin work on what would be her second album for ABC Dunhill, first titled *Elements* and then renamed *Longing*.

Arthur had worked with Janis Ian on the *Stars* album, and was now working on her second album, *Between the Lines*. "Dusty loved Janis Ian," Arthur says, in particular a song called "In the Winter." Arthur asked Ian to come into the studio and play the piano on that session, "which brought me to my concept," he says. *Longing* would consist of a core group of songs that really spoke to Dusty and her life. "There was a new guy in town named Barry Manilow, and he admits that nobody had covered his songs yet and he came up and played, 'I Am Your Child.' Then Melissa Manchester came in and did 'Home to Myself.'" Arthur and his musicians began working around this core group of songs.

I wasn't cutting everybody at once, this was more of a workshop, doing a track, adding the vocal, adding the strings or the backgrounds, so it was like building a little mini skyscraper. It was the New York Rockland County equivalent of Dusty in Memphis, *that's what it was, and it*

could have been, because the songs were drop-dead great. I
was one or two songs away from nirvana.

Once they started recording, though, it became apparent that Dusty's personal problems were overwhelming her life, and she was on the brink of a total collapse. Without Sue Cameron constantly at her side to support her (Cameron visited, but was working back in LA), Dusty was drinking, taking more pills and drugs, and pacing the floor all night worrying. "Sometimes you can overwater a beautiful plant," Arthur says. "She couldn't even get through the vocals at times because of her stuff, and overly caring."

Arthur wanted to build an album that people couldn't take off until the end of side two, "with just enough time to turn the record over and start again; that was the album I was trying to make, and some of her vocals were just gorgeous and some of them she just couldn't get into singing." Arthur now wonders if there were songs that Dusty didn't like, "but on the other hand she uncorked gems on the songs that she loved. 'Turn Me Around' was a killer. 'Home to Myself,' 'In the Winter'—and 'Beautiful Soul,' wow, that was something. But I couldn't get her to finish the vocals and complete my work and I wouldn't turn it in."

As the weeks dragged on, and turned into months, Dusty's relationship with Arthur and the musicians began to break down. "All that personal groove that Dusty and I had, it evaporated, it went away," Arthur says sadly. Dusty wanted to start work around noon, so Arthur would book her in for seven hours or so. "She got a little paranoid about certain things. She would even look at my scheduling book." When Arthur drew one session to a close "she went over to the scheduling book, and said, 'You're making up this name, I never see him, I just see his name every day, so it's just a way for you to leave here and go home and have dinner with your family.'" Arthur told her he wasn't making up the name. "His name is Bruce Springsteen, he decides to come in when he wants!" Springsteen had the room booked out from eight in the evening until nine the next morning, and Arthur refused to move him around, even for Dusty.

What had begun as a "magical" relationship with the musicians also started to turn sour. They had been "like hand in glove with her. They played and lived and breathed on every nuance and mannerism that she threw out vocally," but now they were growing impatient. Arthur says:

> Some of the musicians felt that she wasn't taking care of business . . . Some of those guys picked up on that before I did. I used to keep Dusty's tapes in the vault, in the library shelf in the back of the studio—and one of the musicians crossed out the word "Dusty" and wrote "Rusty."

Sometimes Dusty wouldn't show up, at other times she appeared but was only half ready. "Her voice was very scratchy and tired. The kind of tired that you get by not sleeping too much and pacing the floor, or eating a lot of dairy, which gives you that phlegmy sound, but I noticed that she was just not the Dusty that we knew." She appeared to be disintegrating in front of everyone's eyes. "All the elegance and style was disappearing, it was, like, careless, sloppy looking and not gracious and royal. But she was still Dusty Springfield."

In the summer of 1974 Dusty was indeed facing her demons. Back in England Kay O'Brien was dying of cancer. In the middle of recording Dusty flew home and visited Kay in a hospice near Hove. She was shocked to see that her mother was shriveled on the bed, her face like "a mask," but Kay opened her eyes, looked at her and said "You!," reaching up with a hand "like a claw" and tweaking her nose. It was one of the few moments of physical affection between them that Dusty could ever remember.

When she returned to America she received a telegram from Tom saying that Kay had died. Dusty later told a friend it read "Mummy dead" and then included another sentence on a totally different topic. Dusty found it blackly hilarious, and awful, that her family communicated in such a dysfunctional way. "It's true," Sue Cameron says. "That telegram lay out on the coffee table," shocking everyone.

Back, alone, in Nyack, Dusty slumped into the worst depression of her life. "She was in pajamas sitting on the couch watching baseball, but staring at it in a weird way," Sue Cameron says.

> *I knew she was upset, and I held her and she started crying—and then she told me about how her mother had reached up and tweaked her nose. And she said, "I just have to watch baseball, that's all I can do. You just have to let me watch baseball." So she was there for at least three days watching baseball.*

Later, when her own mother died, Cameron understood Dusty's distress.

> *When you have a mother who's not the mother you want her to be, as long as she's alive, the child still has a hope that they may turn into the mother that they want them to be. When they take the last breath, the hardest thing to deal with is your hope has gone. You have to deal with the fact you never had the mother you wanted, and you're never going to get it.*

Dusty's issues with her parents remained forever unresolved.

She had finally worked up the courage to tell them that she was gay, but they had brushed off her words as though she had said nothing of importance, and blanked it out. Later, Dusty flew her father out to LA for a vacation, but Cameron remembers that she remained "terrified" of him and desperate for his approval—making Cameron get takeouts from several Indian restaurants in the city, so that she could make sure he had the best version of his favorite vindaloo when he arrived.

In Nyack, after her mother's death, there was little to lift Dusty's spirits. Sometimes she would travel into Manhattan to visit Vicki Wickham and Nona Hendryx, who would try to cheer her up for an evening. One evening she met up with John Adams, her former hairdresser, who'd moved back to Australia, and they went to see Labelle playing at the Metropolitan Opera House. Before the show, Dusty recorded an interview introducing *Monty Python's Flying Circus*, which was about to be screened to a US audience. An incoherent Dusty "battled through a series of questions" making little sense, with an interviewer who believed it was part of a plot to showcase how zany English humor could be.

The reality was that Dusty was in the throes of a catatonic nervous breakdown. When she made an apparent suicide attempt, Brooks Arthur rushed over and saved her life, checking her into hospital. It was neither the first nor the last time that this would happen. Arthur says:

> *I checked her into a Rockland County hospital as Mary O'Brien. She was really way under the weather and I knew this hospital was a great hospital. Nobody knew what the story was, and then one nurse was a British woman, and she says, "Mary O'Brien, aren't you Dusty Springfield?" It blew the cover.*

By October 1974, it became clear that *Longing* would never be complete. ABC Dunhill had completed artwork for the cover, and even began advertizing the album's release, but Dusty didn't want to pose for a cover shot and there was no end to the recording work in sight. "She knew that time was running out," Brooks Arthur says. "I was growing impatient because the label was growing impatient, the managers were impatient and her support team was impatient—and her fans were wondering what's going on, but it wasn't meant to be."

Company president Jay Lasker called Arthur and told him that ABC were pulling the plug: "You guys are spending too much money and too much time, and you're wasting my time. Let's cut our losses and we'll move on." The news sent Arthur into a "tailspin." He had known Lasker since he started work in the mailroom at Decca Records and Lasker was the head of Sales and Services. Being unable to complete something as important as an album with Dusty was a huge blow to Arthur's career.

> For the one and only time in my life I did an album that wasn't delivered. I always delivered. If I had one more month or so with her maybe I might have been able to fix "Make the Man Love Me" and one or two other songs. We had great musicians, great arrangers . . . The titles we did were just great, every one of them unto themselves is a standard song. It was the cream of the crop song-wise.

Arthur says he too had peaks and valleys in his life, and his love and respect for Dusty continued undimmed, but their aborted collaboration "was a blur on my track record, and it hurt." He felt that he had let himself down, and Dusty.

> It's a two-sided coin. I feel I let her down because I didn't

capture her quickly enough, I should have had this all
wrapped up in six or eight weeks. Instead it just went on
and on and on and I thought that she would bounce out of
it and that wasn't about to happen. I always had the feeling
that maybe she was looking at me as the guy who let it slide
as opposed to her, who was really the one who slid.

If Dusty had completed *Longing* it would have secured her place in music for at least another ten years, Arthur believes. He had built a masterpiece around her, and she had added some of the most haunting vocals of her career. In the choice of writers and songs, Dusty had also expressed deep truths about her own life—many of them were explicitly about a gay woman who was often alone, and somewhat lost, trying to find her place in the world. "I was spelling her life out in a way, without placards," Arthur says. "'Home to Myself' and 'In the Winter' kind of says it, and 'Beautiful Soul'—those songs talk about the life that she chose, her style. That was ballsy on her part to accept those tunes."

Although the tracks remained unfinished in places, the eventual release of songs from Brooks Arthur's sessions decades later only reinforced the view that Dusty was singing from an emotional depth that she never recaptured. Dusty left Nyack and returned to Los Angeles to enter a recording wilderness. "Nyack was the beginning of it all," Sue Cameron says. "The beginning of the downslide. There was no coming back from Nyack."

When she eventually emerged four years later her next album would include a rerecording of some of the tracks that she'd attempted on *Longing*. Although these new versions sounded slick and smooth, they expressed none of the rawness of that terrible time in her life. Her heart was missing. Brooks Arthur says, "The truth of the matter is those records that she remade lacked the soul that I captured that never got out, because that was the magic, man. We had the magic."

15

IN THE WINTER

"As much as fame was a prison, she loved it," Sue Cameron says. More poignantly, Dusty was lost without it. After her inability to complete *Longing*, Dusty returned to LA without purpose. Royalty checks were getting smaller, even with reissues of her old work, and it seemed sensible to sell the house on Dona Teresa Drive and move to a rental in Sierra Alta Way in the Hollywood Hills off Sunset Boulevard. At the new house she enjoyed socializing with her neighbors Lily Tomlin and Eden Kane, her one-time fake love interest who was now happily settled across the street with his wife and children. Phil Spector lived close by with his girlfriend, and one night Dusty and Sue sprawled on the floor, terrified by the sound of random gunfire coming from his house. Although Dusty's own dramas did not involve guns, her difficult and erratic days were becoming more frequent. "I went to work every day and when I came home I wouldn't know whether she was going to be on the floor passed out, or not—and I eventually just had to ignore it," Sue Cameron says. "I literally would call the paramedics and get back to the work that I was doing and leave the

235

next morning."

At the Dona Teresa house, Cameron had kept a bag packed in the bathroom in case she needed to escape quickly.

> *My bathroom had a door that was an exit to the outside. So I could go in my bathroom quickly if she was screaming and running after me, shut the door to the inside of the house and open the escape door and run to the garage and get in my car before she could catch me. There were times when I was really afraid. I've stayed at every hotel in southern California, I would try to go someplace nice to try to soothe the fact that I had to run away.*

When Dusty drank and took drugs she quickly became distraught and hysterical in what often turned into "harrowing scenes," according to Cameron. "She would scream a lot. She would also threaten to harm herself. She said when she cut herself she knew she was alive, because she could feel it."

Some of Dusty's friends, like Vicki Wickham and Madeline Bell, knew about Dusty's self-harm, but felt powerless to help her. Others, like Riss Chantelle, were oblivious to the evidence in front of them. Chantelle had dropped in to see Dusty on her last dates at the London Palladium, and found her in good form but with her arm bandaged up. When Chantelle asked what had happened, Dusty told her, "Do you know, I was cutting some ham, Riss, and I cut it right through. I've had to go to the hospital." They sat on the floor of the rented apartment and drank a bottle of champagne, and it was only years later, after she'd learned the truth, that Chantelle understood what had really happened. "I realized what the cut was. She'd cut herself, but she daren't tell me. I should have known better because you wouldn't chop ham up your sleeve, would you? And I thought, 'What a terrible thing to do.' She must have been desperate. Why couldn't anybody help her?"

When things got out of control, other friends were often called in to help: Billie Jean King arrived to calm things down when Dusty was running up and down the street smashing car windows, and Dusty's lighting director, Fred Perry, spent an evening in bed with her, trying to soothe her, while she sobbed through the night and dug her finger nails into his arms in despair. This was not a sexual encounter; Dusty just desperately wanted someone to hold her and take away her pain. At around the same time, Lee Everett remembers Dusty creeping into the guest room to ask, "Can I get into bed with you, Lee?" Dusty, and several of her cats, then curled up and went to sleep while Everett lay awake worrying that Dusty's spiky jewellery would do them a serious injury during the night.

It was often too much for Sue Cameron, who was living with Dusty's demons on a daily basis. Just as she tried to remove one bad influence from Dusty's life, a new one would appear. "She didn't have any barometer that could tell her, 'Get rid of this person, keep this person.' She needed bad-value playmates, because that was the trip she was on." Cameron adds, "You can't live with somebody when you don't know if they're going to be sober or not, someone who takes drugs and drinks all the time and someone who was surrounded by the lowest of the low." If Dusty's old friends had sometimes led her astray, her new acquaintances were little more than drug suppliers and celebrity hangers-on. "I wouldn't stand for any crap. She would surround herself with sycophants, and I wouldn't want them in the house and I'd ask them to leave—so it just kept going downhill," Cameron says. "I hated all these people, they were all drug people and all they did was drag her down."

Briefly Cameron and Dusty split up and agreed to live apart for a few months, and Dusty made her first attempt to get sober by joining Alcoholics Anonymous. Even in those days AA meetings in Los Angeles served as a refuge for much of the entertainment industry, with many well-known faces attending regularly. Although a substantial number of people in the room were more famous in Hollywood than Dusty, she fretted that she would be exposed and worried that people would tell her story to the press. Dusty took getting sober seriously, but her greatest fear was that she would be unable to sing as she once had, or that she would lose her creative magic. "I'm different from these other people," she would say in AA meetings. "I need it to perform."

Without a new album on the horizon, and with the catastrophic collapse of her previous sessions, Dusty's fear seemed real. Between 1974 and 1976 she contributed to other artists' work, but created none of her own. Cameron tried to keep Dusty in the public eye, arranging for her to appear on Dinah Shore's daytime TV show, while Dusty's unique vocals can be heard on Thomas Jefferson's Kaye's "American Lovers," "Sho-Boat" and "LA," produced by Brooks Arthur for ABC Dunhill. Dusty also sang with Peter Allen and Evie Sands, and took part in some sessions for Elton John's *Caribou* album, including singing backup on "The Bitch Is Back." On "Don't Let the Sun Go Down on Me," however, her voice gave up completely. While Cissy Houston (who had led the Sweet Inspirations to such heights singing backup on *Dusty In Memphis*) tried to coax the best out of Dusty, and encourage her, she could no longer hit the high notes. Dusty's supporters found the session "grueling to watch" until eventually she stopped midway through and admitted, "Listen, I can't do this."

Working with the Canadian singer Anne Murray for a week in 1975 seemed to be a better experience. Dusty flew to Toronto and sang on "Sunday Sunrise," "If It's All Right with You," "Player in the Band" and "Blue Finger Lou," saying the session had been "heaven"and admitting, "I sang a couple of notes here, there and everywhere."

In her autobiography, Murray mentioned that she, and her husband-to-be Bill, had first met Dusty backstage at the London Palladium in 1973 when Dusty had cleared the dressing room by grabbing Bill's hand, and shouting:

> *"Everybody get the fuck out of here—now!" Then she turned to us and said that we were the only real people there. Her security detail emptied the room in minutes. The three of us sat quietly and talked for a short time—Dusty, it was obvious, was pretty spaced out—and then we said our goodbyes.*

They next met in LA when Anne Murray and Bill invited Dusty to come over to their hotel to discuss her possible contribution to Murray's 1975 *Together* album. Murray writes, "I'm not sure what Dusty was expecting, but she was clearly unhappy to see Bill with me in LA." Dusty had a few drinks and:

> *at one point she excused herself to use the washroom and then, on the pretext of a snag in her zipper, summoned me to join her. There she came on to me verbally and wanted to know, "what was up" with Bill. I spurned her advances, telling her that Bill was the man I planned to marry. When Dusty returned to the room, she physically attacked Bill, scratching his face with her fingernails. It was quite a scene, but she calmed down after that, and Bill ended up driving her home.*

The Toronto sessions, however, turned out to be good for everyone, with Murray saying, "She was clean at the time, and we had the best week together." Dusty told Murray that her pill taking and drinking meant that she could only dimly remember the previous seven years of her life—and they did not discuss their encounter in California.

When Dusty was sober, she reverted to the quiet, serious Mary O'Brien who stayed at home and looked after her cats, but it had become apparent that she was struggling not only with alcoholism but also with living with a mental illness. By the mid-1970s, Dusty was seeing a succession of psychiatrists, and being prescribed the antidepressants Nardil and Marplan, as well as Haldol and Seroquel, which are used to treat psychotic illnesses. She told Sue Cameron she was suffering from a mood disorder, which she later described as a chemical imbalance. "She went through psychiatrist after psychiatrist," Cameron says. "Each one would prescribe a different pill. Dusty used to joke and make a game of it. She told me she knew just what to say to get the pills and that her performances for doctors were her entertainment."

As far as she knew, the pills and psychiatrists were used to treat what Cameron would come to know as an "attack," which was always brought on by a bout of drinking and occurred approximately every ten days.

> The "attack" would always be Dusty sitting in a corner in a dark room, rocking back and forth with her arms wrapped around her knees. Tears would be streaming down her face and she'd be saying, "Demons, demons, they're coming to get me," over and over again. She was terrified.

Afraid and ill, Dusty was not only a danger to herself, but sometimes to others as well. Cameron says that at one point, very late in their relationship, Dusty chased her with a knife.

> I will never know whether she intended to hurt me or not.

She was laughing at my terror as she came toward me teasing
me by thrusting the knife closer and closer as I backed up.
In my heart I think she was playing a sick game that was
almost out of her control. I felt that at the time as well, but
the terror won. I ran out of there to save myself.

A few days later, Dusty was hospitalized, and tried to laugh off the
incident when Cameron went to visit her. "She tried to make light
of it by saying she was teasing me. I wasn't laughing, but I also
wasn't angry." But for Cameron it was "the straw that broke the
camel's back," and the two didn't meet for some time after that.

Despite the very significant hurdles she faced, Dusty was determined not to give up. After three years in the wilderness she was
ready to start recording again, and in early 1977 began work
on her "comeback album," optimistically titled *It Begins Again.*
Later Dusty described the mid-'70s as the time in which "I just
plodded on and made rather unsuccessful pop records," but of
course that was hindsight, and all the projects started with more
hopeful beginnings.

Having terminated her contract with ABC Dunhill a couple of
years previously, she was now working with Barry Krost as her
manager and recording her first album for United Artists in the US
and Mercury Records in the UK. Krost had managed Cat Stevens in
London, and was a straight talker who found Dusty "hard work" but
loved her company, and often went out with her and Sue Cameron
in the evenings to events and Bette Midler concerts. "She was prone
to hysteria if something was hurting her," Krost told Penny Valentine,
but behaved impeccably 90 percent of the time. They would only
argue if Dusty phoned him to say "I've collapsed . . . I'm in [the]
hospital . . . I'm in rehab . . ." and couldn't record, but even then
Krost learned that screaming and shouting at Dusty never won an
argument.

Work on the album began at Cherokee Studios in Los Angeles with producer Roy Thomas Baker, who had previously worked with Queen and Foreigner, and session musicians including Jay Graydon, Jeff Baxter and Joe Sample on keyboards, and Brenda Russell as one of the backing singers. Geared towards an adult-contemporary sound, with a smattering of disco, *It Begins Again* contained a reworking of Chi Coltrane's "Turn Me Around" and "A Love like Yours" from Dusty's sessions for *Longing* with Brooks Arthur, as well as "Sandra," a song by Barry Manilow about a housewife who accidentally cuts her wrists, and "Checkmate," a funky and more feminist number by Nona Hendryx. Cameron recommended the song "Love Me By Name," which was written by Lesley Gore and Ellen Weston.

Lesley Gore had first met Dusty on *Ready Steady Go!* in 1963, when Gore was a newly minted sixteen-year-old pop star visiting Britain to promote her hit single "It's My Party (And I'll Cry If I Want To)," produced by Quincy Jones. Gore says, "I saw her and took a snapshot in my head of the makeup. Her look was very specific. She made an impression, even though we really didn't get to know each other." Gore continued to work with Jones, and had the US hit version of "You Don't Own Me." By the 1970s she had moved out to California, along with most of the music industry, and was working as a songwriter when Sue Cameron reintroduced her to Dusty. Gore and her partner invited Dusty down to their beach house for a couple of weekends, and noticed that Dusty seemed to be up on the 1970s music scene, listening to music, and "pretty involved" in what was happening, according to Gore. As a person, though, she remained private and shy. "She was best at just hanging out, that's when I enjoyed her most, when she was just being herself," Gore says. "I'd had her on a pedestal, so it was not easy to get to know Dusty. You had to back up a little, you couldn't come on loud and strong. You almost had to sit back and wait for her to come to you.'

After spending some time together they found a connection, and Gore was delighted when Dusty invited her and Ellen Weston to the studio to watch the recording of "Love Me by Name." "We were very excited that Dusty was doing 'Love Me by Name' because in my estimation Dusty was the consummate musician," Gore says. "The caliber of her art was always higher than anybody else's. Her musicians were amazing, her arrangers were amazing, and she made incredible choices."

Despite her by now legendary perfectionism, and self-criticism, Gore thought Dusty enjoyed the session, and was in good form. "She was pretty confident about herself as a performer, as much as anybody can be. We all have our anxieties, and I don't think Dusty was without them." Most of all, Gore was happy to see Dusty so energized by recording again. "Her energy levels were really good in the studio. She was really up for it. She was taking it seriously but I was also glad to see that she was also having a really good time."

The session musicians, and producer Roy Thomas Baker, agreed that Dusty was extremely well behaved in the studio and had none of the meltdowns she was now known for. "We would work together right down to every last dot . . . phrase and note," Baker told Lucy O'Brien. "I'd ask her to bend the end of a word up and she'd write it down on her list. There were no ego problems and working with her was really good, but the record did go well over budget for one reason or another." Coming in just shy of half a million dollars, the record companies viewed the album as indulgent, with an end product that didn't warrant the means. Drummer Ed Greene recalled that Baker had gone easy on Dusty, treating her fragile personality with sensitivity—and soothing the underlying pressure that *It Begins Again* was a very important point in both her life and career.

Aside from the sessions, however, things were not going well—

and Sue Cameron decided to end their relationship for good. On the afternoon that Dusty was due to record her last vocals for the album Cameron went to the studio and took Dusty outside to tell her that it was over between them. When she wasn't sober, Dusty's drinking and drug taking were wilder than ever and things had finally gone too far—driving Cameron away much as Dusty had driven away her other partners, always believing, deep down, that she was unworthy of their love. "Mostly she thought that she didn't deserve me," Sue Cameron says, adding that Dusty also envied her relatively stable and successful life. "I think she was also jealous. It was a lot for someone who wasn't sober some of the time to put together."

On that afternoon, in a back alley with a stunned and disbelieving Dusty, Cameron knew she was closing a door on the most important relationship of her life. "I didn't know what to say, except that I had to protect myself," she says. "I'd just kept leaving. But it's no way to live. It killed me to leave her, it just killed me, because I really didn't want to do it—and the night that I did she tried to commit suicide."

Worried that they hadn't heard from her, Dusty's friends from AA Helene Sellery and Suzanne Lacefield spoke on the phone and Lacefield agreed to go over to the house to see what was wrong. Breaking in through a glass door, Lacefield found Dusty unconscious on the floor after taking an overdose. "She had fallen on this potted plant, and she was covered in dirt and leaves. I just grabbed her by the shirt and I just started screaming, 'Goddamn you, don't you dare die on me!'" She was rushed to Cedars-Sinai Hospital where doctors were doubtful she would make it through the night—and Lacefield was later stunned when a psychiatrist asked her, "Does she have any problems?"

Cameron was distraught but, she says, friends advised her not to rush to Dusty's bedside:

top left Dusty in the sea at St Maarten © Sue Cameron
middle left Dusty getting her toes wet, although she couldn't swim © Sue Cameron
middle right Dusty on holiday in Eleuthera © Sue Cameron
bottom At Billie Jean King's condo in Eleuthera, Bahamas in 1974 © Sue Cameron

Dusty and her father in front of Sue Cameron's beach house in Malibu © Sue Cameron

Dusty in Santa Monica during her father's visit in 1976 © Sue Cameron

Dusty and her father in Malibu © Sue Cameron

Dusty and Sue Cameron playing tennis in Strawberry California in 1976. Dusty had just come out of rehab and would sing on stage with Labelle that night © Sue Cameron

Dusty on stage with Nona Hendryx of Labelle © Sue Cameron

Dusty on stage with Patti Labelle, a moment of delight in the dark times of the 1970s © Sue Cameron

Dusty with (*l–r*) Lesley Gore, Sue Cameron and Ellen Weston © Sue Cameron

top left Dusty at Sue Cameron's house in 1978
© Sue Cameron
bottom left Sue Cameron and Dusty's former
manager Howard Portugais in 1990 © Sue Cameron
right Dusty back in Britain for "It Begins Again" in
1978. She had recently split up with Sue Cameron
and was feeling hounded by the press about her
sexuality © Getty Images

Dusty, Judy Stone and John Adams in Australia during the time of Dusty's relationship with Carole Pope around 1980 © John Adams

left Dusty and Teda Bracci's wedding with Tarra Thomas (*left*) and Gloria Del Bianco © Teda Bracci
right Dusty and Teda Bracci clown around in a photo booth at Santa Monica pier © Teda Bracci

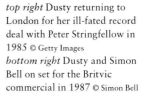

top right Dusty returning to London for her ill-fated record deal with Peter Stringfellow in 1985 © Getty Images
bottom right Dusty and Simon Bell on set for the Britvic commercial in 1987 © Simon Bell

top left Dusty snapped at home on the couch in LA by Teda Bracci © Teda Bracci
bottom left Dusty and Simon Bell sing during a surprise appearance at her fan convention in the late 1980s © Simon Bell

top left Dusty and the Pet Shop Boys, heralding her return to stardom and life in the UK © Getty Images
top right One of Dusty's last faxes to Sue Cameron apologising for an argument © Sue Cameron
bottom Dusty's house at Frogmill, rented when she was in remission from cancer. She loved being close to the river © Sue Cameron

Dusty was in remission from cancer, but photographer Mike Owen thought she seemed thoughtful and fragile in what would be her last photo session © Mike Owen

"Don't go over there, because if you do she'll know that that's
the way to get you and if she ever wants your attention all she
has to do is pull a stunt like this and you'll come running, so
you can't do it, you have to nip it in the bud the first time."
I was awake all night scared to death that she was going to
die. I remember I sat on the floor in my bedroom all night
huddled up in a little ball going "Please don't let her die."

Dusty didn't die, and when she opened her eyes she found an angry
Lacefield at the foot of her bed. "Oh, shit," Dusty said slowly, as
the reality sank in. "I said, 'Listen, you bitch, don't you ever pull
this crap on me again,'" Lacefield remembers. "'I saved you, I own
you. You don't get to do this unless you ask me first!' And that was
the agreement."

A few months later, Sue Cameron married her husband, Bob.
It was a dramatic, symbolic gesture to prove that she could free
herself from the downward spiral and reclaim her life. "I had to do
something really drastic," Cameron says, "because the whole thing
was just too much for me." Dusty, however, wasn't ready to let her
go. "We had these moments of back and forth and never leaving,"
Cameron says. When Dusty recorded "Let Me Love You Once
Before You Go," her first single for United Artists in 1977, she
demanded that Cameron join her in the studio before she would
sing a note.

I drove over, and of course she'd picked the song for me,
because she didn't want me to go, and I stood there in the
studio with her right by the mic and I just held her hand and
she sang it all the way through, it was perfect. She did it for
me. I left sobbing.

Dusty admitted that, coupled with her crippling lack of self-esteem, she had an almost obsessive fear of being abandoned. "My trouble is I get lost in people. I've always thought that they should make up the part of me that I thought was missing. I give people tremendous powers, the power to make me a whole person." Knowing it, and changing her behavior, though, were two different things.

Slowly recovering from the overdose, Dusty was discharged from the psychiatric ward and completed *It Begins Again*. She wrote in the liner notes that it was dedicated to "those who cared." Cameron says, "She was very angry . . . that was a slap at me. Because an alcoholic always lashes out at those who have their best interests at heart." Dusty returned to England to promote her comeback album in a very fragile state of mind.

Despite a massive marketing campaign, the album lingered in the UK charts for just two weeks, peaking at number forty-one, and did not chart in the US. With a more mixed, and some said mediocre, song selection than the usual Dusty album it "probably won't disappoint ardent fans, but it's unlikely to win her any fresh converts either," Patrick Humphries wrote in *NME*. Dave Marsh added in *Rolling Stone* that the album "is marred by its material, which is rarely objectionable but hardly praiseworthy. The one chance she has here to match the potency of earlier masterpieces like 'Son-Of-A Preacher Man' is Lesley Gore's and Ellen Weston's 'Love Me By Name,' but the song is buried by its arrangement."

In general, however, the press were far more interested in discussing Dusty's private life than her musical ambitions. If Dusty had fled England believing she was being hounded over her sexuality, she was shocked by how much worse it was in the late 1970s. Ten years earlier reporters and editors had been reluctant to follow her teasing admissions to their logical conclusion, but now they were ready to bare their teeth. Dusty was no longer the girlish darling of British pop, but a middle-aged singer who had flounced off to LA, and now had the temerity to return and think she could reclaim her throne. At a press conference at the Savoy on February 1, 1978, Dusty looked like a deer frozen in headlights when reporters subjected her to a barrage of questions about why she was still single at nearly forty. "Do I wish I had a man? Not all the time," she answered, adding there was no one in her life at the moment. Did she need a man at her side, the reporter persisted, to which Dusty answered, truthfully, "If you have a hole inside you, you can't have it filled by somebody else's personality." When two women reporters changed the subject to Dusty's music she mouthed "thank you" to them.

Dusty seemed shocked and nonplussed by the reaction to both her return and her album, and to add to her woes she had been presented with an unpaid tax bill as soon as she landed at Heathrow. She commented defensively in one interview that British people looked "pinched and cold" in comparison to Californians, and admitted that the song "I'd Rather Leave While I'm in Love" was in no way representative of her own life, where she said she tended to hang on to relationships far longer than she should. "I'm hopeless," she said, "I'd love to leave while I'm in love but I'm absolutely useless at it, I'd rather leave while something's still happening and it's good but I just can't."

In an interview for *Gay News*, she broke down and wept when asked about her sexuality, despite the fact that she must have known the topic would inevitably come up. Keith Howes, the features editor of *Gay News*, remembers preparing for the interview by playing "In the Land of Make Believe" from *Dusty in Memphis*. He'd specifically asked her record company if Dusty would be willing to talk about her sexuality. The press officer answered yes, and Howes set off for Dusty's hotel in Piccadilly knowing that his readership would be fascinated to read about an icon that they loved. "Gay men loved Dusty because they knew that Dusty loved women," Howes says. "There was massive speculation as to whether she would actually come out of the closet . . . She'd never quite stepped off the cliff."

Howes had been told that his normal photographer would not be allowed to take pictures, as Dusty didn't like being photographed in natural light and only allowed preapproved shots—yet when she descended a spiral staircase Howes thought that she looked like "a diva . . . she was a goddess." At the press conference at the Savoy, he thought that Dusty had looked nervous and almost "enamelled" with a curious new look and hairstyle that made her look like a "straight" businesswoman rather than a pop singer. "It's like a lesbian trying not to look like a lesbian. No trousers, this long skirt and these boots. It didn't suit her at all." She was wearing the same tangerine and brown outfit for the interview, he noted.

For a few minutes, Dusty was charming and funny, and chatted amiably in an Anglo-American lilt about Einstein, her teddy bear, who she said was "very jaded," and her cats back in California. Howes asked her how she felt about her glory days in the 1960s, and Dusty said that most of her hell raising had involved drinking hot chocolate and eating Swiss rolls, and that she had never had hordes of people doing all her chores so it was never a "spoiled trip." Keen to move into more personal territory, Howes asked her if she identified with the lyrics to the song "Sandra," and she admitted that she could identify with the feeling of being trapped, even though she wasn't a housewife. Later Howes returned to the theme, asking what her Irish family made of her unmarried status. She said, "Well, they wonder; let them wonder," adding that her mother had married late in life, and had never encouraged Dusty to do the same. Suddenly sounding very Irish, she added, "There's never been a feeling in the family that I haven't achieved something because I didn't get married, marriage is a state of mind."

Of course, the purpose of the interview had not yet been

broached, and having circled the issue for several minutes, Howes honed in—referring back to Dusty's interview with Ray Connolly in 1970. "The defences went up," Howes says, and Dusty retorted that she didn't give a damn what people thought, and she wasn't going to commit herself to being either homosexual or hetero-sexual, although she loved gay people and her gay following. Howes says:

> *I began to feel really chilled at this point. I heard this sort of stuff from so many celebrities, and this just wasn't good enough, this wasn't what people were expecting. This was Dusty Springfield—and suddenly she's coming over in a very patronizing sort of way . . . She said, "Could you please turn off the tape recorder?" Then she started to cry and said it was impossible for her to come out.*

Turning to the press officer from the record company, Dusty said accusingly, "You promised me I wouldn't be asked this question!" Howes was somewhat aghast, as that question was the whole point of the interview. Dusty said, "I'm sorry—I can't." Howes says, "Dusty was not just angry, she was in tears," and seemingly desperate as she realized that the success of the *Gay News* interview was critical for her fan base.

Howes apologized, decided to salvage what he could, turned the tape back on and continued with the interview. For the remainder of their time together Dusty held forth about the entertainment industry being very closeted and discussed sexuality in a more general way. When Howes told her that there was tremendous homophobia in the emerging punk scene Dusty said, "You see, it begins again. I rest my case."

All questions that veered towards her personal life seemed to create "a little frisson," with Howes gently prodding an admission that she was afraid of being abandoned by her friends. Howes asked her, "Are you a very demanding friend? Do you ring up in the middle of the night?" After a long pause, Dusty said, "No." But Howes thought, "I bet you do ring up in the middle of the night."

The interview concluded with Dusty saying the worst thing she could imagine would be to lose herself, like she had almost lost herself before, and that she was just trying to hang on to Mary O'Brien. Her words trailed off, and Howes walked out of the hotel suite, into Piccadilly Circus and burst into loud sobs, thinking, "Even Dusty Springfield, at this stage of her life and her career, has to live a lie . . . I could see and hear from the tremulous quality of her voice how it was tearing her apart."

After a ten-day promotional tour, Dusty flew back to LA with a sense of relief. In the years since her departure, she had changed and so had Britain. In California Dusty had been homesick for England, but it was no longer the diffident, unthreatening, friendly country she had known so well. Her fans seemed more reluctant to welcome her back with open arms and buy her records, and the press were now ready to pursue her ruthlessly. Neither English nor American, neither in the closet nor out—as she crossed the Atlantic, Dusty must have wondered if there was anywhere she did belong.

16

I'M COMING HOME AGAIN

"It was the interplay between the child and the woman that was so remarkable about her. And in many ways it was so charming, and in many ways it was damn near fatal."

HELENE SELLERY

Whatever demons possessed her, and however low she would sometimes sink, Dusty's talent was the thread that ran unbroken throughout her life, and there were moments, even in her bleakest years, when her star shone out undimmed. Taking to the stage at the Theatre Royal, Drury Lane in April 1979, Dusty tearfully began to sing "I'm Coming Home Again," with the weight of many hard years behind her, and with her confidence wobbling under the added blow that her regional tour around the UK had been canceled due to poor ticket sales. Yet that night, and every night for the three nights that she performed, the packed audience was humming with emotion, and something close to adoration, from those who sensed what she was enduring and loved her all the more for it. When she moved into "Quiet Please, There's a Lady on Stage," in tribute, she said, to "all the women who've been legends in their time," single red roses fell on the stage, thrown by fans who felt the shivers of her tortured fragility.

Dusty's appearances at Drury Lane included a nerve-wracking entrance on roller skates (she was pushed from one side of the stage by Pat Barnett, and caught at the other) which only added to the tension in the audience as everyone wondered if she'd make it through—leading critic Robin Denselow to note that she had appeared "trailing clouds of reputation and the expectation of imminent disaster."

Imminent disaster had long given Dusty's shows an added frisson, and her gay fans loved every moment of it. Dusty's absence had coincided with the growth of the gay liberation movement of the 1970s, and had transformed her from a cult figure of the 1960s into a fully-fledged gay icon—something she was happy to talk about in interviews even if she wouldn't discuss her own sexuality. Now hordes of gay men gave her standing ovations when she took to the stage, and shouted "We love you, Dusty!" between songs. "Give a butch roar or a girly shriek, I don't mind who does what!" she responded.

Dusty triumphed at Drury Lane and could have played to a packed house for a week or more, but beyond London the reception was more uncertain. Posters advertizing her concerts had featured a picture of her with a curly perm that made her look uncannily like Petula Clark—and some believed the regional dates would have been much more successful had they featured an iconic '60s image of the beehive and panda eyes with the words "Dusty's Back!" The question of whether Dusty still had anything to offer to the women who'd once come to watch her, while eating baskets of scampi and taking the weight off their swollen ankles, hung in the air like the smell of stale cooking fat at a northern club, and Dusty was deeply upset by the cancelation of the regional dates.

"She was distraught about that," singer Simon Bell says. "It was a very upsetting time."

Keen to prove that she was more than a '60s relic, Dusty was back in Britain to promote her new album, *Living without Your Love*, which had been hastily recorded at Cherokee Studios as a follow up to *It Begins Again* in the summer of 1978. Produced by David Wolfert, the album comprised what critics called "ten safe songs," the standout being "I'm Coming Home Again," a slow tearjerker by Bruce Roberts and Carole Bayer Sager that moved you either to tears or to cynical dismay—"a heart wrenching warble breaks with risible emotion," wrote *NME*. "The relaunching of Dusty continues on the same satin-finished LA freeway," John Wishart wrote in *Record Mirror*, adding that an "incredibly world weary"-sounding Dusty had embarked upon "the same trip as last year's *It Begins Again* except this time there's more variety, more economy and a couple of possible hit singles."

Living without Your Love also included "Save Me, Save Me," a disco number by Barry Gibb that Dusty tackled with some uncertainty, but the most intriguing song by far was "Closet Man," in which Dusty appeared to be telling a gay man that his secret was safe with her. "Dusty addresses, dare I say it, a large contingent of her fans," John Wishart wrote. "'And the ring that I once gave you, you're now wearing in your ear, but your secret's safe with me, my dear.' Oh yeah?" Dusty's experimentation with different styles and with edgier, more contemporary, lyrics was something that she had begun on *It Begins Again* with songs such as "Checkmate" and then continued with "Closet Man." The results were mixed, but it was something she would push even further on her next album.

During the Drury Lane dates, Dusty had split with manager Barry Krost after a furious argument on the phone, and she returned briefly to LA to hook up with a new manager, Kevin Hunter. In July 1979 she was back in Surrey recording another disco single, "Baby Blue," which provided her first top seventy hit since 1970, back when Dusty and her life had both been very different. As ever, she was disappointed that the song had not done better, saying, "The single was too fluffy for me but it should have done better than it did."

This time her backing singer was Simon Bell, who had first worked with her on her 1978 *Top of the Pops* appearance to promote "A Love like Yours" from *It Begins Again*. Bell was a long-standing Dusty fan who first met her after chasing her through Glasgow streets as a teenager in 1964. He says:

> She did a concert at the Odeon and afterwards she got into a black cab and I chased it through the streets, and every time they stopped at traffic lights I managed to catch up with them. Eventually I got to the motel, and for some reason I didn't have the program—and so she signed my wrist and she commented that I should go in for the Olympics.

Bell was ecstatic, and didn't wash his hand for weeks.

By 1978, Simon Bell was a talented singer himself, and had been working with Madeline Bell (no relation)—bringing him closer to Dusty's orbit.

> I was doing a week's cabaret with Madeline at Caesar's Palace in Luton—very glamorous—and I was staying at Madeline's house. And when we came back one night from the club, Dusty was on the answering machine saying she was coming back to do Top of the Pops *and that she needed backing singers—could Madeline could recommend somebody?*

Madeline turned to Bell and said, "There you are, this is what you've been waiting for."

As a Doris Day fan, Simon Bell had always felt that Dusty was a continuation of the tradition of great singers of the 1940s and 1950s. He says:

> *She was so much better than everybody. She looked like she was having the best time at the best party—which is quite interesting, because it turns out she probably wasn't. But she certainly made me feel like that, and I wanted to be there and be at that party that she was at. It was the sound of her voice and the movement, I loved all the movement. She really was an extraordinary singer.*

Jean Ryder was also one of Dusty's backup singers on *Top of the Pops* that night. She remembered Dusty being relaxed and happier than she'd been for a long time, and Simon Bell being "over the moon" to be performing with her. Much to their surprise the usual *TOTP* backup singers had been given the night off, and they were expected to sing with all the acts—not just Dusty. "Because Dusty had insisted on bringing her own singers in they had given the Ladybirds the night off and we had to sing for everybody else on the show," Bell says. "Even though we hadn't known that or rehearsed the songs, and Lulu was on. She had a new record we'd never heard before. So we had to busk."

His idol looked thin, with a wispy haircut, and Bell immediately felt he wanted to wrap her up and look after her. "The thing I remember most is putting my arms around someone who to me had always been a giant, but suddenly she was this really tiny skinny fragile thing, almost like a little bird," Bell says. "That's the thing that stays in my memory, how you felt you had to take care of her. Immediately I felt like I had to take care of her, it was quite extraordinary really."

After the *Top of the Pops* appearance Dusty asked Simon to work with her again on the Drury Lane dates, where he often stood in for her in rehearsal, and then at her concert later in the year at the Royal Albert Hall. Offstage Dusty was quiet and reserved, and didn't drink much. She also had high standards of professionalism, and dropped another of her backing singers when she was heard chatting up the musical director. "Dusty didn't like that," Bell says.

Dusty's concert at the Royal Albert Hall in December 1979 was perhaps the high point of her outstanding live shows. Organized in aid of the Invalid Children's Aid Association, Dusty appeared following another act and a lengthy introduction by Russell Harty. The reception she received made even the Drury Lane concerts seem restrained. Dave Gelly wrote in *The Observer*:

> *When Dusty Springfield walked on to the Albert Hall stage last Monday the vehemence, even hysteria, of the welcome she received was quite alarming. The crowd rose to its feet and yelled fit to bust, flowers rained down upon her and what should have been a decorous charity gala immediately turned into a pop show of authentic '60s dimensions.*

Dusty responded to the rapturous adoration by laughing, and telling her fans, "It's a big hall to cover, dear, but Mother will do her best."

As at Drury Lane, Dusty did little in the way of rehearsal, making Simon Bell sing for her again while she fretted over other aspects of the show. Bell says:

> *When we came to do the sound check in the Albert Hall she was much more interested in going out front to sort the sound out than she was in rehearsing the songs. She always wanted to do everyone else's job. She went out to the lighting desk to see what the lights looked like, and she went*

out to the sound desk and had me sing "I Close My Eyes
and Count To Ten" so that she could listen to it. And I made
her laugh because I did all the hand movements as well.

Yet, as ever, her performance was spectacular, with Music Week
cooing that the "prodigal daughter of British pop" had returned to
the UK to "prove that she is still the finest British female vocalist
to have emerged during the last three decades."

Wearing a white sequinned body suit, Dusty looked mature
and in command, finding easy responses to the hysteria from the
crowds that threatened to overwhelm her. Gelly wrote:

As she strode purposely about the stage, the cloud of
adoration grew thicker and fans who could no longer
contain themselves stood up with outstretched arms or
rushed to the front of the stage. At the end there was an
awkward moment when the stage-rushers had her in their
grasp and it looked as though she would vanish from sight.

It was hard to comprehend such scenes, *Music Week* concluded—
for they could hardly be attributed to her music, a "curious mixture
of black soul music and sentimental songs of Italian origin." The
answer could only lie in Dusty's stage persona, which she still
employed "to devastating effect."

After the show, an exhilarated Dusty went backstage, eager to
meet Princess Margaret, the patron of the Invalid Children's Aid
Association, who had been watching the show. Princess Margaret
shook hands with everyone in the room, but, to Dusty's dismay,
refused to speak to her about her performance. Shortly afterwards
an official letter arrived asking Dusty to apologize for a joke she
had made to the "queens" in the audience, saying, "It's nice to see
that not all the royalty is confined to the royal box . . ."

Dusty was shaken by the letter and believed, in part, that the snub resulted from Dusty's refusals, years earlier, to accept any of Princess Margaret's invitations to visit her on Mustique—alone. Those around her, including Simon Bell, wondered about the true nature of Dusty's relationship with Princess Margaret, especially as she had been asked to include "Losing You" in her act at Princess Margaret's request, a song Dusty no longer sang because it was so difficult.

After asking everyone for advice as to how to respond to the letter, much to Simon Bell's amazement, Dusty sat down and signed a letter of apology. "I never thought she'd sign it," Bell says. But Dusty was a well-brought-up traditionalist at heart. Later she laughed off the incident, and hung the reprimand from the palace on her toilet wall.

If Dusty's triumphant series of concerts was a sign that she should return to Britain permanently, she paid little to heed to it. A month before her appearance at the Royal Albert Hall, Dusty's father had died, alone in his home near Brighton. "I feel badly because I wasn't there, because no one was there," Dusty told *You* magazine in 1995. "I wonder if he was in pain. Was he incapable of reaching the phone? Did it happen fast? I'll never know." When Dusty arrived at the chapel to see OB's body she discovered that her brother Tom had moved it somewhere else. In fact, Dusty's frequent and desperate late night calls, and an unpaid debt, meant that Dusty and Tom were hardly on speaking terms during these years, and Dusty returned to LA with little to keep her in England.

California was home not only to her many cats, but also to a series of animal charities she was supporting, such as the Wildlife Way Station, and her network of AA friends. Principal amongst these was Helene Sellery, a tall willowy Lauren Bacall figure, who had once been a successful businesswoman. Sellery had met Dusty at an AA meeting in 1976, and credited her for helping her to give up drinking. "My name's Mary," Dusty told her, "here's my phone number. If you want these meetings to help then you have to talk to people, otherwise you'll be back drinking."

The exchange of numbers formed the basis of a brief affair and a friendship that lasted for the rest of Dusty's life, and soon after their meeting Dusty was driving out to Sellery's ranch at Tarzana in the San Fernando Valley where she kept a variety of animals. Despite an unpromising first visit when Dusty had sunk into a hot bath to discover she was being watched over by a goat, Tarzana proved to be Dusty's refuge and was the place she often retreated to over the years when she was at a low ebb.

Dusty also had brief relationships with some of the other women she met in AA, including Tarra Thomas, who she went on to become friends with. Thomas remembers that she was sharing in the meeting one day about having problems with one of her girlfriends:

> *I said something about the blonde tart who lived up the hill, and I noticed at some point that this woman was staring at me. Afterwards she came over and said something about "I liked your comment about the blonde tart on the hill," and I said, "Oh, did you now? This sounds like coffee," and she said, "That's exactly what I was thinking," and that's how we met.*

Tarra Thomas was eager to have a relationship with Dusty, who was appealing, shy with a "gleam in her eye" and a "devilish grin," but their dates were thwarted first by a carjacking at a supermarket, and then by a hunt for a lost kitten outside a Thai restaurant that had Dusty crawling around in a bush for an hour until she retrieved the bedraggled stray. "The best thing was not to have expectations. It would go much better if you didn't," Thomas says, explaining that Dusty cut short any suggestion of putting the cat in the car while they ate dinner. Woe betide anyone who tried to come between Dusty and a stray. "I do believe I was the shortest, briefest assignation in her romantic history. I doubt if it lasted a month, and then we agreed that we were much better suited as friends."

In their brief relationship, and longer friendship, Thomas saw at close quarters Dusty's expectations and demands on those she loved.

> She had a lot of unarticulated requests in an up-close-and-personal relationship, and if you weren't paying attention, you could miss them. And she could get offended at you having missed them, because she intuitively knew you weren't paying attention. She was intrigued by other people's egos. Everybody I knew just thought she had a monster huge ego, but I just don't think that was the case . . . She wouldn't articulate a lot. She would confirm it if you articulated it for her. She had to put a little distance between herself and the really true, deep feelings.

Soon Thomas realized that she was hearing more about another woman Dusty had met, Carole Pope, "and that was that," she says.

Pope was a dark-haired, sultry, punk rock chick from the Canadian band Rough Trade, who oozed an outrageous in-your-face sexiness. She was also an open lesbian working in the music industry—a first for Dusty. Rough Trade were being loosely managed by Vicki Wickham at the time, and when Pope heard that Dusty was performing at the Grande Finale supper club in New York in October 1980 she went along with Wickham to see the show. Rock Hudson was also in the audience that night, and Pope wrote in her autobiography *Anti-Diva* that they sat at a table with Jane Seymour and Fran Lebowitz, who was chain-smoking and muttering under her breath "Is she coming on? When is she coming on?" Dusty was two hours late, "but it was worth the wait," Pope writes, "her voice made me slide off my seat." Although Pope thought Dusty's white-blonde hair and sequinned top was "over the top, in a bad way," she was moved by the way in which Dusty's performance "laid every naked emotion out on the line: love, pain and longing."

Backstage the two flirted, with Dusty managing to look shy while simultaneously stroking Pope's leather trousers. They went out for a drink, and commenced their relationship three months later in Montreal where Dusty was being honored by the Jewish organization B'nai Brith (Dusty had few political affiliations, but generally enjoyed being awarded). Pope made her way to Dusty's hotel suite in advance of the ceremony where, she wrote, the air was thick was sexual tension: "She offered me a drink, and the next thing I knew, we were all over each other. We tumbled onto the bed half-naked. It was the first time I'd been with an older woman. I found the idea very erotic. I fixated on her sensual mouth and her unfathomable eyes." Later they went out on the town to party and Pope discovered that she was "a lightweight, compared to Dusty."

After a considerable period of sobriety Dusty was indeed back on the booze, claiming she needed Grand Marnier to nurse her voice through the two-week engagement at the Grande Finale, and then some shows at Lake Tahoe. As ever, the alcohol and the variety of pills she was taking combined to make her fiercely erratic—and her stay in New York was marked by throwing a heavy painting out of the window of the Mayflower Hotel (she'd drawn some animals on a forest scene for a laugh, and then decided it couldn't go back on the wall that way) and smashing an enamel sink to pieces following an argument with Helene Sellery. Dusty was also smoking heavily, a habit she had taken up for the first time only a year earlier. Despite all of her problems, however, Dusty still loved to have fun and her newly appointed assistant Susan Schroeder, nicknamed "Westchester" because she looked preppy in pearls and sensible shoes, noticed that she loved to clown around: having food fights, barricading herself in her room behind a mattress, and eating hot chocolate fudge sundaes.

It was precisely this combination of light and shade that seemed so appealing to Pope. Dusty was serious, and could seem older than her years, Pope noticed. Although Dusty fretted over their age difference, Pope thought it was her sense of fun and immaturity that Dusty found most appealing. "She acted a lot older than she was. I think part of the thing that attracted her to me is that I can be insanely immature and childish . . . We would just laugh our asses off and be really silly and I don't think she did that with a lot of people."

After spending their first weekend together, Dusty returned to LA, and then arranged for Pope to accompany her on a trip to London and Amsterdam where they ran through Westminster Abbey giggling, ate at expensive restaurants, and toured Amsterdam's red light district, ending up in a gay bar where Dusty was "fawned over" by adoring young Dutch boys. Pope was already learning that Dusty barely functioned in daylight hours, and was awake most of the night. In addition, Dusty's legendary perfectionism over performing reared its head when they went out to record a Dutch TV show in Hilversum. "It took hours for Dusty to pull herself together," Pope wrote in her autobiography. Once in situ she held up taping over many minor details, and drove the producers crazy. "She was just impossible. If there was a way for Dusty to complicate things she found it. I wanted to scream 'Shut up and sing the f***ing song!'"

"She really was a diva when we started dating," Pope says.

I didn't realize how much of a diva she was in Montreal, but then we went to Europe and she had ten suitcases, and we went to the Four Seasons. I'd never seen anyone push so many suitcases. She was like Liz Taylor with all the suitcases. We flew first class always—that was very glamorous and diva-like—and she didn't have to sign into the hotel.

On a trip to LA, Dusty drove Pope around town, making a point of showing her archrival Dionne Warwick's house, and remarking on how hideous it was—before ending up at a party in the Hollywood hills where, she wrote in her autobiography, Pope was aghast to find Dusty drunk on the couch in a passionate embrace with the bass player from U2.

Their relationship lurched dramatically "between Christmas and the seven rings of hell" but, despite early warning signs, Pope was still entranced with the woman whose music she'd loved as a teenager. Within a few months Dusty had made the momentous decision to pack up her belongings and move in with Pope in Toronto. As the day drew nearer, Dusty arranged for Westchester and a friend to drive her things across America in a truck. She would then fly to Detroit to meet them and they would cross the border into Canada together. Driving a truck across America proved to be more taxing than Westchester had imagined, however, and whenever she called Dusty from rest stops on the road, Dusty sounded increasingly like she was getting cold feet. "You're there too soon," Dusty would complain, "Can't you drive more slowly?"

Eventually, in May 1981, Dusty and her belongings arrived in Toronto, where Carole Pope had rented a town house for them in the Cabbagetown area of the city. After paying an immediate visit to the local petting zoo to "commune with the animals" (especially the Shetland ponies, which Dusty felt an affinity towards because of their short stature and irritable nature) Dusty unpacked her collection of Paddington Bears in the bedroom, which she furnished with masses of overstuffed pillows. The rest of her many belongings remained packed up, and the house looked largely unlived in—adding to the sense that her stay there was only temporary.

"I knew right away that she was an alcoholic and there were all these annoying red flags," Pope says. "When we first started living together she wasn't doing anything, apart from hanging out and drinking. We would go out and she would throw up on herself and party in front of my friends." Dusty obviously had lots of issues, ranging from her drinking and self-harm to the kind of low self-esteem that caused her to spend hours sitting in front of a spread-out towel, putting her makeup on, but there were also moments of lightness and vulnerability. Pope remembers Dusty dancing around the living room to R&B, setting her alarm clock to cook a huge fried breakfast and watch the royal wedding between Prince Charles and Princess Diana, and tenderly allowing Pope to strip her make-up off and see her as she really was.

Shortly before her arrival in Toronto, she flew to Australia to open an event for Datsun cars, and met up again with her old friends John Adams and Judy Stone. Stone remembers Dusty being clear headed and happy on the trip, and the two of them spent a wonderful afternoon sitting on the floor playing the guitar and singing. "I didn't really feel that I got to know her properly until she came to Australia and that to me was a totally different Dusty than the one that I saw when I was over in London." Stone also arranged for Dusty to appear on a well-known Australian talk show where, much to everyone's surprise, she announced that she was getting married to a Toronto musician. What was her husband-to-be like, the host, Mike Walsh, asked. Pausing over her words Dusty replied, "*He's* taller than me, very dark and very handsome." Knowing that she was referring to Pope,

Stone sat in the audience with her heart in her mouth, willing Dusty not to reveal too much. "I was thinking, 'Don't do it, Dusty!'"

Afterwards Dusty decided to extend her trip and stay at Adams' house in Sydney, where she spent most of the time engaged in day-long phone calls to Canada, and she delighted in telling him that she loved the raunchy sexiness of her relationship with Pope. "Dusty liked being dominated," Adams says. It seemed a natural development for someone who always felt unworthy and needed to either punish herself or be punished by others. Knowing that she would be flying home on her birthday he went out and bought her a "beautiful leather whip," which he persuaded the actor Anthony Newley, who was on the same flight as Dusty, to carry onto the plane and present to Dusty when they were in the air.

Although Dusty had told the Australian TV audience that she was very happy, back in Toronto she sank back into her worst habits. Now she was staying out almost all night, drinking even more and cutting herself regularly. No matter how much Pope tried to get her to talk about her feelings, Dusty clammed up— reluctant to say anything. Sue Cameron became so concerned at this time that she flew to Toronto just to have lunch with Dusty and make sure that she was all right.

"I just knew the whole time it wasn't going to work out," Pope says. Somewhat against Dusty's will, the pair went to relation- ship counseling for a couple of sessions, but it was clear from Dusty's reluctance that it wasn't going to be a solution. "She was not happy about that. That's what you always do when you are a lesbian, you are always like 'We have to go to couples therapy, because . . .' and then you always break up. It's like the death knell of your relationship when you do that."

Even if their personal relationship was on the rocks, Dusty had absorbed Pope's harder, more confrontational, style that involved bright makeup, leather body suits, clanking chains and Mohawk hairstyle. Pope had also ignited an interest in 1980s music, which Dusty thought sounded vastly better in terms of technique than what she had been able to produce in the 1960s. With her chameleon-like ability to spot and adapt to new influences, Dusty began work on her next album, *White Heat*—something that would necessitate her return to LA only six months after she had arrived in Toronto. Both women gave something of a sigh of relief at her departure, and several months later Pope told Dusty on the phone that she could no longer cope with their relationship. "I told Dusty I was being torn apart by her behavior," Pope writes. "She was very sweet and resigned. It was heart wrenching." Dusty had insisted that Pope build a winter cat shelter in their back garden, but she never returned to see it.

Dusty was "crazy, obsessed, excited, stressed out" about *White Heat*, according to Pope. Fred Perry would pick her up at her apartment and drive her to the studio in North Hollywood, and then collect her at the end of the session "to pick the pieces." When Pope visited she saw a musician frantically chopping up a rock of cocaine on the metal music tape during one visit, while friends from AA would sit with Dusty through the late-night recording sessions trying to help her through and stay sober.

"That was a difficult album because she was trying all these different musical genres," Pope says. She and her bandmate Kevan Staples contributed two songs, including "Soft Core," about the perils of loving an alcoholic (ironically not written for Dusty, but for a previous lover). "Donnez Moi" was what Dusty described as a "funky ABBA" song, written by an old friend, Jean Roussel, who had played her the tape in his Montreal basement. After she heard "Every Little Thing She Does Is Magic," which Roussel was writing for The Police, Dusty asked for her own song too—and Roussel complied by providing her with another song, "I Don't Think We Could Ever Be Friends." On "Blind Sheep," Dusty stomps her way across an aggressive hard rock track, while "Time and Time Again" begins with soft instrumentals, and then breaks into a '60s-style ballad. Most interesting is the inclusion of Elvis Costello's "Losing You (Just a Memory)," which he had written for Dusty in 1977 and coincidentally shared the same name as one of Dusty's 1960s singles. Yet he had never dreamed that she would actually record it. Costello says:

> When I say I wrote for her, I think it would be truer to say I wrote for the dream of having her sing the song. And because I was such a big Dusty fan I wrote this one song at the piano, which to my mind sounded just like she would sing it. And I tried to record it myself and it sounded okay but it wasn't like her.

Costello sent Dusty the demo, and was amazed when she called him up a couple of years later and said she would like to record it. "I was at AIR Studios in Oxford Street and I'd just started work on the record Imperial Bedroom, and this call comes through and, as luck would have it, I had laryngitis the day that she called so I could barely speak. I felt so stupid." Dusty told him that she liked the song, but it was too short. She told him, "It was almost like a little miniature song, and asked if I could write another verse for her specifically." Dusty instructed him "not to make it too mushy," and that she liked the tougher lyrics. Costello immediately wrote another verse, and sent it off to LA.

Although NME cheered White Heat as Dusty's leap into the 1980s, which "feeds on tension from start to finish," the US release was delayed until November 1982, during which time the album's original record company, 20th Century Fox Records, had been bought by Casablanca, and then again by Phonogram. Dusty complained that her first producer had snorted half her budget up his nose, and that she felt like a "tax loss," whose publicity resources were suddenly handed over to Yoko Ono. In the UK, Phonogram decided not to release *White Heat* at all; Lucy O'Brien reported that they said, "We're not sure about it—everything that we've released of Dusty's hasn't really taken off."

The failure of *White Heat*, and her Canadian excursion, meant that Dusty found herself back in LA practically penniless—this time without a place to live or a car that worked. She was essentially at rock bottom, running through record companies and managers until she was almost at the end of the road.

17

WHAT HAVE I DONE TO DESERVE THIS?

The news that Dusty Springfield, shuffling like a confused wreck, was admitted to a locked psychiatric ward at Bellevue Hospital in the autumn of 1985 would have shocked her fans, and seemed like a terrible epitaph to a fabulous, trailblazing, career that had lit up the 1960s. When this episode in Dusty's life was revealed in Penny Valentine and Vicki Wickham's book *Dancing with Demons*, many of her close friends were desperately upset, knowing how strongly Dusty felt about guarding her privacy. Dusty's stay at Bellevue was indeed the lowest moment in her life, but it was also one she staged a brave recovery from—setting her career and life once more on an ascendant and sober path that lasted until she died.

The previous three years in her life had been harsh: she had been almost down and out in LA, getting battered and bruised in fights with a lover, and relying on food stamps from the same woman even while she was incarcerated in prison. They were years that had seen Dusty dress up and take part in a lesbian wedding ceremony, and earn a living miming to her old hits in

West Hollywood gay bars. "They were horrible, horrible years,' says Sue Cameron, but somehow, through it all, Dusty never quite lost the thread of who she was—and their very awfulness makes her determination to recover all the more remarkable.

"I did the whole lazy, self-destructive, California bit," Dusty later told *The Telegraph* in a clear-headed, if understated, assessment of what had gone wrong. "Somewhere—you never know when—I crossed the line from heavy drinking into problem drinking. I was addicted to all sorts of things . . . I'm an addictive personality." Alcohol, Mandrax and finally cocaine had, she said, "scrambled my life"—and almost finished her off. So had her ongoing struggle to live with a mental illness, but she did not mention that.

Following the failure of *White Heat*, Dusty found herself without a recording contract and relying on ever-diminishing royalty checks. She stayed out at Helene Sellery's ranch for weeks at a time, and sometimes with Tarra Thomas, who co-opened a bank account for her at the Mitsui Bank in Hollywood and loaned her an old silver Honda that could at least get her around town while the Jensen Interceptor sat parked in the yard waiting for the funds to repair it. Dusty sold her enormous collection of R&B recordings to Graham Nash from Crosby, Stills & Nash, and filled up on big breakfasts at the House of Pancakes (always one of her favorite meals, and conveniently cheap too).

Vicki Wickham watched Dusty's self-destruction from afar, stepping in from time to time to lend money or arrange a place to stay. "She became—because of drink and drugs—not awfully nice, and she became completely out of control and a pain in the ass. You can't talk to somebody who's doing all that, it's impossible. As things got worse and worse, it just got so sad and so dreadful." Wickham had seen Dusty's career go wrong "from the start" in America, something that Dusty agreed with, blaming, perhaps unfairly, the wrong management—and the world of the American club circuit, which had left her feeling "obsolete" and a "complete nutcase." Now, without a strong support network to buoy her up, things seemed to be getting worse and worse.

Friends from the old days who met up with her during these years noticed that she seemed sad and distracted. "Whatever had held her together before was gone," says Julie Felix, who saw Dusty on several occasions during her time in California. On the first occasion Felix visited the Dona Teresa house when Dusty was having a party with a group of gay Hollywood women—unnerving Felix, who was even more anxious around the gay scene than Dusty. Several of Dusty's cats were sleeping on her large bed, and later Felix could hear the sounds of the coyotes howling in the distance. Another time, after Dusty had moved to Sierra Alta Way, Felix found her walking around outside a club, a little dazed, and they agreed to meet at the house and go out for dinner. When Felix arrived Dusty was frantically going through her credit cards trying to find one that worked so that she could buy dinner—the record company would give her a card, Dusty explained, and she would spend as much as she could on it, then the card would stop, and she would try to get another one issued. Perhaps to Felix's surprise "Dusty succeeded in finding a very nice restaurant that took the particular credit card that still worked," Felix says, "and we ended up having a lovely evening."

"She'd gone through a lot of money. It was drugs and drink, really," Vicki Wickham admits. "She was absolutely broke. She truly didn't have a penny . . . She hated not having money and having to borrow from people." Packing her bags and returning to England still seemed only a distant possibility. "What would she have come back to?" Wickham asks. "It wouldn't have changed. There really was nowhere to go back to."

Dusty's episodes of self-harm meant she made frequent trips to Cedars-Sinai and other LA hospitals, and she joked that the paramedics all knew her by name. After a stay at the Thalians rehab center in 1982, Dusty was living at Friendly House (a halfway house for women getting sober) when she met Teda Bracci, a dark-haired musician who'd featured in *Life* magazine for playing in an all-girl band, The Freudian Slips, in Haight-Ashbury in the late 1960s and hung out with Janis Joplin and her band, Big Brother and the Holding Company. When Bracci returned to her native LA she took on a role in the musical *Hair* and then appeared in a series of 1970s movies including *The Big Bird Cage*, a prison exploitation drama starring Pam Grier that came tagged with the line: "Women so hot with desire they melt the chains that enslave them."

Bracci recalls her first meeting with Dusty at Friendly House as being with a shy, rather aloof, woman who had little to say for herself, except to demand that Bracci carry her luggage from room to room while she found one to her taste.

> I was taking her suitcases up and putting them in the room, and she said, "No, no, I don't like this room." Then she walked into the next room and said, "No, no, the light is coming in too bad here." I was still carrying the suitcases, and finally she said, "How about this room?" I told her to wait, put down the luggage, and went downstairs to talk to someone in charge. I said, "There is a crazy woman up there, she doesn't like any of the rooms and I don't know how to handle this person."

Soon, however, Bracci and Dusty discovered that they knew many of the same people, and started sharing their life stories with each other in their free time at Friendly House and playing music for each other.

> It started because we really liked each other, and she'd bicker

and I'd bicker back at her and we just had this fun, crazy thing. She's eight years older than me, so here's this older woman trying to tell me what to do, and we just hit it off one time. We kissed each other and that was the moment.

One day Dusty left a copy of her *White Heat* album on Bracci's bed, and Bracci played her some of her songs in return. "I played my little stuff for her, and she said, 'Oh, my honey can sing!' and I said, 'Well, thank you, is that a compliment, or are you being sarcastic?' That's how we bickered with each other."

Bracci appealed to Dusty's outrageous side, but even taking into consideration Dusty's diverse range of girlfriends, she seemed a step too far for many of Dusty's old friends, who were more worried than ever. "It was because Teda was sexy," Vicki Wickham says, "and because she was a loose cannon, and Dusty rather liked that.' Dusty ran with a rough crowd, says Suzanne Lacefield, who warned her that Bracci was charismatic but also, she believed, dangerous. Dusty protested, "But she's so alive and so passionate!" It was like a moth to a flame, Lacefield recalls, "something that is absolutely hypnotic." Dusty thrived on drama—"drama in lieu of feeling life," and her choice of friends and people made it hard for her to stay sober.

Bracci admits there was something about their mutual wildness that brought them together: "I fell in love with her because she was the weirdest, craziest person that I loved, and I was the weirdest, craziest person that she loved." Soon they began an intense relationship, based on the strong bond of two alcoholics and addicts struggling to get clean. Dusty was living in a series of apartments around Hollywood, and Bracci soon moved in.

Tarra Thomas says:

This is going to be a disappointment to some people, but she

really cared about Teda Bracci. Dusty was quite a nurturer,
and she was always for the underdog. And she had an ability
when she would meet someone to find their vulnerable parts
and build them up. Teda was woebegone from the get-go.
But Teda also has a great sense of life, and Dusty had the
component of sometimes needing something extremely
painful to be able to get in touch with her feelings.

As far as Thomas could see, Dusty was "crazy about Teda." She wanted to help Teda stop drinking, she wanted to help Teda to get some commercial success, but mostly it was an emotional bond. According to Thomas, "Teda was unfortunately the one who couldn't believe that Dusty was in love with her, and Dusty was. And by the time Teda did realize, it was too late."

If she was drinking, Bracci could be wild and unpredictable—but then so could Dusty. One day she and Thomas were helping Dusty move out of her Beechwood Drive apartment when Dusty went into the bedroom and Bracci began making fun of her behind her back. "Teda started making all kinds of funny faces," Thomas says, "mimicking some of the drama of Dusty, and Dusty walked back in, she said, 'What did you say?'" They both denied saying anything. "One of the things she was packing was a sword. She picked up that sword and, with absolute perfect aim, she threw it right between the two of us. And we got her packed up and out of there as fast as possible."

Often their times together could be tempestuous, such as the night that Bracci says Dusty threw out a beef stroganoff and the bottle of wine to go in it, and they had to go out for hamburgers—or the Thanksgiving dinner that they had to cook with five eggs rather than six because Dusty had thrown one at her in the parking lot, and they couldn't afford another. But there were loving, quiet, times too. Dusty would get up in the morning, pull on her sweat pants, and feed the cats: "The cats always got the best; chicken breast and nice fish. I'd help her, and we'd have a little breakfast," Bracci says. "I'd like to cook breakfast and bring it to bed, and then we'd probably get into an argument. Then we'd do what we had to do that day, and then we'd go to an AA meeting together, and go to a movie." When Dusty did get dressed up and transform herself into "Dusty Springfield," Bracci would watch amazed.

> *When she would get dressed up and do her thing, I'd look at her and say, "My God, you're beautiful!" I'm just an old cave lady, but she'd have her hair beautifully, she'd have everything just gorgeous. When she put her lipstick on I'd watch her in the mirror, and I'd say "I want a kiss" and I'd tell her just to stick her tongue out because I didn't want to mess up her lipstick, and I would just kiss her little tongue.*

Months would pass in relative peace, fulfilling Dusty's longing for a sense of "couple normality." They went for long walks, watched movies, cooked and pooled their money for day trips to Santa Monica pier where they rode the funfair rides and mugged for snaps in the photo booth. "We both were down with the money," Bracci says. "We'd put our money together, and go to a show or go out to eat. We shared everything. She spent money like a wild woman, but she'd spend it on her friends and she was never selfish." Thomas remembers, "When the cannons roared the whole town heard it, but they also had weeks of relative serenity and everybody was happy and relieved. Then the phone would ring at four in the morning . . ."

On one occasion, Bracci was up in court on a public intoxication charge and Dusty begged Thomas to appear as a character witness. Thomas laughed out loud on the phone when Dusty asked her, and said, "Are you kidding me?" Dusty quietly said, "It's really serious, Missy T, will you do it? If Teda loses then she's going to jail." Thomas testified and Bracci escaped jail, giving Thomas a kitten as a thank-you. Bracci had previously done time at the Sybil Brand Prison for Women. On her first visit Dusty asked Helene Sellery to drive her down there, and fretted over her appearance and whether someone would recognize her. As the line for prison visiting often took longer than two and a half hours, Dusty apologetically asked Bracci if she could visit only every other day, telling her, "The longest I've ever stood in line for was for *ET*, and that was forty-five minutes." The visits were also useful as Bracci handed over an allowance for food stamps someone in prison had given her, which Dusty used to buy expensive food for the cats.

Tarra Thomas was also called to assist when Dusty decided to marry Bracci in a ceremony at Helene Sellery's ranch in November 1983. Gay marriage was not legally recognized in any country or state at the time, and some thought it was Dusty's idea of a joke. Thomas believes, however, that Dusty wanted to demonstrate her commitment to Bracci. "She did it for Teda," she says. Bracci believes it followed on from an earlier conversation when she had asked, "Are we going to be together forever?" Dusty had airily replied, "Oh, nothing is forever," and Bracci had questioned whether they should terminate their relationship immediately in that case.

Even if the idea was born of the best of intentions, it was carried out with Dusty's characteristic flair. Dusty called Thomas and said, "I want the whole deal, I want the gown and everything." They set off for a bridal shop on Fairfax Avenue in LA that accepted Thomas's American Express card and outfitted Dusty in a white and foam-green dress, hat, gloves and shoes. "The proprietor was a little Jewish lady who asked, 'So who's the lucky guy?' And without skipping a beat Dusty said, 'Ted.'"

Bracci remembers Dusty said to her a few days beforehand, "Teda, you're getting married on Saturday—and you'd better show up." The wedding ceremony itself would be immortalized in a series of photos that made their way into the *Daily Mail* after Dusty's death. Wearing her white wedding dress, and heavily made up, Dusty hugs Bracci, who was dressed in a black velvet jacket and two ties: "I wore a black tie for mourning and I wore a second tie with animals, because she loved animals. I said, 'The animals is for her and the black tie is for me to hang myself at the end of the wedding.'"

Dusty had wanted the day to be a sober one, and was disappointed and outraged when she discovered that Bracci and some of the guests had been swigging from a bottle of whiskey hanging outside the window. They argued on the drive back to LA, with Dusty later recalling that the vows should have read "Dearly beloved, and barely tolerated," with the "barely tolerated" relating to Bracci's attitude towards Dusty. When Thomas, who was overseeing the service, asked if anyone objected to their union, every guest—including Thomas herself—raised their hand.

Later that night Dusty and Bracci continued to argue, with a violent conclusion. Bracci recalls:

> We get home and she's bickering because it's our wedding night. And so she picked up a pot and hit me over the head with it, and it started bleeding. And I took the same pot, hit her over the head with it, and it started bleeding. So then I said, "Let's fix this up," and I took her to the bathroom and I fixed her head up, and then she fixed my head up and we started laughing. Then we went in the bedroom and we lay down and held hands, and I said, "This is a lovely wedding night."

Despite Dusty's intense feelings for her new lover, Bracci was not universally welcomed by Dusty's old friends. Vicki Wickham says:

> Thank God I missed most of that. Teda must have been a nightmare—she used to call me up on the phone and

threaten me. I used to say, "Okay, let me get this straight—
exactly what are you threatening me with?" She was as bad
as they come. I think she upset everybody. She was great
looking and sexy, but she was just impossible, absolutely
impossible. And nasty and mean.

Bracci admits she was upset at Wickham for seeming to withhold information about Dusty, and had phoned in tears and threatened to blow Wickham's house up. At Dusty's insistence, she later apologized to Wickham's partner. She also disliked Sue Cameron and left notes for her saying, "Why aren't you dead yet?" She insists, however, that most of the jealousy in their relationship was generated by Dusty, who couldn't bear the thought of her going off with another woman, yet often had dalliances with men to make Bracci jealous, especially if she was drinking, and would tell her about them in some detail.

But her heart wasn't in it because she never was in love with
a man, and I know that, but she'd do all kinds of weird things
like with a busboy at a hotel. She was drunk and enticed the
room service guy to bed and then the next morning when
she's walking down from the elevator, everybody looked and
turned around and started whispering.

Bracci says she would also go off with a man to get at Dusty, but never with another woman. "I loved her, and I wasn't going anywhere."

Their volatile relationship, based on mutual attraction and outbursts of temper, led to one of the worst incidents of Dusty's life. According to Bracci, it blew up when she returned to the apartment one day to find Dusty drinking wine and taking Valium, which led to the inevitable fight. "I heard this big crash in the kitchen, and she came in with a cup and said, 'If you want to kill yourself, this is the way you do it,' and she took the broken cup and cut her wrist and the blood just squirted out everywhere." Bracci then says she went to leave and started to put her boots on, at which point Dusty followed her. "She comes over with that same cup and started cutting my leg, the blood was pouring out, and she started hitting me. So I hit her back, tit for tat. I hit her back in the head with my boot because I was trying to get the boot on and she wasn't going to let me go."

Dusty fled from the apartment clutching her mouth, and Bracci was briefly questioned by the police, who then let her go. Dusty's injuries were severe, and she was admitted to Cedars-Sinai with her face swollen and blackened, and missing her front teeth—a sight which reduced those who visited her to tears. When Vicki Wickham visited Dusty she was astonished to see Bracci sauntering onto the ward, like an ordinary visitor. "The fact that she hit Dusty," Wickham says: "you don't do that—you don't hit people, you just don't." Bracci says the story has often been misrepresented and the truth is that Dusty phoned her as soon as she got to hospital saying, "I'm sorry, I provoked you," to which Bracci replied, "Well, Dusty, why were you doing all that?" Tarra Thomas comments, "Despite what happened, Teda was not the initiating physical aggressor in a negative way."

Dusty's role in this highly volatile relationship was "self-punishment," according to Suzanne Lacefield. "She was a cutter and they are usually with violent people or people that humiliate them or demean them. They choose this person, and then that's what happens, and they get to be right and say, 'You see, I am unworthy.'" If, as Bracci insists, their relationship was about love and not "beating up," Dusty's moods often swung wildly between harming herself and harming others. Bracci also says that Dusty was a cutter and goes on:

Her arm looked like a roadmap with all those lines. She never

told me why she did that, and I didn't really want to ask
that question . . . She would say to me, "I'm homicidal and
suicidal." I didn't like hearing that and I made a joke out of
it—who goes first? Because I didn't want her to kill herself.

On another occasion, Bracci says, they were driving in the car when Dusty pulled a gun out of the glove compartment and pointed it at Bracci's head before turning it towards herself. "I jumped out of the car so fast and I looked up there and all of a sudden this gun goes off and this big flare of flame goes out of the car, and she takes off. Then I found that it was just a starter gun."

Dusty's fight with Bracci in the apartment that day had serious consequences, however. Borrowing some money from Helene Sellery, she left for New York where she hired a cheap plastic surgeon to repair her mouth. The result was that her face looked partially frozen, and she lost the characteristic, animated smile that had always seemed to light her up.

"I experienced what battered wives often come up against," Dusty told Kris Kirk of *Gay Times* in 1985. "They're not only afraid to talk because they'll be beaten up again, but the relationship was so disapproved of anyway that people say . . . 'We told you so.'" In truth, she was bitterly disappointed in the failure of her relationship with Teda Bracci and retreated into a series of one-night stands with West Hollywood lesbians who wanted to say they'd slept with her, or, if she was really drunk, occasionally with men. "That was one of the things that was so disappointing about the Teda thing," Tarra Thomas says, "because she was lonely, and then they met and she wasn't lonely, and then it didn't work out and she was very crushed." Dusty could never learn from her mistakes, though, according to Suzanne Lacefield. "She was incapable of examining her part in the cause and effect. She always felt that she was victimized when she was just trying to be this good person and take care of herself."

With her new face in place, Dusty posed for some new publicity shots and agreed to a series of dates miming at gay bars such as La Probe where she would be paid $500 a night. Sue Cameron visited her one night in the back alley behind the club when suddenly they heard gunshots only a few feet away. Cameron grabbed Dusty, pushed her down out of sight in her car, and floored it out of the alley.

Cameron had stayed in touch with Dusty since their breakup in 1977. She had subsequently divorced her husband Bob, and Dusty continued to play a major role in her life. When Dusty got sober she invited Cameron to hear her give the main share in an AA meeting, which was "basically a thirty-minute apology to me," Cameron says.

Dusty was determined to stay sober, and Suzanne Lacefield remembers a few occasions when she would share in meetings. She attempted to follow the steps of the twelve-step program, including taking an honest inventory of what had happened in her life. "She did it as best she could," Lacefield says. "It wasn't terribly extensive because when you have the kind of shame that she had she wasn't willing to humiliate herself, it was too painful." In their one-to-one sessions Lacefield would tell Dusty about her own life, while Dusty sat curled over warily, terrified to open up. She remained convinced, Lacefield says, that her life would collapse, and she was only "waiting for the other shoe to drop."

Sue Cameron was also there when Dusty gave a generous but ill-fated performance for residents of Friendly House. "She wasn't ready and she knew she wasn't good, and it was breaking my heart," Cameron says. After trying to sing for a few minutes Dusty left the stage and returned with a vacuum cleaner. She completed the rest of the show vacuuming the stage and humming.

She didn't know what to do, she knew she couldn't sing well so

*she thought she would entertain . . . I got the joke, but I knew it
came from such deep pain, so I was very, very upset. That was
the most devastating show I've ever seen her do. I was just dying.*

In such tough circumstances it must have seemed like a gift from the
gods when the nightclub impresario Peter Stringfellow announced
that he was setting up a record label in August 1984, and wanted to
sign Dusty with a £100,000 (roughly $124,000) advance for three
songs and an album. Dusty's old manager Vic Billings had overcome
the bad feelings between them long ago, and negotiated the deal
on her behalf, before letting American Jenny Cohen take over the
management. The money more than settled Dusty's financial difficulties, and Stringfellow "wined and dined me, and told me these
stories about how wonderful it would be," Dusty said. After months
of negotiation, she arrived in London in the summer of 1985 ready
to start work with Hippodrome Records. It was a huge coup, but
there were warning signs from the very beginning.

Dusty looked guarded and frozen in a series of TV interviews
to promote the deal—and was clearly petrified that once again she
would be quizzed about her private life and her lovers. Fleet Street
veteran Jean Rook took the bull by the horns in an interview for the
Daily Express in August 1985. When Dusty defensively kicked off
the interview by saying, "You're going to ask me if I'm gay. I'm not
going to tell you," Rook countered, "Then tell me you're not?" Dusty
replied, "God, you've got me into a corner, haven't you, coming
straight out with it like that instead of 'why aren't you married?'
Let's say I have a strong gay following." After further quizzing
from Rook, Dusty admitted, 'Let's say I've experimented with most
things in life. And in sex." Moving away from further discussion
of her sexuality, Dusty described her family and childhood in far
unhappier detail than she had ever given before. Dusty, Rook noted,
looked like "an ancient Greek death mask. Her mouth is a blood

red gash. Her makeup looks bullet proof. She has two terrible black eyes. Or else she's wearing dark glasses with no sides or bridge to keep them on her thin, ivory nose." After admitting that she had self-destructed in America in a fit of "boredom" Dusty said that although the risks of returning to Britain were tremendous, "I really came home because I felt a great need to be visible again."

The question of why things had gone so wrong in California was one Dusty must have been asking herself when she arrived to sing her new single, "Sometimes like Butterflies" (a Donna Summer B-side chosen over a song by Jolley and Swain because they were recording with Bananarama—and Peter Stringfellow loved butterflies) for a television broadcast from the Star Bar at the Hippodrome, once the site of Talk of the Town. Inside, the scene was chaotic with drag artists dressed as Dusty, trained dogs, and dwarves on roller skates wearing gold lamé. Dusty had dyed her hair purple and was wearing a silver space suit that made her look "like something left over from the NASA space probe" according to *The Guardian*. DJ John Peel was equally unflattering, first noting that industry veterans had suspected she would fail to appear at all, and then saying that when she did emerge from behind a screen "flapping her arms around in mock alarm" she looked like "a minicab driver in bacofoil."

Overwhelmed with the press attention that her "homecoming" was receiving, Dusty was backstage in her dressing room throwing things when Jenny Cohen arrived. She passed Pat Barnett in the hallway, who raised her eyebrows and said, "Time for the management, I think." Dusty was coping by taking large quantities of the antidepressant Xanax, but she was still too stressed to sleep, and was holding court over a general melee of cats, friends and ex-girl-friends in a series of rented apartments in Mayfair and Shepherd Market and a house near Hampstead Heath. Predictably, her first performance reflected this, leaving her sounding strained and strung out. Cohen begged the BBC to wait for Dusty to rerecord her vocals before broadcasting the show, but Dusty had by now come down with psychosomatic laryngitis and had been prescribed Ritalin, usually given to children with hyperactivity disorder. The medication had a calamitous effect, giving her the appearance of being "punch drunk," and Dusty was confined to her bedroom under the care of friends from AA.

"She was great at rehearsal," Simon Bell remembers. "She actually did the rehearsal, but the minute she walked out to do the show the voice had gone again. The difference was extraordinary, and it had only been a couple of hours. The next day, she and I went to a BBC studio in Acton to try and repair it. But we couldn't. What we did was we managed to turn her down at the worst moments. They even tried to have me sing in her place at times, but that didn't work at all." Eventually the BBC had no choice but to broadcast the show, complete with the original vocals and surrounding chaos.

Dusty was unhappy with every aspect of her association with Peter Stringfellow—apart from the money he'd paid her—and they had a series of terrible confrontations. Vic Billings recalled sitting through long arguments lasting from eight in the evening until midnight that made him want to scream "Shut up, both of you!" Stringfellow accused Dusty of not working hard enough, and not doing enough to promote the record. "I couldn't get any enthusiasm out of her at all," he said. Dusty shot back that Stringfellow knew "f*** all about the music business" and that she'd like to "punch him on the nose."

Of course, Dusty could be difficult and unreliable (a year earlier she had agreed to take part in a TV recording with Anne Murray at the Royal Albert Hall, and then kept Murray, the orchestra and the venue waiting for eight hours while she dithered about whether she could summon the confidence to sing) but Bell was equally dismayed by the organization of Peter Stringfellow's enterprise. "It was unfortunate, because she wasn't in good shape and the voice wasn't what it had been and she found that hard." The studio engineer was young and inexperienced, saying "yes" to everything and forcing Dusty to produce the tracks herself (not something she usually objected to). Meanwhile Stringfellow was popping back into the studio and remixing tracks himself, picking the original vocal over many subsequent takes without realizing how bad they were (he claimed the others were worse). When Hippodrome Records failed to capitalize on Dusty's press interviews by not getting the records into stores on time, Billings gave up. He later described the whole project as "horrendous," adding, "It was not so much her fault as Peter's. The whole thing was a disaster." Dusty concurred, telling *The Sun* that working with Peter Stringfellow was "one of the incidents that made me feel so fed up with the business, I nearly gave up for good."

If nothing else, her work with Hippodrome had provided monetary relief (although she categorically denied in the press that she was broke, saying ongoing royalty checks meant "I'll never go short") but Dusty returned to America without making the career comeback she'd hoped for. She had been competing for a chart place with Madonna, Whitney Huston and Jennifer Rush, and "Sometimes like Butterflies" was a mediocre offering.

"Shortly after that, when she went back to America, we got to hear that she was really having problems. I think that was what we called her dark phase," Bell says. Bell and Dusty's friends in England discussed going over to help her, but most had family commitments at home, and recognized that there was little, in fact, that they could do to pull her round.

As a result of her own problems, Dusty was often in fact the one other people turned to in a state of crisis. In the midst of her debacle with Peter Stringfellow, Dusty had still found time to help Bell when he cut his wrists in despair over a relationship breakdown. "I had cut myself and sort of gone loopy," Bell says. Two friends immediately rang Dusty and asked her for advice, and she told them to take him to hospital.

> *I got out of the taxi and I was fighting with them, I wouldn't go in. And I started to run down the road—but another taxi pulled up and Dusty got out of the taxi and she'd been in the middle of dyeing her hair and had come out with the silver foil on her hair. I looked at her and all this purple stuff was there. I was so shocked that she had come out like that that I stopped and sort of came to my senses.*

Dusty waited for hours with him in the hospital, and the next morning appeared on breakfast television looking exhausted. Bell was eventually discharged and went on to appear in the Hippodrome show clapping in an odd way because his arms were stiff and infected. Dusty "was a very good person to be around when you were having those kind of problems," Bell says, "because there was nothing you were going to do that she hadn't already done. And she knew all the answers because she'd had all the therapy."

Although Dusty was now managing to stay off alcohol for long stretches of time, the pills, and her underlying battle with depression, were still wreaking havoc in her life. Even sober, she continued to cut herself, unable to find an outlet for her pain. Suzanne Lacefield says,

> *She was always going from here to here to here, afraid of having roots. It felt too threatening. It frightened her. She was probably one of the most frightened women I've ever met. And fear drives us to make choices that are very harmful, because we can't think, so we just go like an emotional locomotive's running through our body, screaming, "Help me, help me!"*

WHAT HAVE I DONE TO DESERVE THIS?

A month after the release of "Sometimes like Butterflies," Dusty pulled together the money for a trip to New York to try and record some demos. On the surface she was smiling and enjoying herself in September 1985, according to Penny Valentine, shopping in her favorite stores and walking around the city. Inside, however, she was feeling utterly desperate, making dozens of phone calls a day to Jenny Cohen and Vicki Wickham, and finding it harder than ever to commit and focus on doing any work. Wickham had already moved her out of a dingy hotel that was overrun with cockroaches and into a friend's empty apartment on the Upper West Side. But being alone was not good for Dusty, especially in the early hours of the morning when there was no one to talk to. The next thing Wickham heard, Dusty had been admitted to Bellevue after calling the paramedics late one night—telling then to come quick, she'd had an accident and cut herself.

The locked psychiatric wing at Bellevue had a notorious reputation, but when Wickham visited Dusty there she was amazed to discover that Dusty considered it a refuge rather than somewhere she wanted to escape from. Psychiatric units were places where Dusty knew she would be safe and looked after, and she was in no hurry to leave—explaining that she had to stay because she was a manic-depressive and the doctors couldn't get her medication right. In retrospect, Dusty's illness had been something she had struggled with since the 1960s, and a series of wrongly prescribed medications, combined with a lack of understanding of bipolar disorder at the time, had only made her condition worse.

"I think she was both a manic-depressive and an addict," Vicki Wickham says. "The combination was absolutely lethal. Nobody really dealt with the manic depression, because everyone thought it was the drink and the drugs. She never went to a doctor or anybody who would have helped her deal with that first."

When she got back to California, Dusty laughed and pulled the straitjacket out of her suitcase to show Helene Sellery. Without a hint of embarrassment or shame, she announced she wanted to keep it as a memento—just like her convent school girl uniform and her dresses by Darnell, it was a potent symbol of where she had been.

18

SINCE YOU WENT AWAY . . .

Walking down Sunset Boulevard one hot afternoon in 1987 Tarra Thomas was debating with Dusty where they could buy a burger on her American Express card, when somewhere, from a store or a car window, the light breathy tones of "What Have I Done to Deserve This" floated across the hazy traffic fumes. "Hey—that's you! That's your song!" Thomas said, startled once again by the realization that the woman she sat next to in meetings, and spoke to on the phone in the early hours of the morning, also operated in a parallel universe of talent and fame. Dusty ducked her head down, but broke into a shy beaming grin. After years in the wilderness, at the age of forty-eight, she was enjoying the second biggest hit of her career, and it had "dropped in her lap" out of nowhere.

Dusty later said she had been sitting under a tree in Helene Sellery's backyard in California, pondering what direction the rest of her life should take, when the call had come through from Vicki Wickham asking if she was interested in recording a song with the Pet Shop Boys. Wickham often called Dusty with various offers and proposals—and Dusty invariably declined. That day, though, something piqued her interest. "Who are they?" Dusty asked. They were the band that recorded "West End Girls," Wickham told her—but she would need to decide fast. Dusty later said that hearing "West End Girls" on her car radio had made her practically swerve right off the side of the freeway because it sounded so real; so edgy and unique. She still had an innate sense of who was making good music, and what direction musical tastes were moving in. When the demo arrived from London the next day Dusty listened to it, and said yes.

Although this version of events is often repeated, it is unlikely in several respects. Dusty had already turned down one offer to work with the Pet Shop Boys when she signed up with Peter Stringfellow, saying they "weren't the sort of group I wanted to be associated with"—and she almost never listened to music on the car radio, immediately tuning it to talk radio or turning it off. And the option of singing on "What Have I Done to Deserve This" had not cropped up overnight, as Dusty's story suggested, but had been brewing for three years, at the ongoing insistence of songwriter Allee Willis. "I've rarely read an accurate depiction of 'What Have I Done to Deserve This,'" Willis says.

They had first met in LA in the early 1980s after Willis had achieved a long string of hits for Earth, Wind and Fire, and they spent an afternoon together, chatting in Dusty's house, which was later plunged into darkness by a power cut. "Our connection was the music itself, and the hatred of the industry," Willis says.

> I was very similar to Dusty, and I guess that's what brought us together. I hated the music industry, I hated everything about it, and even when all I was doing was writing music and I was selling ten million records a year I never ever enjoyed it. I hated hustling, I still do. You know, it was a

pure experience for me and Dusty. It didn't have to do with
making money, it didn't have to do with beating people out.

Dusty had recorded two of Willis's songs, "Send It to Me" and
"I Wish the Love Would Last," by the time Willis found herself
working with the Pet Shop Boys. Neil Tennant was a huge Dusty
fan, and he told his fan magazine, "Nikke Slight in our office said,
'You're always going on about how much you like Dusty Springfield—why don't you ask her?'" Their record company, EMI, was
less enthused, citing all the usual reasons to avoid her, but Tennant
was not easily dissuaded.

"When we first started working together they said, 'You know
Dusty Springfield, we love Dusty Springfield and we want to do this
for a duet with her,'" Willis remembers. "Then there was literally
three years of me calling Dusty, them calling Dusty, Vicki Wickham
calling Dusty . . ." Finally Dusty relented and spoke to Willis on the
phone. "She just said, 'Everyone is pushing me to do this, I know it's
a good song, but the music business absolutely repulses me and if I
do it I don't want to go through the shit!'" Willis reassured her that
"West End Girls" had been a big hit, and that she thought the Pet
Shop Boys were a great group to work with. "I said, 'This is a really
extraordinary opportunity and it's with a classy group. I think you
should do it.'" Much to Willis's and Wickham's relief, Dusty agreed.

Wickham was now negotiating so much of Dusty's work that
she said, "I'm doing all this, I might as well just be your manager."
Dusty thought about it for a moment and said, "Okay, let's just
shake hands on it." After they shook hands Wickham added,
"I'm not going to make any money from you." Dusty admitted,
"Probably not." They agreed that if Dusty did make any money
she'd give Wickham a percentage. Wickham muses that she doesn't
recall exactly what prompted her to become Dusty's manager. "I
must have been out of my mind."

Managing Dusty was "not easy," Wickham says, "but I like challenges, and the Pet Shop Boys record was such a wonderful opportunity for her to start again, without any pressure, because the pressure was on them. I'd known her for so long, I just thought, 'Somebody's got to do this, or it will slip away, and I don't want her to have to deal with all that again and feel bad about it.'"

Dusty appeared for the first day of recording looking her best in a black leather designer jacket and high-heeled boots, with a lyric sheet covered in her usual marks and notes tucked under one arm. If she was wracked with nerves it didn't show, and she proceeded to work through the vocals, giving them a breathy transcendence that thrilled the Pet Shop Boys and the studio engineers sitting in the control booth. "Is that what you're looking for?" she asked—not realizing that the Pet Shop Boys only wanted her to sound like herself. "It's a bit more me than them," she said of the final recording. "They write songs that don't have a lot of interpretation . . . I had to unlearn my vocal mannerisms to get it right because that's how Neil sings."

Although she refused to take part in publicity for the single, she did make her first music video, shot at the Brixton Academy, and found the process strange and amusing. In the final video Dusty appears, smiling knowingly—somewhat apart from the rest of the video, just as she sounds somewhat apart from the song.

Reaching number two in the UK chart, and number one in America in August 1987, "What Have I Done to Deserve This" was Dusty's biggest hit since 1970—and something she had feared would never happen again. Yet however grateful she was, Dusty felt that she was an appendage to the popularity of the Pet Shop Boys, rather than successful in her own right. Simon Bell says:

> Dusty was not as excited about it as she might have been.
> I don't think she felt it was her career. I think she thought

she was just playing a bit part in theirs. I don't think she
thought her career was taking off at all. And in a way it
didn't particularly, there were a couple of hits, but they
weren't ground-breaking. I think she was savvy enough to
know that it was never ever going to be the way it was.

With Bell singing alongside her, Pat Barnett on hand to soothe
frayed nerves, and Wickham managing her career, Dusty was
beginning to rebuild her support network—and look to the
future. "Dusty was very demanding about the pettiest things,"
Wickham says. "She would call me fifteen times to ask, 'Are you
sure you've got the right makeup mirror?' I'd say, 'Dusty, I've got
the right makeup mirror.' Then she would call me again." When
fax machines became widely used Wickham gave her one, so that
Dusty could write faxes instead of calling all the time.

Wickham also faced the unenviable task of trying to make
money for her client. "She truly didn't have a penny. So that was
another challenge—to get her some money so that she could get
a place and start up again." A deal with EMI was in the works
after Dusty's success with the Pet Shop Boys and Wickham secured
her an advance on the advance so that she could have some
immediate funds.

Later it was often a question of "Okay, you want me to do
this, what am I going to make?" Sometimes I'd say to her
"We are going to make nothing, but, if you do this it might
lead to something else so I'm sorry, you've got to do it, and
I'll make sure it doesn't cost you."

Dusty felt, in an undefined way, that she should have got more
out of her deal with the Pet Shop Boys, and also from "Something
in Your Eyes," a duet she recorded a few months earlier with

Richard Carpenter. Although she was initially delighted to sing with Carpenter, and felt overawed by the legacy of his sister Karen, Dusty was devastated when she did not appear on the cover of the record, which only mentioned in small text "lead vocals by Dusty Springfield." The feeling that she had been turned over once again was so strong that friends in AA feared that Dusty would drink on the disappointment—but she remained sober. "I don't remember her ever drinking because she was disappointed about her career," Tarra Thomas says. "It was always because of her love life, never because of a record." Richard Carpenter said he and his sister Karen had always loved Dusty's voice and that he was thrilled with the single, saying Dusty had a great sense of humor and was an "absolutely terrific singer"—an appreciation that certainly wasn't reflected in the final product.

The success of "What Have I Done To Deserve This" and the prospect of more work in England, including an ad for Britvic (a popular British softdrink) that had raised her onscreen profile and the upcoming release of her *Silver Collection* compilation album, confirmed that it was the right time to move back to Europe, something her old friends had been advocating for years. Dusty had enjoyed one of the most significant relationships of her life in Los Angeles with Sue Cameron, and had formed deep friendships with people in AA that her friends from the 1960s did not always fully understand or appreciate. Even so, by the mid-1980s she was tired—tired of California, and tired from everything she had been through. "She was ready," Vicki Wickham says. "The only problem was the damn cats."

Dusty's family of cats which had once numbered six and more, had now been reduced to only two—Malaysia and Nicholas, but she baulked at the idea of putting them into quarantine for six months in Britain. One solution seemed to be to move to Amsterdam, where the cats could be in residence immediately and from where Dusty could easily commute to London, which was less than an hour away by plane. Eventually this plan of action was decided upon but, as ever, Dusty dithered, with most of her anguish revolving around what she could take with her and what could be left behind. It took her weeks, she admitted, just to decide which records to take, especially as she often had to listen to each one to remember why she had bought it in the first place. She recalls, "It took months to get out of that house because of the amount of decisions over that bloody record collection . . . In the end there's this gibbering idiot in the corner going 'I can't make one more decision.'"

Eventually, Dusty locked up most of her possessions in a storage unit under the care of Helene Sellery, and left LA in early 1988 after fifteen long and eventful years. Her friends in AA, including Tarra Thomas, were sad to see her go and offered to accompany her to the airport. Dusty declined, saying Sellery would want to do that—and the emotion would probably be too overwhelming. After living briefly in a rather dark apartment that overlooked Anne Frank's attic, her final destination was a penthouse at the top of a town house on Herengracht where she spent a year staring at the rain-lashed landscape of canals and the church spires, crying to booming renditions of Tchaikovsky.

If the year Dusty spent in Holland seemed a rather peculiar interlude in her life, it gave her the space and anonymity she needed to come to terms with her recent past—and decide what she wanted in her future. Still chain-smoking and drinking gallons of Diet Coke, Dusty decided to lose weight by eating only cauliflower and ice cream. This made her unpopular at dinner parties, but had been brought about by her appearance at the BPI awards where journalists had dubbed her a twelve-stone "giant of pop."

"Part of the uneasiness with dinners also came from not wanting to drink," says Pieter van der Zwan, who owned the house on

Herengracht with his partner, TV producer Edwin Prins. "She was very determined that alcohol was not going to ruin her life again, so she tried to stay away from situations where other people did drink. Partly not to be tempted, but also because people who drink can get pretty boring for someone who is sober and tries to stay that way. She always said that since she stopped drinking her attention span was smaller."

Dusty became friends with van der Zwan and whiled away many afternoons and evenings chatting to him, playing clips of Madonna and Tina Turner and explaining what she would have done differently, or showing him places she had looked up in the atlas and wanted to go to. On one occasion van der Zwan introduced her to Miep Gies, one of the people who had hidden Anne Frank in an attic only a street away, and they spent an evening discussing the war and the Holocaust.

If Dusty was closer to van der Zwan than to Prins, van der Zwan surmised it was because she felt more comfortable with people from outside the world of entertainment. She once said to him, "We are both equals, you in your job and me in mine." After that van der Zwan noticed that many of Dusty's friends were actually people who worked for her, "and however friendly, for them she stayed Dusty. I think one of the advantages we had was that I did not need anything from her and she did not need anything from me, except each other's friendship." When her friend Leon Shaier, a long-time fan and travel agent from London, came to stay in the Herengracht apartment, he remembered that Dusty was amazed when he wanted to pay for his own meals. "She expected to pay for everything for everybody. I told her, 'I can pay for myself, I can pay for both of us. I earn my own money, you know.'"

Those who visited Dusty from England thought she seemed visibly calmer and more settled. When Pat Barnett came to stay, she noted that, although Dusty was finding it hard to get used to the fact that Amsterdam did not have drive-ins and 24-hour super-markets like LA, she enjoyed showing Barnet's sixteen-year-old son Lee around the red light district. Dusty was Lee's godmother and had first met him on one of her visits to England when he was a small boy. Barnett had found them both lying on her bed at the Hilton, propped up on their hands, chatting away. Madeline Bell also met up with Dusty when she was in Amsterdam performing in *A Night at the Cotton Club*. Bell was pleased to see that Dusty was doing better than she had been by previous reports, but she was shocked to discover that her friend was now a heavy smoker, and that "California had turned her into a wreck."

Although Amsterdam was pleasant and calm, Dusty was becoming bored waiting to restart her career and entertained herself by playing with the cats and looking broodingly out of the window. Although she had been in touch with an American woman in AA called Nancy Fox-Martin, she did not go to AA meetings in Amsterdam, and formed few new friendships. She admitted that sometimes she and Malaysia and Nicholas "stared at each other for hours" and that, although she liked the city, she wished that it would occasionally stop raining.

In November 1988 she was back in London and once again recording with the Pet Shop Boys—this time "Nothing Has Been Proved," the theme song for the film *Scandal*. Neil Tennant remembers inwardly groaning when Dusty, armed with a cup of coffee in one hand and a cigarette in the other, took to the micro-phone and proceeded to sing the very first syllable of the first word: "Ma—" Dusty then stopped, the tape was rewound, and she began again with the next syllable. "She recorded her vocals very slowly," Tennant said, "though the end result usually flowed together seamlessly." Looking at the two pages of vocals that had to be double-tracked, Tennant remembered, "I thought I'd go insane," but Dusty got through them. At the end she added a surprise lift and twist to the line "It may be false, it may be true" that added all the drama to the song she feared it was lacking. "It really was a fantastic moment in the studio," Tennant said, "I never thought you could make this song sound like that." Dusty of course was an appropriate choice for the song since the events of the "Profumo affair" had occurred just as she burst onto the scene as a hugely popular solo performer in 1963. She remembered that time very well, and seemed to have great sympathy for Christine Keeler and Mandy Rice-Davies. The intervening years had been difficult for both of them, and for Dusty—something she couldn't help but be reminded of.

On her fiftieth birthday on 16 April 1989, Dusty exchanged brief greetings with Pieter van der Zwan and spent the rest of the day alone. But her situation was far from bleak—she was certainly "hungry to be working again," according to Pat Barnett, and van der Zwan remembered how excited she was about the upturn in her career: "She would often mention colleagues who had offered help to write lyrics or music, saying, 'They all want to be part of it, it's wonderful.'" "Nothing Has Been Proved" had reached number nine in the *NME* charts when it was released in February 1989, and she performed it at the British Academy Awards the following month. In May she was due to record another Pet Shop Boys song, "In Private," and then start work on a new album. But fifty was a big milestone for a woman who'd always feared getting older, and who now appeared to be in a temporary hiatus between the glories and horrors of the past and the possibilities of the future. Those who knew her in LA had heard her speak of a weariness with life that extended beyond an exhaustion brought about by the dramas of the last few years—and a sense that she didn't have much time left. Regardless of quarantine restrictions, Dusty decided it was time to return to England.

Padding about in her pajama bottoms and a T-shirt, without

makeup, Dusty occupied the night hours, sitting up watching TV at Pat Barnett's house for the first five months after her return. "She'd creep down in the night and pinch a packet of chocolate digestives, because she was wide awake, make herself a cup of tea and then I'd get a note in the morning saying 'IOU one packet of chocolate digestives,'" Barnett says. Dusty arrived at the end of August 1989 and was sleeping in her godson Lee's old bedroom in the house Barnett shared with her husband in Southgate, north London. "It was the only time I've known her to be completely at ease," she says. Dusty only needed a bed and a television set, she told her secretary of almost thirty years, and would eschew sitting on a chair to curl up on the floor in front of the radiator, ready to chat. Dusty had always loved Barnett's homeliness, calling up in the old days to see if she could pop over for Sunday lunch with roast parsnips, and Barnett now offered the kind of everyday normality and security she needed. "Pat looked after her," Vicki Wickham says.

In those months they talked about many things, including how Dusty felt about the years she'd spent in California. "She'd learned more who to trust and who not to trust, and she said it was a great learning curve," Barnett says. "She never touched a drop of alcohol. I couldn't even buy cough medicine if it had any alcohol in it—she'd say 'Please check the bottle.' She was absolutely brilliant about that." When the comedian Bobby Davro presented Dusty as a stumbling drunk in a sketch in March 1991 she successfully sued him on the basis that she had not touched alcohol for more than eight years, and won a settlement of £75,000 (just under $100,00).

Returning to England was something Dusty had greatly looked forward to, but found difficult in practice. In phone calls to Pieter van der Zwan she sounded tense—and talked about how much the country had changed in her absence. It seemed at first that she was unsure about where she belonged, or what to do: her appearances included a solo visit to open a housing estate named Springfield in Plymouth, where new residents found her to be extremely nice but so nervous she trembled like a leaf. After a few months, Dusty moved out of Pat Barnett's house and rented an apartment around the corner in Fox Lane. She continued to drive out to visit the cats almost every day, and surprised locals by dropping into Asda (a British supermarket chain) or picking up a takeout from the fish and chip shop. A more permanent solution was needed, however, as it soon became clear that it would be easier to move out into the country, giving Dusty the tranquillity and peace of mind she increasingly craved.

The first home she had bought for many years was a nondescript 1970s terrace house in the village of Taplow, Buckinghamshire—not far from where she had grown up in High Wycombe. Dusty was physically and spiritually coming home, and she often drove around the countryside in her new silver Citroën XM, stopping to cry when she saw a typically English landscape like a field of corn, or enthusing to Pieter van der Zwan about the beauty of Cotswold stone when he came to visit. Simon Bell says:

> The house in Taplow was absolutely nothing like you would expect her to be living in. It was really quite unattractive from the front, but it had the most wonderful view from the back, and that's what she liked about the house. Not that she ever sat outside and looked at it, because she built a cat cage on the back so you couldn't see the view.

Dusty renovated the interior in her own style, adding a metal industrial staircase, and making Simon Bell rearrange all the furniture in a branch of Habitat until she could imagine how it would look in her living room. "The people in the store let me do it," Bell says, "so they must have known it was her. And that's the kind of thing she would do. She just thought that it was normal to be able to do that." (Dusty undertook a similar exercise in Harrods with Bell and Pat Barnett when she was contemplating whether to buy a Nordic ski machine. Much to the delight of onlookers, an embarrassed Barnett tried out the machine, and reported back to Dusty—who was standing alongside—on how it felt. The machine was duly purchased, but never used.)

Dusty "kept herself very much to herself" in Taplow, Barnett noticed. She still went to AA, but not nearly as regularly as she had done in LA, and she introduced herself to her new neighbors as Mary O'Brien. It was as if Dusty was undecided what identity to occupy now that she was back in Britain—or maybe it was because she felt that her house "wasn't good enough for 'Dusty,'" Simon Bell speculates. When nearby resident, and another '60s survivor, Sandie Shaw knocked on the door one day on behalf of a local charity, both were so short sighted they initially didn't recognize each other.

Despite an innate restlessness that still led her to drive to Heathrow just to sit in the café beside the arrivals gate and watch people coming and going, Dusty was more peaceful than she had been in many years. She made good friends with two local women, and enjoyed organizing excursions for them, even though she never went herself. Sometimes she met up with old friends for tea, just "like the old Dusty," Vicki Wickham says. At Christmas she invited Simon Bell for dinner, and attempted to cook it herself, although the final meal was not ready to be served until Boxing Day. To the astonishment of her friends, she appeared sanguine even in the face of one her greatest fears—one of the cats being killed on the road. Having survived LA, it was tragic when Malaysia was run over by a passing motorist in Taplow, but Dusty appeared accepting of her fate, if sad—saying that she had "gone to the giant litter tray in the sky." Dusty brought Malaysia inside, squeezed her into a baking tray "like in a black comedy" and called Bell to deal with her remains. Ultimately, Dusty wanted to bury her in the garden, but for some reason couldn't do so immediately. In the interim Dusty asked Bell to put Malaysia in the freezer, but unfortunately the cat was by now stiff with rigor mortis and wouldn't fit. "Can't you just cut her legs off?" Dusty asked—taking a practical approach. "I'm not doing that!" a horrified Bell replied. Dusty mourned Malaysia, but her one remaining cat, Nicholas, was delighted to be the sole object of her affection.

Notably, she refrained from embarking on a new relationship, knowing perhaps that they had always been her downfall in the past. Women had often immersed her in trouble and drama, and Bell thinks her restraint came from applying the principles she'd learned in AA to the rest of her life.

> I think she knew that she had an addictive, destructive personality, and learned that she couldn't have relationships . . . I observed that she didn't believe she deserved to be loved, and when she was being loved she behaved as badly as possible to make the other person stop loving her, and then she could say "I told you so."

Dusty often mused on her own solitariness, but said she wasn't prepared to put up with bad relationships any more. In 1990 she told the *Daily Mail*:

> I do care [about what people whisper], I go through very vulnerable stages. I don't know why I put up with California for so long . . . It was bad but I put up with it. But I won't any more. The same with a relationship. I used to think I had to put up with the pain, not any more. I care terribly about me again.

Vicki Wickham believes that Dusty's chances to find another partner were also hampered by her fame back in Britain. "She didn't really get a chance to meet that many people." Back in England Dusty was often recognized and, as Wickham puts it, "That's the other problem of being known. You don't meet people, you meet fans. She was extremely attractive. I was always amazed she didn't settle down with somebody, or have more girlfriends."

More immediately, Dusty had her new album, *Reputation*, to think about. Originally she had planned for the Pet Shop Boys to produce the entire album, but as negotiations stretched on they began other work and could only complete half of it—something Dusty claimed to be pleased about as it gave her more creative freedom. In October 1989 Dusty began recording the Pet Shop Boys tracks "I Want to Stay Here," "Occupy Your Min" and "Daydreaming." After a break for Christmas she completed the recording, enjoying working with Dan Hartman in his Connecticut studio to complete "Born This Way" where she could look out of the window and watch the snow falling and the flocks of wild geese.

The first single to be released from the album, in June 1989, was the title track. Dusty said she found the lyrics "so sort of campy and relevant that I couldn't resist it"—but the song fared poorly in the charts. When a New Zealand radio interviewer asked her how she felt about "Reputation"—both hers, and the song—Dusty was heard to give a long pause before replying. In November the follow-up ballad "Arrested by You" was released, but struggled to reach number seventy in the charts. *Reputation* contained none of the stand-out singles that had launched her comeback, but it was a nevertheless a strong album that peaked at number eighteen in the album chart, and was awarded a silver disc.

It seemed that her success had put her back on an upward track, so fans were outraged when Dusty announced in December

1989 that she would once again be parting ways with her record company, EMI. Chagrined, she replied that people failed to realize that she still had to make money from recording, and had been unable to secure a favorable renegotiation of her contract. Whatever the origin of the dispute, Dusty's collaboration with the Pet Shop Boys was over, and she would once again have to find another way forward for her career. It was 1990, and she was back out in the cold.

19

GOIN' BACK

The trees that fell did so in almost eerie silence, with only the faintest creaks, as they littered the frozen fields and roads. In the early morning of February 9, 1993 office workers, farmers, telephone repair men, housewives and thousands of other bleary-eyed citizens of Tennessee woke to the slow snap of boughs breaking and falling. During the night an ice storm had swept across the state, coating the landscape in a beautiful frozen glaze that cracked as the day wore on, bringing massive trees crashing down across cars and through the roofs of houses. In Nashville, Dusty and Pat Barnett emerged from the studio and stood, smoking and shivering, to survey the scene. The day before it had been seventy degrees.

After exhausting the mileage of her "rent-a-diva" days of the late 1980s, Dusty was in Nashville to record an album she finally felt she could mold and call her own. *A Very Fine Love* had brought her back to the roots of country music, and the state where she had recorded her first US album with Shelby Singleton and The Springfields. That trip had been the catalyst for her career, and for her love of America. Had she stayed in 1962 the arc of her life and work would have been very different. Now she had returned, full circle, not realizing that it was almost all at an end.

"I'd either be enormously rich or I'd have blown my brains out by now," Dusty told *Mojo*, considering the different course her life might have taken had she remained in Tennessee. "I understood I would not be comfortable there because they don't like women who fight their own case too hard. I was a very combative person and I couldn't have won there."

After parting ways with EMI, Dusty had occupied herself on personal projects at home, adopted various animals at animal sanctuaries, wondered—slightly despairingly—about where her life was going, revisited the old days by singing a duet with Cilla Black, and taken part in a documentary about her career with French and Saunders. If the part-serious/part-spoof result was rather strange, it did at least allow fans to hear Dusty talking in depth about her life.

A Very Fine Love was a big step forward. Dusty's first album with Sony Columbia, it had come about because the new boss was a huge fan of her music. One of his first acts upon being installed in the job was to demand that the company sign Dusty Springfield, whatever the cost. "On July 19, 1993, I started my job as MD of Columbia in London," Kip Krones told Lucy O'Brien. "I called Vicki Wickham on that first day and said, 'I wanna do a record with Dusty.'" She was "the best female pop singer of my generation."

Overseen by writer and producer Tom Shapiro, most of the recording took place in the converted dining room of Bennett

House, a colonial home in the historic district of Franklin, Tennessee (with additional recording at the Recording Arts Studio in Nashville itself). The original title of *Dusty in Nashville* was considered to sound too much like a country album, and was dropped in favor of *A Very Fine Love*, but Dusty was thrilled by the song choices, which she believed reflected her evolution into a mature performer and musician. She told *Mojo*:

> *I'm not a dance act. I felt if I was to do music again I'd have to be where I felt comfortable and I was allowed to be less of a diva. Where it wasn't necessary for me to sound as if I was about to explode if I changed key one more time . . . I am the age I am and I've learned a lot. I wouldn't make a bloody record unless I were enthusiastic, because it's a lot of hard work.*

Dusty had asked Barnett to accompany her, but the trip seemed destined to be difficult from the start. The weather was bad, their baggage was delayed by two hours, and then they had to take a sixty-mile cab ride between airports in Washington DC to catch the connecting flight. As the storm wreaked havoc across the state, knocking out power for weeks and freezing fish in their tanks, Dusty and Barnett were forced to relocate to a motel miles away that had an electricity generator. The six weeks of the recording session soon stretched towards twelve.

Shortly before the storm struck, Dusty had been planning a visit with Sue Cameron, and Cameron believes they were on the brink of making an epic decision.

> *We had been talking on the phone a lot and this was the time that we both were ready to say, "All right, stop the games, this is silly, we are supposed to be together forever,*

we're just going to do this." So I was all excited and I was a few hours away from leaving for the airport, and she called me and she said, "Nashville has had the worst storm that they've had in a hundred years, we have no electricity, the airport is closed, there's no way you can get here."

Cameron was terribly upset and could hardly believe that after all they'd been through a mere storm could keep them apart. Eventually, they agreed that Dusty would call when she got back to London, and they would be reunited in England. But as Barnett, and her producer and musicians in Nashville, had already realized, Dusty was not well.

"She couldn't believe these wonderful instrumentalists that were playing on the sessions. She just thought they were so great, they would get the sound she wanted in about two minutes," Barnett says. With K. T. Oslin and Bonnie Raitt delighted to sing backup on the bluesy-sounding "Where Is a Woman to Go," recording should have been a dream. Dusty, however, was taking hours to get her vocals right and, unlike sessions in the past, she was clean and sober and ready to work. Despite her best efforts, her voice just wouldn't oblige—and she seemed to have a series of awful colds and throat infections that left her exhausted. Simon Bell says:

It was good work, she sang really well. But I think she found it all a bit of a slog by that time. It didn't come easy. And she knew that people had expectations of that voice and she knew equally that her voice wasn't there in the same way. So it took her longer in the studio to get anything down on tape that would be acceptable to the people who had those expectations.

Eventually, Barnett and Leon Shaier, who was also visiting from

England, persuaded her to see a specialist, who gave Dusty a thorough examination and could seem to find nothing wrong. Nonetheless, he suspected that she was not in good health, and asked her to consult with a doctor as soon as she returned to the UK.

If Dusty did not have a confirmed diagnosis, she was certainly moving into a more spiritual and reflective realm, indulging her interest in the Civil War by visiting battlefields with Barnett and Helene Sellery and contemplating the ghosts that still hovered there. Fulfilling one of her long-standing ambitions, she rented a car and drove the Shenandoah Valley, where she stood crying beside a river thinking about her place in the world.

When she returned to England, Dusty did not see a doctor, but immediately began a diet to lose the extra pounds she had piled on in Nashville eating Southern fried breakfasts. Within a few days, while taking a shower, she noticed a large indentation in her left breast—something she casually dropped into a conversation with Vicki Wickham. Wickham told her to go to her GP right away, but Dusty confessed that she had never bothered to register, adding, "It's just not convenient, Vicki, I've got all these things to do . . ." Wickham insisted, and arranged for her to see a female doctor in Harley Street who immediately referred her to the Royal Marsden Hospital for further tests.

While everyone waited for the results, Dusty returned to the studio and finished her vocals for a "duet" with Daryl Hall on Diane Warren's "Wherever Would I Be" (the vocals were recorded separately and they never met) that was later used in the Sandra Bullock film *While You Were Sleeping*. Although she had written for, and got to know, some of the biggest artists of the decade, Warren idolized Dusty and was thrilled to have a brief phone conversation with her: "No one had a voice like Dusty Springfield. There was so much soul in her voice, she had so much in her voice that compelled you." Dusty finished the call, delighted by the honor, but joked to Leon Shaier, "I bet she said that to Céline Dion half an hour ago!"

After Dusty finished her work, she returned for her follow-up appointment at the Royal Marsden. The doctor was sitting chatting about her cat, called Moses, when, as Dusty told *Woman* magazine, "I saw her face change, and I thought, 'Hell, that's it,' and eventually she said, 'I'm afraid it's a tumor, and one we just don't want.'" Dusty put a brave face on the news, taking Barnett and her brother Tom to lunch on the King's Road, but later she went home and wept over Nicholas. "At first it was as if it wasn't happening to me, it was happening to that person over there," Dusty told the *New York Times*. "I was numb, and I had a record to finish. Then I was sitting at home and my cat was sleeping and I thought, 'Who will look after you?'"

Sue Cameron says:

> *Dusty died of alcoholism, not breast cancer. Alcoholics, even though sober, still have self-destructive behavior, and she'd never had a physical, she'd never had a mammogram, and it wouldn't matter whether she was sober or drunk if you don't fix that behavior. She got a lump and it was too late from the very minute she told me.*

Cameron was a doctor's daughter and asked for the full diagnosis, including her rating. Dusty told her. Cameron says, "She didn't understand too much. I knew it was over, but I never said anything. I was obviously very, very encouraging until the day, much later, when she called me and she said, 'I'm going to die.'"

After the initial shock of the diagnosis, Dusty was determined and optimistic about beating the disease, undergoing chemo-therapy to shrink the tumor within a week and then having a lumpectomy. "Apparently my body still likes poison," she joked. "It was saying, 'Yes! Give me some poison.'" She'd feared that Sony would cancel the album when they heard the news, but instead they agreed to put the release and promotion on hold until she recovered. Barnett says:

> I know stress is what cancer feeds on. They wanted her to go and promote the record. Now she got very stressed doing that. It's not like getting up and singing. You never know what questions people throw at you when you're doing interviews. I said to Dusty, "You're not doing it, it's stressful." I think Vicki Wickham was very surprised. And Dusty went, "Oh, okay," and nodded.

A Very Fine Love was released a year later in June 1995 with "Wherever Would I Be" as the first single. "I really like this album," she concluded—"and that's a first for me." Promoting it in a series of interviews and performances, Dusty seemed willing to talk about recovering from cancer. "I'm all right now," she insisted to Mojo, "definitely in remission." In television interviews she praised the staff at the Royal Marsden, and explained that they had given her the news and told her to go home and think about it for a few days. "That's when you realize that you're not going to die today." Although she would not have chosen to have cancer, she told The Times, "it has turned out to be a learning curve. It's a long time since being a star was the most important thing to me, but it's even less so now. I don't need to be adored, to hear that applause. If I never heard it again, I would still be fine." Even so, Dusty was still capable of thrilling her fans, appearing on Later... with Jools Holland with Alison Moyet and Sinéad O'Connor on backup. Giving it her all—and loving every minute of it—she proved she was still Britain's queen of soul.

The release of the album, combined with the huge success of "Son of a Preacher Man" on the soundtrack for *Pulp Fiction*, appeared to have willed Dusty back to life "by her legend," the *New York Times* noted. Talking to her in October, around the time of the US release of the second single from the album, "Roll Away," reporter Rob Hoerburger asked why she was still smoking when she had not only her voice to protect, but also her health. "I know it's stupid, and it will go," Dusty replied, rather wearily. "But a bit at a time. I've already had to give up so much." With the first stage of her battle with cancer behind her, and the album released, Dusty seemed calm, reflective . . . and worn out. Those wishing for the crockery-throwing tirades of old seemed bound to be disappointed. "People expect to get drama from me," she said. "I just get tired." Later the *New York Times* caught up with her again, over tea by the Thames. *A Very Fine Love* was not selling particularly well, and there were rumors that despite Kip Krone's staunch support, it might be Dusty's last album. Dusty looked wistful at the prospect and said, "Well, no matter. I shall still have my house on the river."

Never settled for long, Dusty had left the modern terrace in Taplow and was renting a converted barn in Frogmill near Henley-on-Thames. The house was dark downstairs, but opened up into a double-height living room on the upper floor that looked straight out on the river. When *Mojo* asked her if that meant England was now her permanent home she answered:

> *I would say so . . . I haven't forgotten how I missed England. For now, this is where I am, but my restlessness will take me somewhere else. I don't know where. My life seems to take me where I'm meant to be, sometimes for disastrous episodes, but all of it is necessary. If it took me to Ireland I would be very happy.*

The previous year, she had filmed the video for "Roll Away" on the

Galway coast, creating nightmares for producers Sean O'Hagan and Seamus McGarvey when her enormous Winnebago got stuck in narrow country lanes, and she asked them to "do something about the wind," which was wreaking havoc with her hair (they explained there was little they could do short of building a windbreak around the whole of the west coast of Ireland). Dusty seemed tired, and lonely, on the shoot—but it had connected her to her family roots and she returned proclaiming that "Irishness is a state of mind," and that she was proud of her heritage and the fact that she could weep watching *Riverdance*.

When she returned on vacation with Helene Sellery in early 1996, they stayed at the same location, Cregg Castle, which she had loved the year before. While Dusty's hair-raising driving caused many arguments, the two friends enjoyed sightseeing— but once again Dusty was not well, this time complaining about a cough and a pain in her collarbone. Sellery insisted she see a doctor in Dublin, who referred her back to the Royal Marsden in London. This time the diagnosis was that the cancer had returned and spread to her bones—and Dusty's condition was terminal.

When Suzanne Lacefield visited her at the Churchill Hotel Dusty confessed that there were times when she didn't think she was going to make it. "Do you want to make it?" Lacefield asked her. Dusty replied, "Some days yes, some days no."

"She was frightened and I think she was very angry; there was an awful lot of anger in her," Simon Bell says. "But once she knew she had something that was going to kill her she wanted to fight it." Bell had worked with Dusty since 1978, but it had taken her time to trust him. "She didn't let me in at first; we weren't very close right away. It took quite a long time, even after the Drury Lane concerts," he says. Once, when she was passing through London with Carole Pope in the early 1980s, she called him in the middle of the night and asked him to go to her hotel. "That was the first and only time I had one of those legendary phone calls saying 'I need you to come.'" When he arrived Bell found Dusty quite well, but tipsy. "There was nothing wrong with her, except she was drunk. She was drinking Cointreau—which I thought was a horrible thing to get drunk on." Pope stayed in the bathroom during his visit, and Bell couldn't work out why Dusty had summoned him. "I never really figured out why she had sent for me. I thought about it afterwards and decided that she was testing me to see if I'd come. I passed the test, and that was all she really cared about."

Their friendship grew and, after she returned to live in England, he often drove her into London for appointments, or took her out for the day when she felt like going sightseeing or shopping. Sometimes she just wanted to drive around Ealing, or High Wycombe, and see where she grew up. On another occasion Bell drove Dusty to the polls to vote on election day and was dismayed when she emerged and announced that she had still voted Conservative, despite Bell's pleas to switch to Labor. "I couldn't go through with it,' she told him sheepishly.

Dusty never called on the day that she wanted to go out (that would not leave her enough time to get ready—a process which still took several hours). Instead she would usually call at 11 a.m. the day before and suggest somewhere she wanted to visit. Bell says:

> I think she just wanted company. But she always paid me. She had a thing about that. I think she felt everything was all right as long as she gave me twenty quid or something. It came to a point where my life was really on hold just for whenever Dusty would decide she was going to do whatever it was, and that went on for a long, long time. It got quite frustrating at times, but it was Dusty so I didn't mind.

Sometimes their outings involved long drives, but Bell noticed that

Dusty much preferred to be on the move, and was rarely interested in her chosen destination once they got there. As ever, Dusty was friendly, and generous—but reserved. She remained silent about her family—"she never spoke about them, never," Bell says—and about previous relationships, and once they finally got back to Henley, she would smile and send him on his way. "When I got her home she would immediately say, 'You'll be wanting to get up the road, then.' And I could never be sure whether it was that she was sure you couldn't possibly want to stay with her, or whether she wanted rid of me. I never knew."

Dusty, he noticed, wanted very much to be liked, but was also acutely aware of her own limitations. One day, in town for a manicure, the woman who did Dusty's nails complained that she couldn't go on holiday because there was no one to look after her cat. "I'll look after the cat," Dusty replied immediately. The woman was immensely grateful, but when they got out to the car, Dusty bashfully said to Bell, "You will go and look after the cat for me, won't you? I'll pay you. You know I won't do it."

Bell was also closely involved with Dusty's musical career, singing with her and attending recordings—and he was often the person either backing her up and validating her decisions, or calming her down.

> We were doing one of the TV shows and we were rehearsing round a piano. She didn't like what the musical director was playing on the piano, and she said, 'That's not the way it goes at all, I'm fed up with this, why don't you get over here?' And she walked out of the room and slammed the door. I went after her and said, "Dusty we are in his house!" And then she burst out laughing.

The recurrence of the cancer brought a change, and new depth, to their relationship, with Bell breaking the news to her that her condition was terminal. "I think she was able to be open with me on a lot of different levels because of being gay, and also because our relationship wasn't just a friendship, it was also musical, so I think I was involved in more parts of her life."

By now Dusty was clearly unwell. With press photographers trying to take pictures through the windows, her friends fretted that she needed someone to live with her and look after her. Bell seemed by far the best choice: he was loyal and supportive, and he also had the kind of calm and quiet personality that Dusty needed on a day to day basis. In addition Bell had nursed someone he cared about through AIDS—something he had often talked to Dusty about—and she knew he could handle the emotional and physical demands of her illness. Even so, he expected that one day she would prefer a woman to look after her. "I even said to her, 'Look, I know there's going to be a time where you think it's time for a woman to look after you and it's okay to tell me when you don't want me around.' But it didn't happen."

At first Bell stayed in the house at Frogmill, but it was becoming clear that its accessibility made it a nightmare. Not only were the attentions of the press such a problem that the curtains had to be kept closed all day, but Dusty was also feeling that she needed to withdraw from her friends' many phone calls and messages of support. "She needed to shut herself off to die," says Carole Pope, sadly.

Using funds Vicki Wickham had arranged from the sale of the back catalog of Dusty's songs to Prudential Insurance, Lee Everett found Dusty a new house to rent on the other side of Henley in Harpsden Bottom, surrounded by grounds and a locked gate that made it private and impossible to be overlooked. Everett was now regularly visiting Dusty too, and was administering healing sessions. When Dusty raised the prospect of a "miracle cure" in America, Everett says she told her, "Dusty, this is it. There is no miracle cure. It's going to take you this time."

The money ensured that Dusty would have enough to live on comfortably for the rest of her life, and to pay for any exploratory treatment she might decide on in America, despite what Everett had told her. "The money was really for any treatment in America," Bell confirms. "But that day never came." When she discovered that the total raised from the sale of her back catalog was less than a million pounds, Dusty was deeply upset. Money had always been important to her, giving her an often false illusion of safety. "I explained to her, that was a monetary value put on it by an insurance company, and in no way reflected her true worth," Bell says.

The original prognosis was that Dusty had only four months to live, but with intensive treatment, including three month-long courses of chemotherapy, as yet unlicensed drugs from America and full blood transfusions, she carried on. One day Dusty poignantly wrote herself a little note that read, "A year to the day since my diagnosis and I'm still here. Haven't I done well!" On several occasions Dusty was desperately ill, seemingly comatose and at the point of death, but somehow she would always rally. Bell would watch each return from the brink with mixed feelings. He cared deeply about Dusty, but with her death inevitable, he wondered if it would be better for her to slip away in her sleep rather than struggle back, prolonging her suffering.

Dusty was terrified of dying and whiled away the dreaded night hours when Bell was sleeping by calling her old friends in California and watching television. During the summer of 1998 Bell would leave her wearing her Brazil football shirt and big glasses, watching the World Cup. On the first night he stayed over he was amazed to come down in the morning to find Dusty sound asleep with her eyes wide open—something he surmised might have been due to an earlier facelift. Often he would leave her sleeping until late in the morning and go food shopping, hoping that some roast potatoes with rosemary and garlic would tempt her to eat a little, even though she rarely felt like it. Then they would sit and talk and watch TV—"Her favorite thing was to watch *Bonanza* on satellite TV in Germany"—or Dusty would read some of her favorite books, especially Bill Bryson's popular travelogues, which cheered her up.

Simon Bell was now not only her friend and companion, but also her protector from the outside world that she feared would sap her energy. "Once she moved into the house at Little Hill she never went out," Bell says, but even there people swarmed around who did not necessarily have her best interests at heart. "The whole thing was like a nest of vipers. All of the people she was surrounded by were behaving in extraordinary ways."

Many people wrote, called and faxed but Dusty marshalled her resources to fight her battle with cancer, and couldn't cope with so much emotion and sadness from people who'd once been close to her. When her old friend Martha Reeves wrote letters, Dusty was too upset to read them. Doug Reece, her bass player from The Echoes, sent a long fax explaining how much she'd meant to him. Pat Barnett told him Dusty had read it, and had been quiet for a long time. Mike Hurst from The Springfields wrote a letter too, and received a reply that said, "It's very sweet of you to write, but I don't want to see anyone." Pieter van den Zwan was upset that Dusty had changed her phone number, and he had to wait for her to call him, which she did, leaving two messages on his answering machine. Julie Felix very much wanted to see Dusty too, but was told that Dusty was too ill for visitors.

In her inner circle, perhaps Barnett was the one who found it most difficult to come to terms with the fact that Dusty was dying.

Dusty had kept the news from her for quite some time, knowing that she would be devastated. Upon hearing the truth, Barnett was so overwrought that she developed irritable bowel syndrome and was too ill to drive up and down the motorway to visit for many weeks.

It was Barnett, however, who had to break the news to Dusty that Linda McCartney had died in April 1998. Dusty had come to rely on phone calls with McCartney to buoy her up and support her, and McCartney had always sounded so positive and encouraging that Dusty simply could not believe she had died. "Dusty started screaming, 'No! No! It's not true!'" Barnett remembers. Helene Sellery was visiting at the time from California, and Barnett told Dusty to put the phone down and tell Sellery what had happened. It was the only thing she could think of to calm her down.

Even though she was ill, visits with Dusty could still be as tempestuous as of old. Simon Bell remembers Helene Sellery waking him up shouting, "She's gone!" At first he thought Dusty had died, but Sellery explained they had been having a big argument when Dusty had run out of the house and driven off—heavily medicated—into the night. Eventually Dusty returned, with the side of the car scratched from driving it into a hedge. Bell was more than used to Dusty's temper, but as her full-time carer he now often had to bite his tongue when she had no one else to take her frustrations out on. "There was one moment when I walked away and left her and went home," Bell says. "I came back and let myself in the next morning. And when she woke up I was there. She never mentioned what had gone on the day before." On one occasion she threw a heavy old-fashioned phone at him. Another time when he complained about feeling ill, Dusty retorted, "You feel ill? Try having cancer."

Dusty was now also suffering from a form of obsessive-compulsive disorder which meant that all the carpets and furniture were covered in plastic and, even though the sofas were wrapped in dust sheets, Bell still had to sit on the floor. Cups and dishes had to be washed immediately as Dusty was nervous about anything leaving water marks in the sink, and she insisted that all the rubbish was torn up into small pieces of identical size. Under strict instructions, Bell usually had to buy the grocery shopping in three or four different supermarkets to get exactly what Dusty knew she wanted. "It took about half a day, because she just had to control it all. It was all insane." Dusty was also often worried sick about Nicholas the cat. On advice from the vet, Nicholas was stuffed with pills and subjected to enemas, and taken for walks on a lead. When he escaped from the house at Little Hill, Dusty issued a large reward and prowled the area for two days frantically calling for him, until he returned. Powerless in the face of so much, domestic life was the only area left within her control.

Much as he cared for her, Dusty told Bell more than once that she regretted that she was living out the final stage of her life with him, and that she hadn't been able to have a successful, lasting, romantic partnership. While she was in remission she had wistfully told *The Times*, "There are days I'd like to retouch my entire life," something she reflected on even more when the disease returned— telling Lee Everett that she was embarrassed by so much of what she'd done.

When Suzanne Lacefield visited from California, she sat down with Dusty in private and asked her if there was anything she wanted to talk about. Dusty thought about it, and said, "I don't think there is a lot that I regret. I regret the feelings of my childhood, I regret that I didn't make better choices with my career and the people that I had around me, but I just couldn't help it—I just don't know how to do it differently."

At heart, Dusty had always felt a fraud, Lacefield says. "I don't think she was ever really in love with anybody. She was in need.

And if they were nice to her for a minute and looked like they were going to give of themselves to her and be her best friend or helper or what have you . . ." Sometimes Lacefield had felt that self-hatred exuded from Dusty's pores, and she was incapable of taking in the love and support that she was offered. "You have to create a space to take love in, and if you have no forgiveness of yourself, and self-hatred, you'll never believe it. She couldn't take it in." When they parted, Dusty gave her an astrology book that Lacefield says Dusty "practically looked up by the hour. There were so many notes along the edges, twenty years of notes along the edges about her concerns and hoping that this would happen or that would happen. There was a lot of magical thinking in her life."

Of the former lovers who did still care for her (and there were many), it was Sue Cameron who did the most to support her and help her through her illness. After they had come so close to being reunited in Nashville, Cameron had immediately volunteered to come to England and look after Dusty when she heard the diagnosis. Dusty said no, her illness was something she was ready to fight alone. "You are at the mercy of someone like that. If someone is dying you have to do exactly what they say," Cameron says.

Later, Dusty phoned her in a panic and said, "I'm going to die and I've never done it before, I don't know how to do it." Cameron told her, "You'll do it very well." The way that Dusty came to terms with death "was a gift to her," Cameron believes. "It made her happy that she finally believed it wasn't about singing, it wasn't about religion, she finally believed that she was a stellar human being." Quietly, Cameron began calling all Dusty's old friends in California and asking them to call her or write to her. Angie Dickinson and Ann-Margret called, and Bette Midler wrote a card that said, "Every time I go onstage I think of you, and I know I'll never be as good as you." Both Dusty and Simon Bell wept when they read it, and later, when they were watching the film *Beaches*, Dusty asked Bell to sing Midler's song "The Wind Beneath My Wings" at her funeral. Overcome with sadness, Bell tried to lighten the moment by saying, "No—I'd rather sing 'By the Light of the Silvery Moon.'" Even in her final months, Dusty knew what people wanted and needed from her, and she still wanted to give it. "It was part of her nature that she would do things for people because she knew she could give them something," Bell says. "She did that. I'd seen her do that on other occasions. I think that's why she had me sing at the funeral. I think she thought, 'I can do this for him.'"

Sue Cameron also helped to arrange Dusty's induction into the Rock 'n' Roll Hall of Fame. When she saw Ahmet Ertegun (who had so memorably signed Dusty to Atlantic Records) in the Peninsula Hotel in Los Angeles, Cameron told him that it was time for Dusty to be inducted. "I said, 'She needs to be in the Hall of Fame now,'" Cameron recalls. "'She didn't make it last year, she's not made it again this year. Now, Ahmet, do you understand?'" Ertegun replied, "Yes." "Dusty never knew I did that, but she did know she made it," Cameron says. When Dusty complained that they were only inducting her out of sympathy, Cameron told her, "Just enjoy it."

Dusty's inability to sing anymore was something that both women found indescribably sad. Dusty had phoned Cameron every Christmas for twenty-five years, and they would sing "Angels We Have Heard on High" together, with Cameron taking the lead and Dusty singing the choir. "A year before she died she called me, she tried to sing and she tried to hit some notes—and she said, 'I can't do it, I can't sing any more,'" Cameron says. "It was just the saddest, most horrible thing."

Despite dire warnings not to visit and enact any emotional deathbed scenes, Cameron phoned Dusty when she was passing through London towards the end of 1998, a few months before her death—and told her she would be coming to see her. Simon Bell remembers that when he left to pick Cameron up, Dusty looked terribly ill, but by the time he returned she had made an enormous effort to pull herself together, get dressed and put on her makeup. "And there she was—she was Dusty Springfield again," he says. Dusty would make a similar effort every time she went to the hospital. "She'd turn up fully made up, and they never knew how ill she was," Bell says.

"Seeing her that last time was the most difficult thing I've ever done in my life," Sue Cameron says. "She looked beautiful. She was not too thin and she was covered up with larger clothes. Her hair was pretty much grey rather than blond, her skin was so clear, and her eyes were so beautiful. She just looked like an angel." At first, they walked around the garden and the woods, "just so happy to see one another," and then went and sat inside, where Cameron was astonished to see many of the things she recognized from the houses they had shared in California. Later Cameron found out that Dusty had asked Bell to put things out for her to see, and gave her a favorite pair of shocking pink boots.

As they talked, Dusty became more tired, and fell asleep on the couch. Cameron says:

> It was like I left my body. The insides of my body were shaking like Jell-O. It was all surreal, because I couldn't believe I was going to lose her, I couldn't believe it, and so I knelt down at the couch and I started kissing her cheek, and she started crying—and we both started crying.

Cameron recognized the familiar smell of Dusty's favorite perfume, Chanel No. 19.

*When I first knelt in to kiss her the Chanel 19 was over-
whelming and I literally said, "Oh my God, that smell."
I don't know how I lived. And she was crying and I was
crying and I said, "You're the love of my life" and she said,
"Oh sure," trying to be funny and throw it off.*

When the time eventually came for her to go, Cameron left the
house in a daze. She desperately wanted to stay "but that wasn't
the deal, I was supposed to go." Dusty walked Cameron to the door.

*I couldn't believe I was walking out of the house knowing I
wasn't ever going to see her again. I don't know how one foot
went in front of the other. I stood by the car and I looked at
her at the front door and the look in her eyes, it was just like,
argh! And then she looked at me and she smiled and she went
like this—thumbs up—like "we have to do this."*

Before she died, Dusty would speak to Cameron, sometimes from
her hospital room at the Royal Marsden, where she had a private
phone line. On one of the last occasions Cameron phoned her and
broke down, saying, "I love you, I love you." But to the end Dusty
wanted to conceal the truth about her private life—"Shh!" she
told Cameron, "they might be listening in." By now Dusty was on
heavy medication, and often repeated herself—but that night she
kept telling Cameron over and over again that she was worried
about her; Cameron was too trusting and naïve and people took
advantage of her. "She kept saying she couldn't go unless she knew
I'd be taken care of and that I would take care of myself," Cameron
says. Her final words to the woman who had loved her longest
were, "God bless."

Dusty spent her final Christmas at the house in Harpsden Bottom
with Simon Bell and Nicholas the cat. Even then she couldn't escape

from the attentions of the press, all wanting to put a picture of "dying Dusty" on the front page. "Towards the end we had the *Daily Mail* flying helicopters over the house with telescopic lenses, and photographers climbing over the fence," Simon Bell says. Her brother Tom came to see her and, although they had spent long periods of their lives estranged from each other, they shared a nice visit. Bell noticed how unfamiliar and polite they seemed with each other and, as he got Dusty up and dressed, he wondered if she wished it was her brother helping her instead.

Early in the New Year, Dusty's health began to deteriorate quickly, and Lee Everett says she believes Dusty's true spirit departed, leaving behind someone who was frightened and angry. "I say to people that when someone is so ill their spirit leaves and all that is left is the fear, and nastiness. But that's not the real person, that's the fear."

"Control was important," Simon Bell says. When the doctor told Dusty she needed a medical air mattress to stop her getting bedsores, she insisted she needed two. Sleeping on two would be dangerous, the doctor said; she would be too high and might fall out of bed. "She had to have the two," Bell says, "and I saw a look in her eyes; it was like something she wanted that had to be done, so I went and bought two." Dusty slept on both mattresses, and did not fall out of bed. "It was about her being able to keep control of something," Bell says.

Throughout her ordeal, Dusty did not waver from her decision to stay sober, something that amazed and impressed Simon Bell. "I always thought that I wouldn't blame her if she started drinking. But she never did. She even felt guilty about taking the medication for the cancer. I used to think I might come down one morning and find that she had killed herself." Dusty was ready to fight to the end but she knew it was nearing, asking Bell when his next tour, with the James Last Orchestra, was scheduled to start. He told her it began in April. "Well, I'd better be gone by then," Dusty said.

Lee Everett did not visit again, but Pat Barnett came to see Dusty, and found her restless and distressed. Dusty was only truly bedridden for the last three days of her life, but by now she couldn't speak. "She looked troubled," Barnett says. She asked the local vicar to visit and say a blessing over Dusty, who had never returned to Catholicism. After the blessing was over, and everyone left the room, Barnett leaned over and said to Dusty, "You go. Don't worry about anyone else. If you want to go—go." Then she left too, closing the door and weeping inconsolably because she knew that she would not see Dusty again.

Later that night, the nurse came and asked Bell to come downstairs to sit with Dusty. The end was near, and Bell sat beside her, holding her hand and stroking the top of her head. After a few minutes, he felt a puff of air blowing against his hand and he had the strongest sensation that it was Dusty's spirit leaving her body. "She's gone, isn't she?" he said to the nurse, who nodded.

"I wish I could remember her last words," Bell says, "but I didn't know they were going to be her last words." Instead he remembers how, the day before, he had found some old videos of Dusty's BBC shows from the 1960s. The two nurses who had come to look after her were young Australians, and Dusty was disappointed they didn't really know who she was. "She knew she was on the way out, and she wanted to let them know they weren't dealing with any old so-and-so," Bell says. He pushed the video into the machine, and the nurses watched in amazement with their mouths wide open. And Dusty sat propped up in bed with her big glasses on, watching the nurses and watching herself—so fabulous, and perfect and young—and Bell saw that she was beaming with delight.

EPILOGUE

O n the night that Dusty died, Simon Bell had called Tom Springfield, Pat Barnett and Vicki Wickham, and arranged for her body to be quietly taken to the funeral home under cover of darkness. After a lifetime of ambivalence about being in the public eye, Bell wanted to ensure her one final moment of privacy. It was March 2, 1999, only six weeks away from what would have been Dusty's sixtieth birthday—but Dusty had always said she didn't want to turn sixty.

Dusty had missed seeing her induction into the Rock 'n' Roll Hall of Fame by a few weeks, but she had lived long enough to receive her OBE, which was delivered to her a few weeks earlier at the Royal Marsden Hospital. At first, Dusty had been unsure about the award, saying, "Isn't that the one they give to cleaners?" Nonetheless she had been delighted when Wickham brought it back from the Palace, wrapped up in a Fortnum & Mason shopping bag. Her status as a national icon seemed cemented, after a career that had included a long stretch when she had fled from her country, and the announcement of her death was greeted by wall-to-wall media coverage and an outpouring of public sadness.

In California, friends pulled over to the side of the road, shocked to hear the news on their car radios as they drove to work. Norma

Tanega, who like Sue Cameron considered Dusty to be the love of her life, found out when a reporter from *The Sun* phoned up and said, "How do feel about Dusty dying? Weren't you involved with her once?"

Depending upon whom you asked, Dusty's funeral was either the kind of high kitsch that she would have loved, or the epitome of bad taste punctuated by speeches from people who barely knew her. Both Neil Tennant and Lulu gave an address, but Pat Barnett did not—although she admitted that she was so upset she would not have been able to. Old friends such as Kiki Dee and Mike Hurst attended, as did Carole Pope and Fred Perry. Sue Cameron had warned Dusty that she would not come—she couldn't cope with the idea—and Dusty had replied, "It's all right, I wouldn't come to yours either." Madeline Bell had not seen or spoken to Dusty since their last meeting in Amsterdam, but burst into tears the moment she walked into the church and saw the coffin. Just as she had wanted, Dusty stopped the traffic in Henley, arriving in the rain in a horse-drawn carriage. She was seen off to the strains of "Goin' Back." Later, some of her ashes were interred in the church at Henley, while the rest of her remains were scattered off the Cliffs of Moher—her favorite spot in Ireland. She asked her brother Tom to oversee her final journey.

There was protracted wrangling over Dusty's peculiar discretionary will, which meant that she had listed the people she wanted to leave money to, but not the amounts or proportions. Lee Everett received a substantial sum to care for Nicholas the cat and feed him the expensive baby food that Dusty flew in from California. (Nicholas lived happily for many more years, running around Everett's garden and adopting Everett's other cat as his girlfriend.) Money was also willed to animal charities that Dusty had supported over the years. In the end, probate and tax deductions meant that most people received little.

Dusty had made a lot of money, and spent a lot of money, and whatever her worth, it could not be measured in monetary terms. Instead her friends remembered a fragile, sensitive, kind, intelligent and loving woman. When her funeral was over, Pieter van der Zwan returned to the house at Harpsden Bottom, indescribably sad that he had never visited her there. Her presence was the one that everyone always wanted to be close to, but now she was not there. Looking out of the window he saw "the beautiful view that she loved of the green fields and the sheep," and he hoped that she had found peace at last.

Dusty's life had rarely been peaceful. She had always fought for the underdog, whether it was promoting black music, standing up to apartheid, fighting her corner as a female recording artist, or looking after stray cats. And as a person of fierce intelligence and integrity, she had struggled courageously with illnesses both physical and mental, as well as the dilemma of how to live in a world that would never let her be honest about who she really was.

Above all, those who knew her, and those who didn't, were joined together in remembering her iconic talent and charisma — and her immense contribution to music. "All British artists are hugely indebted to Dusty Springfield, whether they know it or not," Diane Warren says. "She was so influential, her vocal footprint is vast. She was simply the greatest blue-eyed soul singer."

Even amongst her contemporaries she remains above the rest. "Her records still stand," says Lulu. "A lot of records don't stand today that were made in the '60s. They were for that time and so should be left there. Or when they're played, they're 'Aww, so sweet.' But she had gravity. She was very articulate too—she was a heavyweight."

After describing the ups and down of Dusty's life, stretching back to their days together with the Lana Sisters, Riss Chantelle looked wistful, and said with simple poignancy, "You know, she did have a lovely voice."

ACKNOWLEDGEMENTS

I would like to thank Simon Bell for encouraging me to write this book, and for spending so many hours talking about Dusty and leading me in the right direction. Sue Cameron also spent much time and care sharing her memories of Dusty, and her photographs, with me.

Maggie Vanderschoot's research into Dusty's bipolar condition provided much food for thought, as did Nancy Young's PhD thesis and contributions from other Dusty fans and the *Let's Talk Dusty* community, including Carole Gibson who shared some fascinating photos from the 1960s.

Special thanks also to my agent Gaia Banks, who was an enthusiastic and determined Dusty fan from the beginning, and to Jeremy Robson and Sam Carter at The Robson Press and Jonathan Wadman.

For spending endless hours discussing this book with me and encouraging me, thanks to my parents Margot and Brian Bartlett, to Amna Khwaja for spending hours discussing Dusty and to Colleen Witkin, Eric and Wendy Adler, Pam Alcock, Pete Gordon and Bernadine Gregory.

Most importantly, the following people who agreed to be interviewed for this book: John Adams, Brooks Arthur, Jeff Barry, Madeline Bell, Simon Bell, Marcelle Bernstein, Shelley Bovey, Teda

Bracci, Sue Cameron, Riss Chantelle, Martine Collette, Ray Connolly, Elvis Costello, Kiki Dee, Julie Felix, Kenny Gamble, Lesley Gore, Keith Howes, Mike Hurst, Suzanne Lacefield, Dennis Lambert, Lulu, Peter Miles, Carole Pope, Peter Rand, David Redfern, Doug Reece, Pat Rhodes (Barnett), Jean Ryder, Leon Shaier, Judy Stone, Tarra Thomas, Diane Warren, Vicki Wickham, Allee Willis and Pieter van der Zwan.

SOURCES

As well as a huge collection of newspaper articles and interviews, the following books were particularly helpful...

Burt Bacharach, *Anyone Who Had a Heart* (Atlantic Books 2013)

Cilla Black, *What's It All About* (Ebury Press 2003)

Laurence Cole, *Dusty Springfield: In The Middle of Nowhere* (Middlesex University Press 2008)

Richard Davenport-Hines, *An English Affair: Sex, Class and Power in the Age of Profumo* (Harper Press 2013)

Sharon Davis, *A Girl Called Dusty* (Andre Deutsch 2008)

David Evans, *Scissors and Paste: A Collage Biography of Dusty Springfield* (Britannia Press 1995)

Robert Gordon, *It Came From Memphis* (Pocket Books 1995)

Peter Guralnick, *Sweet Soul Music: Rhythm and Blues and the Southern Dream of Freedom* (Canongate 2002)

Peter Hennessy, *Having It So Good: Britain in the Fifties* (Penguin 2007)

Paul Howes, *The Complete Dusty Springfield* (Titan Books 2001, revised 2007)

David Kynaston, *Family Britain 1951–1957* (Bloomsbury 2009)

David Kynaston, *Modernity Britain 1957–59* (Bloomsbury 2013)

Simon Napier-Bell, *You Don't Have To Say You Love Me* (New English Library 1982)

Lucy O'Brien, *Dusty: A Biography of Dusty Springfield* (Pan 1999)

Carole Pope, *Anti-Diva: An Autobiography* (Random House 2001)

Annie J. Randall, *Dusty! Queen of the Postmods* (Oxford University Press 2009)

Martha Reeves, *Dancing In The Street: Confessions of a Motown Diva* (Hyperion 1994)

Mark Ribowsky, *The Supremes: A Saga of Motown Dreams, Success and Betrayal* (Da Capo Press 2009)

Dominic Sandbrook, *White Heat: A History of Britain in the Swinging Sixties* (Little Brown 2006)

Penny Valentine and Vicki Wickham, *Dancing With Demons: The Authorised Biography of Dusty Springfield* (Hodder and Stoughton 2000)

Dionne Warwick, *My Life, As I See It* (Atria Books 2010)

Jerry Wexler, *Rhythm and the Blues* (Alfred A. Knopf 1993)

INDEX

INDEX